THE STRAIGHT-A CONSPIRACY:

YOUR SECRET GUIDE TO ENDING THE STRESS OF SCHOOL AND TOTALLY RULING THE WORLD

BY
HUNTER MAATS AND KATIE O'BRIEN

ILLUSTRATED BY
LINDSEY GARY, ANDREW GOULET, AND TRAVIS STANBERRY

At the time of this book's publication, all facts and figures cited are
the most current available and have been verified as of May 2012.

Cover Design by Lindsey Gary

Illustrations by Lindsey Gary appear on pgs. 2, 33-36, 39, 52-53, 55,
71-73, 77, 80, 124, 128, 135, 176, 204-207, 220, 234, 265-268, 272,
275, 277, 286

Illustrations by Andrew Goulet appear on pgs. 11, 18, 91, 201, 222

Illustrations by Travis Stanberry appear on pgs. 85, 86, 88, 89

Sherlock Holmes silhouette p. 139: © The Sherlock Holmes Mu-
seum, 221b Baker Street, London, England www.sherlock-holmes.
co.uk
Graffiti font: Lars Håhus
Handwriting fonts: Kimberly Geswein

Scientific Research Consultant: Quinn Ho
Copy Editor: Andrew Goulet
Author Photo: Keegan Uhl Photography

www.thestraightaconspiracy.com

Hunter and Katie would like to acknowledge the following people for their support:

For being there from the very start, through every page of every iteration, and helping us take this book from mere words to an engaging and creative visual experience far beyond what we could have imagined alone, we owe boundless thanks to Lindsey Gary.

For ensuring that every page of this book is scientifically supportable, grammatically accurate and in every other way ready for publication, we would like to acknowledge Quinn Ho, Jean S. Perwin, and Andrew Goulet.

For reading draft after draft (after draft) and for giving invaluable advice from the parents' perspective, we would like to thank Laurie Abkemeier, Trish Babtie, Robin Steiner, Lisa Florence, Stan Rogow, and Harald and Sharlene Ludwig. We also owe a huge thank you to our publicist, the endlessly creative Kim-from-LA, for being the best thing since Mexican chocolate ice cream.

We also owe a special thank you to Bud Vana and Laura Weidman, our very first partners in our journey of figuring out how to help students fall in love with school again.

Thank you to Dave Holstein for his tech support, joke support, and for munificently allowing us to appropriate the top floor of the house for hours on end in the name of this book. Katie feels lucky to be marrying you. Hunter feels lucky to be able to raid your fridge. (By the way, you're out of milk.)

Thank you to the countless friends, family members, and near strangers who have patiently and helpfully listened to us discuss, share, and test out this book over the past few years, at every dinner party, birthday party, New Year's party, backyard barbeque... You are too many to list, and you have enriched this book more than can be measured.

Thank you to each and every one of our students, past and present. You have taught us as much as—if not more than—we have taught you.

And finally, we owe the greatest thanks of all to the people who have dedicated the most day-in and day-out support to this book—our very first and very best teachers, our moms and dads, Job and Peggy Maats and David and Karen O'Brien. Thank you for raising us to be the type of students who love learning, giving us the confidence to take risks, pushing us to never settle for "good enough," and cheering longest and loudest for everything we've ever done.

CONTENTS

PART ONE

Chapter 1

<u>Worst. Idea. Ever.</u>

Hey! What's new with you? I mean, besides the fact that every moment of your entire life is based on a lie...

What? Oh, wait...too soon? Well, we thought you deserved to know. Knowledge is power, and all that.

That's right. Your entire life—or at least all of the hours that you're awake—is based on a big, fat lie. The lie affects the actions you take every day, the dreams you have for your future, and your entire opinion of yourself. And to see why that's true, you need to look no further than school. If you're like most teenagers, you probably find school somewhat annoying. You spend your days learning things that you think you'll never use as an adult. You feel like you'll never get your parents and teachers off your case, because you're already doing the best that you can. And to top it all off, some kids just breeze through school, getting great grades and never feeling stressed. If you've ever had any of these thoughts—or others like them—then we can tell you, straight-up: the lie is running your life. You deserve to learn the truth. Actually, you *need* the truth, and quickly.

Most people believe that being smart is about being born with the right brain or being a slave to your books. In reality, it's much, much simpler than that. And when you learn the truth, you'll never be able to look at school in the same way again. It will instantly be possible for you to become one of the smartest people who ever lived. You just can't let yourself play victim to the lie any longer.

Actually, if we're really getting into the nitty-gritty of it, the word "lie" doesn't do this betrayal justice. In fact, you are caught up in a full-fledged, centuries-old conspiracy. Yeah, yeah, we know. Usually people who talk about conspiracies are "questionably sane" and "deserve to get strange looks in restaurants," but we're not necessarily saying that there are creepy druids or mysterious government agents involved. It's not exactly like that.

What we *will* say is this: the conspiracy to which you've fallen victim is so big that we can't even tell you how big it is, because you wouldn't believe it. It's so big that it's bigger than all of the other conspiracies that you know combined. It's like finding out that Elvis was an alien who crash landed at Roswell, assassinated JFK...and then faked his own death to go live with Bigfoot. If you are a person who prefers math to reading, it's like this:

R = ROSWELL
K = KENNEDY ASSASSINATION
Є = ELVIS'S FAKE DEATH
A = STRAIGHT-A CONSPIRACY

All of these conspiracies have one goal in common: they cover up the truth and keep the public believing lies. The difference is that while the existence of aliens may or may not affect you (or even occur to you) on any given day, the Straight-A Conspiracy actively makes your life worse—less fun, more stressful, and less successful—every single day. And the worst part of all is that it has been going on right in front of your face—in front of all of our faces—for centuries. And we've all just let it keep going.

That's because the Straight-A Conspiracy didn't start with a big event like a UFO crash landing or the death of a huge public figure. It was far subtler than that. Centuries ago, a small group of people took some small actions, trying to help themselves and their friends get ahead. They never could have predicted how much the results of their actions would snowball, or how many millions of lives they would affect. But thanks to those people, an idea was born that became the root of the conspiracy...and poisoned education for everyone.

Worst. Idea. Ever.

Genius. Giant-brained, unexplainable, awe-inspiring genius. *What* is more amazing than being a genius? Maybe you prefer the term "prodigy" or "gifted," or if you're German, "*wunderkind.*" Whatever you call it, the potential to have an idea or to discover a skill out of the blue one day and have that special idea or skill bring you guaranteed fame, fortune, and a place in history books for all eternity...*that's* the life.

Of course, part of what makes genius so exciting and intriguing is that most of us will never have it. We can all marvel at the inventive talent of Thomas Edison, the mathematical brain of Sir Isaac Newton or the musical abilities of Wolfgang Amadeus Mozart, but we can't imagine being lucky enough to be born with brains like theirs. Genius is effortless. Genius is unattainable. Genius is only for a special few. And the fact that we all think this way is exactly why those "geniuses" achieved success that was so legendary.

Pretty much everything that you've been told about history's most famous geniuses is no more than a highly successful ad campaign.

How to Sell Absolutely Anything

Pop Quiz: Who invented the light bulb?
a) Thomas Edison
b) Alexander Graham Bell
c) Humphry Davy
d) Cuthbert O'Lightbulb

If you picked a), you're wrong. That may seem unfair, because you've likely heard from *lots* of different sources in your lifetime that Thomas Edison invented the light bulb. That's a classic story about the super-genius inventor from Menlo Park who churned out innovation after innovation from his amazing brain. The *actual* inventor of the light bulb was Sir Humphry Davy. So why is it that we all think, "Thomas Edison invented the light bulb," when actually, Humphrey Davy invented it forty-five years before Edison was even born?

Advertising.

First of all, Thomas Edison was *definitely* awesome. He just wasn't awesome for the reasons you've heard. Let's get the real deal on his accomplishments. In the 1880's, electric lights were already in department stores and on city streets, but because they were hugely expensive and unreliable, most people had to use gas to light their homes...which was great if you like your lights with a side of potential fireballs in your bedroom. A lot of inventors knew that gas lighting was less than ideal and that there would be big money for whoever solved this problem. Edison had already had his first taste of fame with the gramophone, and so he promised all the newspaper reporters that he would solve the problem of the electric light in no time at all. Fortunately, Edison wasn't working alone. He had assembled a giant team of top inventors to work in his Menlo Park laboratory, and together, *they* attacked the problem. It was obvious to everyone that the quick-to-burn-out filament was the one thing keeping the light bulb from being in every home. So, Edison and his many colleagues carefully tested over 10,000 different types of filament until they found success with one of the most unlikely materials: carbonized bamboo.

Having the resolve to

Even a Genius Can't Do That

On April Fool's Day, one reporter wrote a fake article about Edison's "Food Creator," a machine which could turn dirt into any dish you could imagine. When people eagerly wrote in to place advanced orders, it was clear that the hype about Edison was out of control; people believed that the great Edison could even do the impossible.

Let's Make a Deal

When two unknown inventors approached Edison's team with a revolutionary new movie projector, they were offered a deal: they could make a fortune, but they had to put Edison's name on the invention. This basically meant they had two options: a) fortune, but no fame or b) no fortune, but, wait, still no fame. Wisely, they agreed to the deal. Edison got the glory, and they remained silent. It wasn't ideal. But everyone involved knew this was the best way to sell the maximum number of machines.

stick with this problem through *ten thousand* different attempts is, in itself, an impressive feat. But if the light bulb was going to take America by storm, people would not only need to buy the bulb, but also wire their entire homes for electricity. In other words, it wasn't an easy sell. What's more, while patience is certainly a virtue, the slogan "Hundreds of men spent thousands of hours figuring out how to make this thing work a little better than before!" wasn't really as catchy as, say, Nike's "Just do it." Edison needed a good advertising campaign.

Fortunately, Edison knew how to use the newspapers to his own advantage. To generate buzz about his inventions, he paid the newspapermen with shares in his company; in exchange, they would write stories about how the answer to America's lighting needs came to Edison in a sudden flash of inspiration. There he was, just sitting at his workbench, when suddenly, his geniusy self *just knew* what to do. "Oh! Partially burnt Japanese panda lunch! It's so obvious!!!" This was the start of an ongoing media blitz that secured Edison's genius status and earned him the nickname, "The Wizard of Menlo Park."

As Edison's notoriety skyrocketed, so did the sales figures. If the product came from a wizard, then everyone wanted it. Suddenly, Edison's genius reputation wasn't just motivated by vanity, but also by business strategy. The other inventors at Menlo Park were quietly kept out of the public awareness. By the end of Edison's life, his team had patented hundreds and hundreds of inventions, but as far as America knew, all those inventions came from Edison alone. Having a genius as the face of your company was *great* for business, and to keep the profits rolling in, it was crucial to make Edison seem superhuman.

Over time, people's awe of Edison became a part of the country's lore, and just like a game of Telephone, the story of Edison was passed down, simplified, and changed. That's why what you hear generations later is simply, "Thomas Edison invented the light bulb." That's why what you know is a lie.

Once you start recognizing lies—or, at least, obvious "adjustments" to the truth like this one—you'll find that many famous geniuses throughout history have relied on clever advertising to make themselves seem more "geniusy." Perhaps the next most impressive example is everyone's favorite boy genius, Wolfgang Amadeus Mozart.

Mozart's work is amazing. No one can question that. But although his adult performances and compositions are totally worthy of being celebrated for the rest of human history, there are other parts to his story that have been embellished *far beyond* what actually occurred. And it all begins with the world's most overzealous stage dad. His kind, fatherly face looked like this:

As you might be able to guess from his picture, Wolfgang Mozart's dad, Leopold, wasn't really into organizing themed slumber parties for his kids. He was intense. As the author of Europe's most popular book on teaching violin, Leopold knew how to do one thing for kids: turn them into musical prodigies. And he planned to use every scrap of what he knew to transform his own kids into little eighteenth-century cash machines.

It started with his oldest daughter, Nannerl, who by the age of seven was really catching on to Leopold's teaching. She could've had a great career. The only problem was that a better "product option" came along. Basically, it boiled down to this: Nannerl was skilled, but Wolfgang was a boy. (This was eighteenth-century Europe. "Girl Power" didn't exist until much later.) So Leopold shifted focus and set out to make Wolfgang a star.

It's All An Act

To really blow the wigs off people's heads, Leopold would challenge a local composer to come up with a totally new piece that Wolfgang would play unrehearsed and without missing a beat. One composer, however, tells us that the feat rested on a simple trick: when Wolfgang got stuck, he played passages he already knew by heart in place of the ones in the new composition. The audience saw him playing flawlessly from start to finish—it just wasn't the exact piece that the composer had written.

For the rest of Wolfgang's childhood, Leopold devoted himself to making his son look like a genius. What's more impressive than a twelve-year-old who plays piano? A twelve-year-old who plays a sonata that he composed himself! Only a *genius* could do that! Sure Leopold may have "helped" a lot with the composition work, but it's better publicity to say it was entirely little Wolfie's creation. And if Leopold said his son was younger than he really was, that was no biggie. It all just made for a better show. Leopold dedicated his life to "spinning" the truth in a way that made Wolfgang look like he basically was born composing masterpieces, and all of Europe ate that advertising right up. Wolfgang quickly rose to fame, playing for kings and countless sold-out concert halls, because no one could explain how he was so good; they just knew that they had to see it.

Of course, it's not like Wolfgang Mozart was a complete *fraud*, either. Fortunately, during that period of Wolfgang's youth when Leopold was busy spinning and truth-stretching, he also was giving Wolfgang an excellent musical education. By the time Wolfgang was twenty-one, he actually was as good as his reputation. At that point, he had been playing for eighteen years, and his skills had fully caught up to the stories of his feats. That's when he began to create the real masterpieces.

So that's the real deal. Mozart became amazing because he rehearsed so much, and in the meantime, he needed his father-turned-publicist to spin the truth a bit in order to sell concert tickets. But just like Edison's story, the myth of Mozart has been passed around the world and down through the generations until it no longer resembles the truth of how Mozart actually became so good. Today, Mozart is known for "composing his first masterpiece at the age of five"—a feat that none of us could ever imagine doing. But if we said, "Do you think that you could play the piano every day and then take credit for your dad's work?" then you'd be more likely to see Mozart's accomplishments as something you could do too.

These stories are good, but the genius myth that really takes the cake, both for ridiculous plot and shady motivations, is that of the great Sir Isaac Newton. Isaac Newton has hands-down the most absurd genius myth out there. You've heard it—the one where he's, like, half-napping under a tree, and then an apple plunks down onto his head, and in that instant, Newton discovers gravity. That certainly sounds impressive; the idea that the entire understanding of the world's most powerful invisible force could "come to you" instantaneously would lead anyone to believe that there was something magical about Newton's brain.

But *come ON*, people. There are so many problems with this. Let's break it down: 1) Newton did not "discover" gravity. After all, long before Newton was even alive, people had certainly noticed that things always seemed to fall *toward the ground*. 2) Being hit on the head doesn't make people revolutionize the entire field of physics. It makes them say, "Ow." The truth is that in Newton's time, people already knew that the planets revolved around the sun and how their orbits worked. What they couldn't figure out was what kept the planets going in circles. Why didn't the planets fly off into space? It's not even certain whether Newton had any encounter at all with an apple, but even if he did, it simply gave him something to think about...and then he essentially locked himself away for *twenty years* until he figured out the equations to explain how gravity might be responsible for holding the planets in their orbits.

Now, a mathematical equation is not exactly a hot-ticket item like a new light bulb or box seats to the hottest concert of 1765. Newton wasn't set for stardom, even with the history-making greatness of his work. What's more, telling a story of taking twenty years to figure out one problem might be honest, but it's not particularly sensational. Not to worry. Newton was in the middle of a high school cafeteria-style popularity contest, and the apple story was the key to becoming the scientific equivalent of prom queen.

Science in Europe at that time had all the cattiness, backstabbing, and notoriety of today's celebutantes. The scientists may have made more significant advances for the human race... but both sets of people still wore lots of long, fake hair. One of Newton's greatest supporters was a guy named Voltaire. (P.S. Voltaire is an extremely important writer and philosopher in his own right, with many groundbreaking written works, which you should look up. It's just that for the purposes of this story, we're focused on his lesser-known role as the Queen Bee of the gossipy intellectuals.) At that time, there was a scientific rivalry between the supporters of a French scientist named Descartes and the supporters of Newton, and Voltaire was *definitely* Team Newton. Voltaire really wanted to crush Descartes. Unfortunately, that was slightly difficult, because Voltaire was no match for either of them in science and math. So, rather than resorting to "Descartes' mama is so fat..." jokes, Voltaire focused on making Newton look so amazing in the public eye that Descartes would be yesterday's news.

Voltaire may not have been a top scientist, but he was an exceptional writer, and so step one of his plan was to write a popular book that explained Newton's work to the public in an accessible way and made Newton look like a god. This became *Eléments de la Philosophie de Newton*. Step two was to take Newton's nerdy image and make him over into a studmuffin (or at least the eighteenth-century version of one). For your viewing pleasure, here is the "illustration" of Newton that Voltaire included in his book:

Step three was to make sure that even people who wouldn't read that big mathy book still knew that Newton was the bomb. To do this, Voltaire came up with a subtle and devilish idea: create a sensational story that gossips could spread like wildfire. World, meet "the falling apple."

Voltaire must have known that the apple story was the best way to make Newton look like a genius, because in addition to its appearance in *Eléments de la Philosophie de Newton,* there are numerous different records of him telling it over and over again. After all, if you are trying to become famous, then you need a lot of fans. Think about it. In his time, Edison couldn't reach millions of people by doing a Super Bowl ad, so he needed a good story that people would spread. Mozart couldn't get discovered off YouTube, so what's a stage dad to do? And Newton couldn't just go on a reality show like *So You Think You Can Explain Gravity?* (This was partly because he was unattractive and potentially crazy from mercury poisoning, and partly because there were no TVs.) For thousands of years, creating stories of impressive, innate genius was the one way to a guaranteed victory.

Eliminate the Competition

Newton had more than one scientific enemy. Around the time that Newton's book was coming out, Robert Hooke reminded the scientific community that he—and not Newton—had been the first person to suggest the basic form of the law of gravitational attraction. Always Mr. Maturity, Newton responded by finding every single mention of "the very distinguished Robert Hooke" in his book and, one by one, crossing out "the very distinguished." Boo-yeah! Then, after Hooke died, Newton mysteriously "lost" Hooke's last remaining portrait and all of Hooke's records about his accomplishments. Had you heard about the scientific accomplishments of Robert Hooke before this? Exactly.

The World Looks Flat from Here

One trait that makes human beings so awesome is our strong desire to understand and explain the world around us. Of course, we don't always get it right. That impulse to jump to an explanation can lead us astray sometimes. Look out the window. The world should look flat. Do this exercise again at someone else's house, or at a grocery store, or at the post office. Unless one of the places you went today was the space station, all of your evidence should suggest that the world is indeed flat. And when we see *multiple* pieces of "evidence" to support a particular idea, then, try as we might to keep an open mind, deep down we become convinced that it's true.

In the same way, the genius myths *began* as relatively well-intentioned advertising campaigns, but people quickly latched on to the fact that their underlying message was the same. Sure, the details varied: Mozart played piano and Edison invented things and Newton hated his friends. But at the core, what do all of their stories have in common? They all say that these "geniuses" achieved everything by doing nothing. Thanks to some sort of miraculous mental superpower, their accomplishments arrived out of the blue. Seems like they all must have been *born* with "genius brains."

This is the Straight-A Conspiracy—little white lies and innocent omissions that weren't necessarily meant to be harmful, but that poisoned everyone's idea of intelligence. Over time, the web

Did You Need That Blood?

For over 2000 years, doctors believed that the best way to get rid of disease was to drain blood from the patient's body. Sometimes, they would use leeches, but when a person was really sick, the doctors would just open a vein in the patient's wrist. In 1799, George Washington caught a cold. So, his doctors bled about half the blood from his body. Then, he died. We can't say for sure that his doctors killed him, but we now know that they certainly didn't help. Bad theories lead to bad choices.

of lies grew bigger and bigger, far beyond the famous geniuses. Soon every time that someone was quick to solve a problem or accomplished something impressive, people assumed it was because he or she was "lucky" enough to be born with a great brain. Smart went from being something you *made* happen to something that happened *to* you. The idea that you have to be "born smart"—*this* is the Worst Idea Ever.

But there was no stopping the conspiracy. In fact, if you tried to go against the idea of the "born genius," people didn't even want to hear it. This problem became endlessly frustrating to the man who is known as the biggest "genius" the world has ever seen: Albert Einstein. The name "Einstein" is synonymous with genius...the outrageous, big-haired, theory of relativity sort of genius. Genius beyond what any of us could possibly comprehend. Einstein is like double-Newton with a side of fries. And he spent his entire career telling people things like, "It's not that I'm so smart, it's just that I stay with problems longer." He didn't think he was a "genius," and he didn't want anyone else to either. But at the beginning of the twentieth century, Arthur Eddington, a British physicist, was trying to promote the new thinking on relativity, and in the spirit of Newton's apple, he knew that a compelling story would sell much better than a bunch of math. So, he depicted Einstein as a boy wonder with ideas that threatened to destroy the man who had for centuries been the Goliath of scientific thought: Sir Isaac Newton. Which was more compelling? An all-out intellectual cage match or "staying with problems longer?" The public already knew which of those two perspectives they wanted to buy. They'd rather hear about a "born genius" any day.

"All manner of fable is being attached to my personality, and there is no end to the number of ingeniously devised tales. All the more do I appreciate and respect what is truly sincere."
—Albert Einstein

How the Conspiracy Affected You

Alright, enough talk about *other* people. Dead dudes are interesting and all, but what about *YOU*? What is the Straight-A Conspiracy really all about, and why should you care?

Well, it's bad enough that the adults who heard stories of geniuses started feeling bummed about having been dealt ordinary brains. No one likes a bummed-out adult. But the Straight-A Conspiracy goes far beyond just affecting people's feelings; when we mistake beliefs for facts, then that can affect the choices we make. In essence, those beliefs affect the way we live our lives. And in school, that's downright destructive. After all, if you have the completely wrong idea of smart, that's going to change the way you feel and what you do every day. If you think you're terrible at reading, how excited are you going to be for English class? If you're sure you'd never get an *A* anyway, how hard will you study for tests? But here's the worst part: if you believe the ideas of the Straight-A Conspiracy, then school *actually is* harder for you than it is for someone who's conspiracy-free.

Wouldn't it have been nice if, for your whole life, you knew you could have the following things—and you knew *exactly* how to get them?

- Straight *A*'s
- A stress-free school experience
- Having your parents off your case about school
- Actually feeling as if the things you learn in school *matter* for your future
- The ability to do all of this and still "have a life"

You know that those things are possible, but you probably don't think that they're possible *for you*. You've been taught— more like brainwashed—to accept that school is naturally easy for some people and hard for everyone else. In reality, all of the things in this list have been *well* within your reach since the very first day that you stepped into a classroom.

Fighting The Conspiracy with Facts

The only reason you don't feel like a super-amazing, rocket-science-level genius every day that you're in school is because you do know the genius myths, but you don't know how learning is really supposed to work. No one would ever put you in a car with no license and no driver's ed training and expect you to drive on the highway. So why would anyone put you in a classroom with no training in how to use your brain and expect you to get straight A's?

You need facts. Fortunately, in the last three decades, science has gotten closer than ever before to figuring out exactly how your brain works. And the news is going to blow you away.

At this point, scientists have identified over 300 specific genes that play a direct role in mental retardation. That link between genes and intelligence is pretty clear. However, scientists have *not* found a gene for *A*-level math ability or a gene for having a "natural ear for languages." In fact, so far, scientists have found *zero* genes that cause people to have above-average intelligence. In other words, the idea that someone can be born a genius just isn't true.

But that's not to say that the people who we see as geniuses are just a random selection of well-advertised historical types. What science *has* discovered is that all geniuses have one thing in common: practice. Not like your soccer practice. Not like half an hour of guitar. What it takes to become a genius is about 10,000 hours of focused practice.

That's right...we said 10,000 hours. After studying experts in fields from sports to science to music to writing, scientists have determined that 10,000 hours is the amount of practice needed to take anyone to the top of his or her field. Remember, Edison, Mozart, and Newton really did achieve some pretty impressive feats. The lie is in how we *think* they achieved them. Edison's huge team of inventors tried *ten thousand* different filaments for the light bulb before they got it right—and that's just for *one* of the many technologies they created! You don't think that got frustrating at times? Mozart wasn't born composing masterpieces; his great works didn't begin until he had been playing *every day for eighteen years*! And you probably glossed over that part in the Newton story where he *worked on the same set of equations for twenty years*!!!! There's a guy who made a lot of mistakes.

The difference between finding a super-complex answer through doing twenty years of work and finding it during a sudden apple attack is, well, pretty big. What is amazing about Edison, Newton, and Mozart's accomplishments is not that they did what no one else could do. It's that they took what just about anyone could have done, and they worked at it until they were the ones to get there first. In fact, if you were to look at every little step they took in pursuit of their goals, you would realize that anyone who followed those same little steps could have done the exact same thing.

Because we've all heard that great ideas just pop into people's heads, most of us would say, "There's no way I could invent a light bulb." But it seems reasonable that any of us could sit down and test out replacement parts on an invention that's been around for over seventy-five years. Things only seem as if they're not doable when you're looking at the end result (something awesome) without seeing all the little pieces (the practice) that happened along the way.

The point that we want you to take from this is not that your life needs to be miserable for decades in order for you to do something cool. It's that to achieve their real accomplishments—which absolutely were amazing—these "geniuses" had to start with their totally average brains and work at it. All of these guys were just ordinary people who let nothing stand in the way of getting the results they wanted.

In fact, there's proof of that. Advertising slogans and genius myths aside, deep down, Edison, Mozart, Newton, and especially Einstein still wanted to be recognized for the *effort* they put into their work:

"I never did anything worth doing by accident, nor did any of my inventions come by accident. They came by work."
—*Thomas Edison*

"It is a mistake to think that the practice of my art has become easy to me. I assure you, dear friend, no one has given so much care to the study of composition as I. There is scarcely a famous master in music whose works I have not frequently and diligently studied."

—Mozart

"If I have ever made any valuable discoveries, it has been due more to patient attention than to any other talent."

—Isaac Newton

Einstein Agrees

"It strikes me as unfair, and even in bad taste, to select a few individuals for boundless admiration, attributing superhuman powers of mind and character to them. This has been my fate, and the contrast between the popular assessment of my powers and achievements and the reality is simply grotesque."
— Albert Einstein

What's more, these guys certainly didn't let themselves fall for the genius myths that already existed when they were alive. Seriously, there is no one who would *ever* willingly spend 10,000 hours practicing the same thing if they at all doubted that they had what it takes to succeed. If Edison had believed in "natural genius," he may have given up after two or maybe three unsuccessful tries, and you'd be reading this book by gas lamp and dodging fireballs in your bedroom. Thank goodness he had the confidence to keep at it.

The Conspiracy Is All Around You

So, what does this really mean? Well, all this time, you've had the potential to achieve greatness on par with the "geniuses" and you didn't even know it! School is supposed to be the place where people gain confidence in their intelligence. The conspiracy reversed that effect, however, and the idea of "natural ability" has tricked students into doubting their intelligence instead.

Once they're in that mode, students spend years coming up with "ability"-based ways to explain why certain things in school aren't going well. Here's a list of some classic "theories" that students have told us about their brains. The students came up with these theories and then completely bought into them—the same way that they bought into the story of Newton's apple:

> I'm just not a math person.
> I'm good at vocab but bad at spelling.
> I don't have an ear for languages.
> I'm only good at speaking Asian languages. (Note: This was said in English.)
> I have to get it on the first try, or I never get it.
> You can't be good at both math and English.
> I'm just a bad test taker.
> I have a really bad memory.
> I have to be in the right mood to write.
> Some people are just good at grammar and some people aren't. I'm "aren't."
> I can't do standardized tests.
> I've just never been very creative.
> Boys are good at algebra, girls are good at geometry.
> I'm bad at word problems, because I can't do math and English at the same time.

Really? When you hear these theories out of context, they seem pretty ridiculous. You can't just *invent* a gene that makes you bad at word problems! That's not how science works; you have to have *evidence*. Then again, these students had all kinds of bad grades to serve as "evidence" that these problems were real, and they couldn't see any other way to explain why they were happening. By coming up with theories, they were declaring that there was something wrong with some parts of their brains. Here's the thing, though. None of these students had a degree in neuroscience. So how could they be so sure that they had defective brains?

"Girls Aren't Good at Math"?

Do you remember the lady covered in creepy angels from the front of Voltaire's book? That's Émilie du Châtelet, Voltaire's girlfriend... and his math and science tutor. She was really, really smart and was the only reason that Voltaire was able to understand the math and science well enough to write Eléments de la Philosophie de Newton. Beyond this feat, she also predicted infrared radiation, made sense of kinetic energy, and wrote books on everything from rational linguistics to the nature of free will. But over time, while Newton and Voltaire both became famous geniuses, Émilie du Châtelet and her accomplishments dropped off the radar. Today, instead of her story, we have wild and crazy ideas floating around, like the one where "girls aren't as good at math and science."

Having theories like these is not only ridiculously unscientific, but it's also toxic. If you really believe that you were set up at birth to consistently fail at grammar or spelling or algebra, how motivated do you think you're going to be to get better at them? "Oh! I know this will totally not pay off, but let me sit down and practice this for 10,000 hours! That's a *fantastic* use of my time!" Um, we don't think so. Any way you look at it, these theories hold you back.

We also know that not everyone feels this certain that his or her brain has limitations. But even if you feel smart in school most of the time, you probably don't have rock-solid confidence in your intelligence. Certainly not enough to say, "Hey! I can be just as smart as anybody who has ever lived." That's exactly the kind of confidence that's going to help you be a stress-free straight-A student—and that's exactly what the Straight-A Conspiracy has taken from you. It's time for you to take that confidence back.

THINK ABOUT IT

Are you bad at math because you hate it? Or do you hate math because you think you're bad at it? Your perspective on your schoolwork has a huge effect on how hard you work and ultimately, on how you do.

Who Says You Can Be a Straight-A Student?

We do. (For the record, so does your brain. More on that later.) In fact, we are *certain* that you have everything it takes to get the grades and the school experience that you've always secretly wished were possible. That's because we've seen so many students just like you turn their educations around, more simply and more quickly than they ever thought possible.

Here's the deal on us, Hunter and Katie, the authors of this book. Despite being totally different from each other in our high-school lives, we ended up in the same class at Harvard, where we moved in very different circles. Hunter had graduated from Eton, a boarding school in England, where the atmosphere was super-competitive and the school uniform made everyone look like a butler. When he got to Harvard, he majored in biochemistry and minored in ridiculous stunts. Katie, on the other hand, hailed from a public school in rural New Hampshire that was as American as apple pie. At Harvard, she was an English Literature major who did musical theater and performed regularly with the hip-hop dance company. Here are some rather unfortunate high-school yearbook photos of us:

Anyway, the point is, despite going through a few phases of horrible awkwardness, we both grew up really liking school. Sure, we didn't always find it "easy," and we both preferred some subjects to others; but on the whole, we both found a way of working that helped us to get great grades and enjoy our time in school.

And then, something interesting happened. We started a tutoring company with some of our friends from Harvard, and we got to look at the high school experience from a new perspective. And now that we weren't students anymore, we got a *whole new view* of what school was like for most people. It wasn't pretty. Those theories that we mentioned before—those are all *actual things* that our students have said to us. At first, we just thought, "Um, are you serious? How can you only be bad at *standardized tests*?" But in time, we noticed a pattern. Pretty much all of our students had these bogus ideas and worries about their brains, and *that* was what got in the way of them doing well. We had always known there were ideas like this out there, but the problem was bigger than we'd ever imagined. Each time we helped our students to get rid of these totally unfounded theories and their beliefs in born genius, the good grades naturally followed.

So, we set a goal for ourselves. We wanted to figure out the simplest way to make school straightforward and totally stress-free for students everywhere. And guess what? We found it! We tutored for thousands and thousands of hours. We studied what's out there about the brain and what it can do. Then we applied it to high school, and got a straightforward, no-nonsense approach to learning that has worked wonders for the students we know. We think you deserve to know it too.

You'll hear more about our individual experiences and those of students we've helped as the book goes on. In the meantime, if you're willing to stick around to hear how we uncovered the conspiracy, then we can promise you'll get a whole new perspective on what has been holding you back.

Are You Sure You're Ready for the Truth?

For the first time ever, the human race is uncovering the truth about what our brains are capable of achieving...and it is mind-blowing. Learning *any* new skill, *any* new material, *any* new subject works in the exact same way. So, the truth is this: if your brain has learned everyday skills like walking, talking, reading, and basic math, then that is a clear indicator that you can also master quantum physics, Shakespeare, Chinese...anything. Whatever your reaction just was—that scoff, that smirk, that roll of your eyes—that will be gone by the end of the book.

Once you learn the truth, here's what will happen:

1) You will have the tools to ace any subject.
2) You will know how to eliminate stress from school.
3) You'll never have to feel stupid again.

You lucky dog, you. You have it better than Newton, Mozart, AND Edison ever did. That's because you're alive at the best time in history to be a student. You don't need to read every neuroscience journal. You don't need to wait to have a medical degree. You now have the simple, step-by-step manual for systematically unlocking your brain's phenomenal potential until school is not only easy—it's also fun. You're not wrestling with the formula for gravity, you're just going from *B*'s and *C*'s (or even *D*'s and *F*'s) to getting all *A*'s. Just like the world seems flat until you see a picture taken from space, the new perspective that you're about to get on your brain is going to completely shake up your view of school. Raising your grades only seems like a lot of work when you let any of that old-school thinking get in the way. After reading this book, you'll wonder why you ever thought there was anything you couldn't do.

Life beyond The Straight-A Conspiracy is good. Really good. The days of dreading school, being stressed, and getting results you aren't proud of are behind you. You're about to be smarter and more successful than you ever thought possible. Getting great grades and loving school are just the beginning of the awesome life that awaits you.

Of course, maybe you *want* to stay stressed out. Maybe you *like* dreading school and feeling just so-so about your grades. No problem. If you want to keep living life in the dark, then *don't turn the page*. Seriously—put this book down. Put it away in a box and never look at it again. Once you know the truth, there's no going back.

If you *are* ready to turn the page, then you're ready to step out of the dark ages. Welcome to learning in the twenty-first century.

PART TWO

THE THREE THINGS YOU SHOULD KNOW ABOUT YOUR BRAIN

You have chosen wisely. We're glad to have you on board. Let's get started.

All it takes to do well in school is an understanding of how to use your brain? "Oh, yeah, sure, no problem. I'll just get right on that PhD in neuroscience and get back to you in about a bajillion years. Sounds real easy, guys." No worries. When we say "understand" the brain, we mean that you need to understand the brain in the way that you understand your iPod. You know how to play songs, skip tracks, upload music and do everything that you need to be a successful iPod user. You don't need to understand the function of each microchip; you just need to know enough so that you can control the device.

That's exactly what we're going to teach you about your brain. To win in the game of high school, you don't need to know every cranny of your cranium. You just need to know enough to be in control when you're learning. In fact, just by knowing three simple things about your brain, you will have the power to become as smart as you want to be.

The biggest surprise you're going to have by the time you finish this section is that, to some extent, you already know how to do each of the three things that we're going to teach you. The little actions that your brain naturally takes every day are exactly the things that would help you get straight *A*'s if you did them more often.

Once you know these three things about your brain, you'll be able to recognize how some kids seem to always get perfect results, and how you've gotten your results—both good and bad—too. It's your job, as you go through these sections, not only to read about our students' experiences, but to think about how they might be similar to your own. Much of what you've been through in school will start to make a lot more sense. That also means you don't have to worry about what's in the past anymore. You'll understand why it happened and how to move forward. It's time to find out how smart you really are.

Chapter 2

Automaticity

Only Effort Can Make It Effortless

"If people knew how hard I had to work for my mastery it would not seem so wonderful."

—*Michelangelo*

Pop Quiz! Try the following problems:

$2 + 2 =$
$3 + 4 =$
$1 + 5 =$

How did those go? Were they pretty easy? That's automaticity in action. Automaticity is just the ability to make something automatic. For example, once upon a time, adding was a challenge for you. You counted on your fingers, you had no idea what answer you might get, and even single-digit problems required major focus. Yet now, adding doesn't seem like an enormous challenge; you can do it with ease. In fact, without automaticity, you wouldn't even be able to read this sentence.

Actually, let's get even more basic than that. Walking. Billions of people do it. They don't have to think about it while it's happening, and yet they do it really well every day. But when you started to learn to walk, you were bad at it. Seriously, you, we, and everyone else did a horrible job. We fell, quite literally, flat on our faces. But, there was never a question that you were going to get it. The act of walking, which you now make look so easy, is actually incredibly complicated. It involves a very, very precise coordination of movements. Watch a toddler's face while he tries to walk. His or her full attention is on how to avoid a face plant. Although you don't remember that learning to walk once felt like work, it is a skill that you acquired and now use all the time. Skills like walking, which you take for granted, are actually the product of thousands and thousands of hours of practice. It's just that a) at the time you didn't think of that practice as work and b) that effort happened so long ago that it's very common to incorrectly assume that walking, talking, and adding have always been easy.

So, how does this happen? Well, it's just like exploring the Amazon rainforest. Let us explain.

Imagine that you are standing at the edge of a scary, uncharted, snake-infested jungle, and we tell you that somewhere in the middle, there's a giant gold mine. You can have all of the gold in it, if you're willing to go get it. Then, we point out a faint, little path heading straight into the jungle. It's visible, but it's totally overgrown with huge jungle plants. At first, you'd probably think, "Yeah right. I'll just end up getting lost...and eaten." Maybe that's true, but we're talking a LOT of gold here. So you decide to go find it, and you set out for your treasure. With every setback, you keep reminding yourself how much you really want the gold. The bottom line is that it won't be easy. But by the time you reach that huge gold mine, your footsteps and your chopping action have cleared a more noticeable path between where you are and where you started. It's not a great path, but it works.

The only thing is, this gold mine is huge. There is definitely more gold than you can carry with you on one trip. So, you're going to need to go back and forth through that jungle a lot before you have all of it. Each time that you make a trip, the path gets smoother and clearer, and it's easier and easier to stay on it. Better yet, it becomes less and less likely that you'll ever get lost again.

What a Bonus!

Note: Unlike strip-mining the Amazon, no monkeys need to lose their homes in the making of your brain.

The real question is, when you've already made squillions of dollars from the gold that you carried out by hand, how are you gonna spend all of that money? By expanding the operation and getting even more gold! You hire some trucks to start carting loads of gold out of the jungle. But they can't pass each other on your little one-lane dirt road.

Time to pave it. You do pave it, but pretty quickly, you realize that even that paved road isn't fitting as much gold as you would like to transport. You know what that means... superhighway!!! (Yes, there's that much gold.) As you stand on the mountaintop, watching hundreds of trucks full of gold pass each other on the multi-lane Gold Expressway, you think back to where you began with that one little footpath, and you feel great about what you did and how quickly things are now going.

This is how learning works in your brain. You have billions of cells called neurons, and these neurons are ready to help you master an endless set of skills. But when you are born, the paths connecting them aren't very clear.

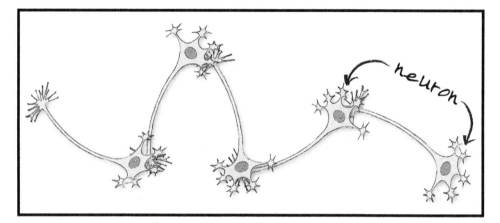

Every time you do something new, it's like going to the gold mine for the first time. 2+2 takes a while on that first journey. But each time you do 2+2 again, that path gets clearer and faster, just like the road to the gold mine. Your brain "paves" your neurons with a substance called *myelin* (MY-uh-lin). Each time you do something, your brain wraps that pathway in a little bit more myelin.

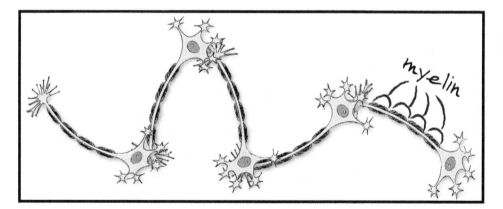

The more layers of myelin your neurons get wrapped in, the faster the signals in those neurons can go. Now that you've done 2+2 as many times as you have in your life, that pathway has become wrapped in lots of myelin, and you can do that addition at superhighway speed.

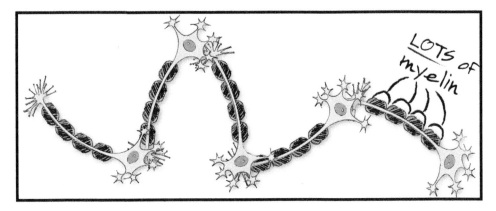

Every time you do something new, your brain takes notice and makes changes, so that it is easier to do that thing the next time. Your brain is ready for action, whether you're walking, talking, reading Shakespeare, or doing calculus. Whatever you're doing, your brain makes it so that eventually you can do that thing without even thinking about it. This is why scientists call this brain function "automaticity." Your brain makes whatever you do automatic, so that you are free to focus on the next new thing that you try.

Automaticity makes life *so* much easier. Imagine how it would feel if you were sitting in algebra class and trying to learn about the FOIL method, while also having to remember how to write the number 4, what multiplication is, and what the best way to hold a pencil might be. Thankfully, those skills that were so challenging when you were little are now easy. Your brain put those skills in the bank so that you only have to focus on what's new. That means constant progress.

So, more repetitions of new info = stronger pathways in your brain. Sounds kind of like, "practice makes perfect." We've all heard that a million times, but just in the last thirty years, research has demonstrated that an extreme amount of a *very specific kind of practice* is all it takes to make ordinary people into geniuses. Now here's the really cool part. You can actually see those changes in your brain.

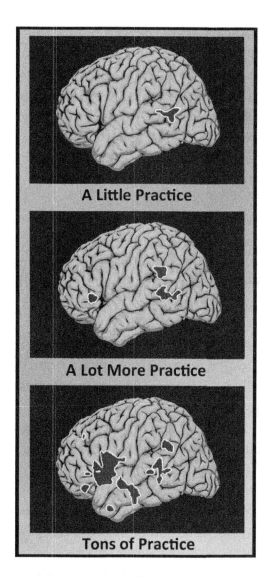

A Little Practice

A Lot More Practice

Tons of Practice

These images show the brains of people who are all practicing the same skill. The first is what the brain looks like after a little practice. The second shows the brain after a lot more practice. The third one shows what the brain looks like after a ton of practice. As you can see, with practice, more and more sections of your brain get involved in that skill. Keep in mind, each of these little areas is made up of millions of neurons. All these neurons have formed a massive network of superhighways. So the difference between someone with a little practice and tons of practice is huge.

So, what skill were these people practicing? Reading. If you are reading this book, then you've already trained billions of neurons to help you in the reading process. And every time you read something—a newspaper, a book, a billboard, a comment on your friend's Facebook wall—your brain is actually changing itself to make reading easier. What this means is that you're getting smarter, right now. And right now. And now. And now... still getting smarter.

You could scan the brain of any professional and see that what they've done to reach the top is literally to condition their brain to be amazing at a particular skill. Their extra brainpower comes from repetition. But as you saw in those images, the brain doesn't change overnight.

More importantly, the beginner and the pro both have to work very hard to get better; they are just working on different parts of their skill. In other words, beginners have to practice the basics: learning letters, sounding out syllables, and recognizing words like "cat." But at the expert level, you've gotten so good at those things that you don't have to think about them anymore. The brain makes the basics automatic by wrapping more myelin around your neurons. That way, you can put your attention on the more advanced things, like learning bigger vocabulary words or interpreting something you read more deeply.

Ultimately, it's not essential that you become an expert on neurons and myelin. What is essential for you to remember is that the first time that people learn anything, they often have no clue what they're doing. It's a weird, awkward, slow, and confusing journey to find an answer. Fortunately, a picture is worth a thousand words. We'll take all of this neuroscience and sum up everything that you need to know as a brain user in this diagram:

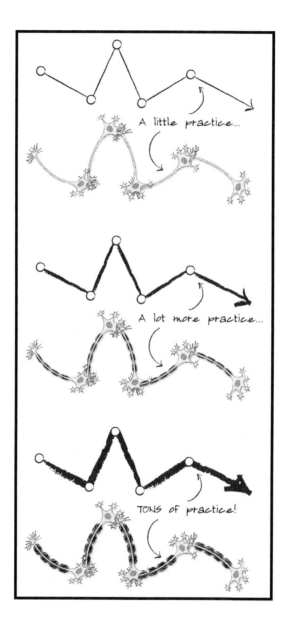

That's all automaticity is—the process of doing something over and over until that faint, little jungle path becomes a superhighway. Automaticity is responsible for every great performance in every field. In the next section, you'll find out why automaticity is not only the basis of becoming a genius, it's also the reason why people have gotten tricked into *thinking* they were stupid.

Unfair Comparisons: The Birthplace of Stupid

See if this scenario sounds familiar: You're sitting in class, and your teacher asks a really tricky question. You just start to figure it out when, *BAM!*, one of the other students has a hand in the air and is answering the question correctly. Here's the worst part: it's the same kid who always gets it right. We've all had this experience at some point, and it makes us ask, "How are they so fast?" The real question to ask is this: Why do we even care if someone else is a bit faster or smarter? Simple. We see that rapid-fire answer, assume that it's the sign of a "naturally amazing" brain, and conclude that our brain doesn't work the same way.

All along, there has been a huge problem with that assumption, and it's the fault of automaticity. You're making a comparison between that other student's brain and yours, but that comparison is totally unfair. Think about it this way. No one can do something impressive without putting in a lot of practice. Automaticity's job is to take all of that practice that people do—hours and hours of it—and train the brain to get better at that specific activity until finally, it can be done at top speed. That other student may do super-speedy mental calculations now, but that's because automaticity is hiding all of the work that he or she did to get there. Automaticity made the work invisible.

School is the *ultimate* place of invisible work. For example, you don't see what kind of practice another student is doing at home. You don't see what kind of practice they're doing in study hall. Sure, you can sit near somebody in class or do your homework together. But even with

> **As You Wish**
>
> Having one extra-sensitive finger may not seem that useful. But for people who can't see, it's the key to reading. If you look at the brain of someone who has spent many years reading braille, a huge portion of their brain is connected to what they feel with the specific finger that they use to read. Your brain makes any changes that it can in order to make your life easier.

that close angle of observation, you still can't see the kind of work they're doing *inside their heads.* And the more mental work they do, the more automated that work becomes until eventually, the student "just knows" the answer right away. And all of that happens where you can't see it. There's no way you can *ever* know how much work a person has put in, because it's invisible. So, trying to compare your brain with someone else's is only going to cause you problems.

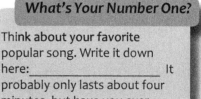

Your Brain is Like Your Biceps

Kids who play sports or take dance lessons or play video games are always quick to recognize that practice is responsible for them getting better at fielding grounders or doing pirouettes or beating the final level. Those kids think that they are only training their muscles or their hand-eye coordination, but actually they are training their brains. The same kind of practice pays off just as much in school.

Meet Phil Callahan. Phil doesn't know much about automaticity, but he does know that girls have cooties. Phil is eight. As summer ends, Phil is really excited to get back to school, his friends, and a bunch of new classes. On the first day of third grade, Phil's teacher introduces multiplication. Everyone is a bit confused. Phil thinks multiplication is sort of weird, but everyone is having a hard time, so it's okay.

By the end of the first week though, that's no longer the case. While Phil is still trying to figure it out by counting on his fingers, Jenny says the answer at lightning speed. She knows it right away. How does she know all the answers? Why can't Phil do it that quickly? When the teacher asks Phil, "What is 7 x 2?," he panics. *Jenny just knows it right away. I should*

What's Your Number One?

Think about your favorite popular song. Write it down here:_____ It probably only lasts about four minutes, but have you ever thought about how much time went into making those four minutes of music? Write down your estimate of how many hours of work went into making that awesome tune happen. _____ hours. When you're done, look at the end of the next page.

know it right away. Okay, here goes nothing: "Uhh, twelve. Thirteen. Fourteensixteenteneleven. Twelve. Twelve." When the teacher asks the class which of those answers is correct, Jenny sweetly says, "Fourteen!" Phil thinks to himself, *Curses! How did she KNOW! Why didn't I? I must be bad at math...I hate multiplying!*

Let's get real. Jenny didn't get all the answers right on the first day. She's not a "multiplication natural." There's no such thing. Phil has no *idea* what Jenny's been doing for the past week. When she is home, Jenny's dad helps her to drill her multiplication tables and even teaches her some tricks for remembering the answers. She's not as fast as her dad or her teacher yet, but she's working toward that. At home. Where Phil can't see her. But Phil, like most of us, only thinks about what he sees going on right in front of him. And all Phil sees is Jenny in class, spouting off answers and making it look like she did no work at all.

To Phil, it looks as if Jenny was born with super-strength math neurons that allow her to be an amazingly fast learner. "Super-strength math neurons" is a pretty ridiculous idea, but Phil's not wrong to think Jenny's brain is better at multiplication. It *is* better. That's right. Jenny has *made* her brain better at multiplication through lots and lots of practice. Every time Jenny practices her times tables, her brain makes changes so that each of those paths is clearer and faster. The more she practices, the more Jenny's multiplication pathways become like a superhighway.

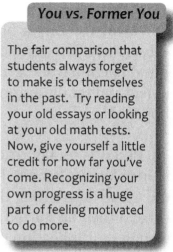

You vs. Former You

The fair comparison that students always forget to make is to themselves in the past. Try reading your old essays or looking at your old math tests. Now, give yourself a little credit for how far you've come. Recognizing your own progress is a huge part of feeling motivated to do more.

Unfair comparisons are pretty much always the source of why people feel stupid in school. That's right. If you feel stupid—ever—it's because you've made an unfair comparison. Phil has taken a perfectly ordinary experience and used it to convince himself that he's bad at math. That's the first step on the road to thinking you're not so smart or even downright stupid. The bottom line is that Phil has no clue what Jenny has been doing. Phil can definitely master multiplication. (And with our help, he did.) But he can never make a fair comparison between his brain and Jenny's. You can never, ever know all of the invisible practice and automating that goes into making someone else amazing at a certain kind of work. Why put your energy into making a meaningless comparison when you could be putting it into making actual progress?

Unrealistic Expectations: Why Trying to Look Smart Makes you Dumb

The best learners alive today are all under the age of two. Babies see their parents doing things like walking and talking, and they want to do those things too. But when they start to try to walk or talk and aren't perfect right away, they don't give up. Maybe they cry a bit or get angry, but it doesn't last. Those setbacks are just temporary. Babies reach those goals because they diligently work at these things every day until the skills are perfect and totally automatic. They don't settle for living without those skills.

Phil was totally ready to give up on himself. Comparing his brain to Jenny's left him feeling like a loser. The unfair comparison was a bad move, but the ways it affected his work were even worse. When he started paying attention to Jenny, Phil had done enough multiplication practice to be able to figure out the right answer in about twenty seconds. Phil hadn't done *nearly* enough automating to give lightning-fast answers that were correct. But Jenny had, and when Phil watched Jenny, he wanted to put the pedal to the metal. This expectation was totally unrealistic. That's like being on that first path through the jungle and trying to drive at superhighway speeds. That's asking for an accident. Each time someone like Phil can't get the right answer as quickly as someone else can, they get more and more frustrated until eventually they decide they must be bad at math, and give up on multiplication entirely.

Why couldn't Phil provide the correct answer as quickly as Jenny could? Because, in trying to match Jenny's speed, he had to rely on guessing. Guessing is the most immediate consequence of unrealistic expectations. When Katie met Jasmine Darzi, she was in her second year of French. At one time, Jasmine had dreamed of standing under the Eiffel Tower, baguette in hand, but lately, French had become kind of a drag. Jasmine had worked so hard, and it had gotten her nowhere. That's why she called Katie. When Katie asked Jasmine to practice by reading the sentence, "Qu'est-ce que vous cherchez?" (In French, that means "What are you looking for?"), she read it very quickly. The problem was that while Jasmine was speaking another language, it definitely wasn't French. For over a year, Jasmine had been guessing. She wasn't really sure how she was supposed to pronounce "Qu'est-ce que," so she just sort of said whatever seemed close. She also wasn't really sure how to pronounce "vous" or "cherchez." So, she made something up for those too. That's like trying to find the gold mine in the jungle by just running in whatever direction you feel like. You may end up in a swamp, you may end up facing a tiger. But the chances you'll guess your way to the gold mine are slim. Until you've carved a solid, reliable path, you need to keep checking that you're going exactly the right way. From Jasmine's perspective, it hadn't *seemed* like guessing; she really had been putting a lot of effort into this, and she was genuinely stressed out.

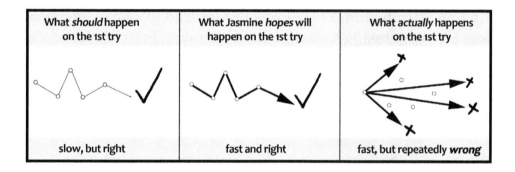

What *should* happen on the 1st try	What Jasmine *hopes* will happen on the 1st try	What *actually* happens on the 1st try
slow, but right	fast and right	fast, but repeatedly *wrong*

So, what was Jasmine's unrealistic expectation? Well, she was speeding along because she thought she should be able to read French like she reads English. But it's totally unfair to compare the way you read French after *one* year to the way you read English after *over ten years of practice*. Jasmine needed to get over that unrealistic expectation. So, she started reading French as though it was the first time she'd read *The Cat in the Hat*. That meant going slowly, sounding out the words, looking new words up, and going one sentence at a time, until she was sure that she was pronouncing every single word in exactly the right way. Jasmine doesn't have to go that slowly anymore—in fact, she's getting faster all the time. And best of all, she's able to make sure it's 100% correct.

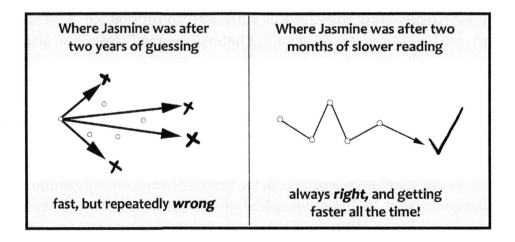

Unrealistic expectations are the reason that we all stop finding learning fun. These expectations lead to a lot of guessing, and a lot of guessing leads to a lot of mistakes. Pretty soon, you've got the bad grades to "prove" your initial assumption that you're not so smart. Students who get trapped in this cycle get more and more frustrated until, ultimately, they just give up. Fortunately, breaking the cycle is easy. You only need to do one thing: fix it.

What Does My Brain Need From Me? Fix-It-Focused Practice

Even when you're taking a break, your brain is hard at work. Your brain is constantly automating the new things that you're doing. Whatever those things are, it automates them. Practicing your violin? It automates it. Picking your nose? Yeah, it automates it. If you're doing reliable, methodical work, it automates it. And if you're guessing, it automates that approach too. Phil was so concerned with being as fast as Jenny was that he made learning his multiplication tables way more stressful than it needed to be. Your job is to make sure that your brain is automating the *right* way of doing things. At first, you're going to need to work slowly enough to ensure that you're getting it right. No rushing.

No guessing. No fudging. You need to do fix-it-focused practice.

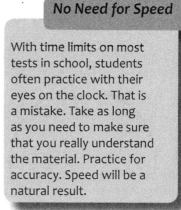

Jasmine was practicing—she was working really hard. But she wasn't fixing her mistakes as she went, and so even after two years of hard work and stress, she still wasn't getting it right. Fix-it-focused practice is the only way that anyone's brain learns something correctly. You start in on something new. At the first sign that something's not clear or might be wrong, you fix it. You figure out exactly what's not working, and then you look it up, double-check your answer, or clarify what you're doing. Then, you keep plugging along until you see something else that's not totally clear. You stop, and you fix it. Then you keep going until you reach the end with guaranteed success. Whatever needs fixing, you fix it.

As you do more and more fix-it-focused practice, you're going to realize something totally crazy: your mistakes are your new best friend. A mistake is any result that you didn't want to get. A wrong answer is a mistake, getting stuck is a mistake, and bombing a quiz is a mistake. And in school, a mistake is like a giant flashing arrow pointing to exactly where you can do fix-it-focused practice. The instant you see a mistake, you should jump at the chance to fix it. Get it done and move on with your life.

In school, everyone makes mistakes all of the time. The difference in people's results comes from how they react when things aren't going the way they expected.

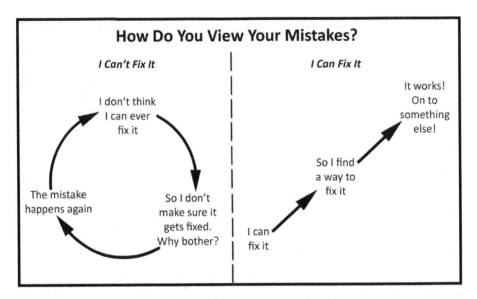

The thing to which you have to pay the closest attention on the "I can't fix it" side is that final arrow—the one that brings you right back to "I can't fix it." As soon as you think a mistake happened because you're just not smart enough, you feel like there's no point in trying to fix it. You do a classic eye roll, let out a pained sigh, maybe do some more stalling, and finish it off with some halfhearted textbook page flipping. But if you don't fix the mistake this time, you're going to have to go through this process all over again the next time this topic comes up. This is a recipe for wasting a ton of time.

Students who get *A*'s don't see every single mistake as a reflection of their intelligence. They did something that didn't work, and they'll do it differently the next time. Just look at the word "mistake." It's a "mis-take." You took the wrong path this time, but next time you don't need to. You got points off because you wrote "definately." Look it up, learn that it's "definitely," and get it right on the next paper.

Actually, we're kind of telling you something that you already know how to do. Everything that you already do to make your life better happens through fix-it-focused practice. If you try on a few outfits before deciding what to wear in the morning, *that's* fix-it-focused practice. If you go grocery shopping, hate the kind of cookies you bought, and get different ones next time, *that's* fix-it-focused practice. You wouldn't settle for eating totally disgusting cookies forever just because you didn't want to look for a new option. **But thanks to the conspiracy, you do settle for grades and experiences in school that are less than your ideal.** Take those fix-it-focused practice skills that you already use, refine them, and then apply them to your work.

> **Why Stop Fixing?**
>
> Fix-it-focused practice is exactly what Edison did. He took a light bulb that burnt out too quickly and was too expensive and fixed it until he ended up with one that people would actually want to buy. Even though that was a great light bulb, people are still fixing the light bulb today. Consider this: Edison's best light bulb lasted for 50 days before burning out. Today's energy-saving light bulbs last for over ten years.

Once you're doing fix-it-focused practice, you'll be amazed at how quickly you can turn all of your grades around. Students often get annoyed when they realize they need to stop and look something up or check their answers. They think of it as "extra work," but that's because of the unrealistic expectation that some people *never* have to look *anything* up. That couldn't be further from the truth. Looking things up when you're not sure of them isn't an extra step in the process; it is the very heart of the process. We can guarantee you that anyone who gets great grades achieves those grades through fix-it-focused practice.

Each time you fix something now, it means that you're making the rest of your life easier. You can make unfair comparisons, develop unrealistic expectations, and spend tons of time feeling stressed out. But the only thing that your brain needs in order to move closer to genius results is fix-it-focused practice. You may not be a math whiz or a French ace yet, but you can train your brain to do that math or that French amazingly. We're going to show you exactly how to do that, and it will help you save yourself years of frustration. Your new mantra is, "Whatever it takes, just fix it now."

Chapter 3

Attention

Make the Most of Your Most Valuable Resource

Now you know how automaticity works, and you've seen how you can use fix-it-focused practice to know any answer correctly at lightning speed. That's awesome, but it's not the whole deal. What you need is a way to control *what* your brain is automating. Meet Attention. In terms of what you need for high school, your attention is the most valuable tool in your brain. Fortunately, the jungle that just taught you about automaticity can teach you a lot about attention too.

On your first day in the jungle, when you initially set out to find that gold mine, you have to take the most basic actions in order to make progress. You chop your way through vines, avoid quicksand and animals, and constantly check your map. That's your job right now, and *you* have to do all of that work yourself. Once you've actually found the gold mine, then you have a totally new set of tasks to complete. You need to figure out how to extract and purify the gold, make the road bigger, and set up transportation to and from the mine.

But come on. You can't possibly do everything at once! There is *way* too much gold. If you're going to build a gold mining empire, you're going to need some help. So each time you figure out the best method for doing one of these tasks, you hire employees to run that part of the operation.

Not So Fast

Note: Remember to provide your employees with a competitive retirement and healthcare plan.

Once you've figured out the mining well enough to teach it to others, you can train a whole team of miners. Because they've got the mining covered, you can leave them to their work and shift your focus to a new task: figuring out how to build the best road. You set some more people to work paving that road, and while they do that, you can shift your focus again to the next task.

Eventually, all of the parts of your operation are running on their own. You can check in with them from time to time, to make sure things are going smoothly. But now, most of your day is free to think about the really big-picture things like figuring out your sales pitch. What can people possibly do with all of this gold? You can put your focus on designing the world's first golden toothbrush, and then solid-gold baby diapers...and then you can make a deal with Nike to create the new all-gold running shoe: the Nike Gold Rush (sure, you won't be quite as speedy at your track meet, but, dude...your shoes are made of solid *gold*).

So, yeah, gold is awesome, but the important part of this example is that if you tried to do all the work yourself, it would take *forever* to build this empire. Yes, you created the vision and the game plan. But you could never come this far without such fantastic employees. By taking over the day-to-day work, they leave you with the time to really focus on each new challenge, so that you can figure out the *best* road to build, and the *best* way to mine...and the *best* all-gold shoelaces to complement your all-gold running shoes.

BRAIN AREAS RECRUITED FOR READING	WHERE'S THE BOSS?
A Little Practice	Basic Words and Sentences
A Lot More Practice	More advanced vocabulary, metaphors, imagery
Tons of Practice	Literary Analysis

This is exactly what happens in your brain. As you can see, whenever you encounter a new challenge, you use your attention to focus on one part of it and break it down until you understand it completely. As you automate your ABC's, the paths in your brain get stronger so that you don't have to think about each individual letter when you read. Then, you put your attention on reading words; once they're automatic, you are free to focus on the meaning of the entire idea. Attention and automaticity have the same relationship as you and your employees have. Together, they can make huge accomplishments possible.

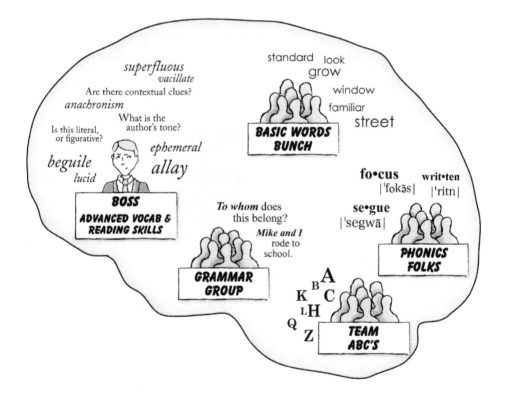

But the lies of the Straight-A Conspiracy aren't limited to your automaticity. And if you don't know exactly how your attention is meant to work, then you're probably making school far harder for yourself than it needs to be.

Problems with Production?

When business is going swimmingly in your gold-mining corporation, the employees in all of the departments are doing what they're told and making simultaneous progress. The boss—the brains of the operation—is there to jump in and fix problems or redirect efforts as needed. That's exactly what is happening with your brain when you're sailing through a homework assignment. Your automaticity is doing what it's told and breezing through the parts that you know, and your attention is doing the troubleshooting. But just like the best bosses, your attention has its limits, and when it gets spread too thin or takes on a task for which it is not prepared, the whole operation can grind to a halt. When that happens, nothing gets done until the boss figures out how to get the process back on track.

Overwhelmed: Why Trying to Impress Leads to Stress

One of the most misleading ideas of the Straight-A Conspiracy—at least when it comes to Attention—is the idea that multitasking is the most efficient way to work. Multitaskers see themselves as members of a super-productive elite. In reality, multitasking is one of the best ways to work *against* your brain.

Here's a basic, inarguable reality about how the brain works:

Your attention cannot effectively multitask.

You just can't do it. Just like overloading any machine, when you try to deal with too many things at once, you're asking your brain to do something it's not equipped to do. Commonly, students get into a state in which they feel stressed because they have so much work and "no time." They think that multitasking is the solution to much of their stress, when actually, it's the cause.

If you just thought to yourself, "No way! I'm so good at multitasking. It makes me so productive," then let's do a little thought experiment:

Can you walk and chew gum at the same time? Yeah.

Could you walk, chew gum, and talk to your friend on the phone about what you're wearing to prom? Of course!

Great. Could you walk, chew gum, talk to your friend on the phone about what you're wearing to prom...and read *Huckleberry Finn* at the same time?

Nope. In order to *sort of* pay attention to your friend and *kind of* get the meaning of the book, you need to switch your attention between the two tasks. That means you're not going to be dealing with either of the tasks well. Your attention can only deal with one *unautomated* task at a time. The idea that your attention can multitask is a *major myth*.

When you're trying to do all four of these tasks—walking, chewing gum, talking to your friend and reading *Huckleberry Finn*—the first two won't be affected, because you've automated them. You can keep walking and chewing gum without even noticing they're happening. But each of the other activities— holding a new conversation and reading a new book—requires your full attention in order to go well. Think about it this way: how long do you think it's going to take you to get through *Huckleberry Finn* (by the way, it's about 320 pages long) if after every sentence, you stop to listen to your friend and respond? Then, when you go back to the book, you have to remind yourself where you were and what was going on before you jump back in. Good luck getting it done in time for class.

Red Pen Alert!

Multitasking doesn't only make work take longer. Researchers have found that people who regularly multitask make about twice as many errors as people who don't.

But the more important point is that you just don't want to put yourself through that! It's totally manic! And that's exactly how you start to feel when you choose to make your brain work this way. You can't do more than one *unautomated* task at once, but school is all about doing *unautomated* tasks; you're learning brand-new things all the time. The more stuff you pile on at once, and the more time pressure you add to the situation, the more you start to feel really overwhelmed.

When you get overwhelmed, that's when things get really un-fun, because not only are you not getting the work done in time... you also feel terrible. You know what we're talking about. It's that tight-chested panic that comes when you think you'll never get a handle on the situation. It's the feeling of having a million things to do and thinking that you'll never get them done in time. We all have had this experience before, and for much of her junior year, our student Aaliyah Davis was spending most of her days feeling like this.

Aaliyah is one of those students who is always busy and is very proud of that fact. She works on the yearbook, designs the set for the play, and competes with the dance team, just to name a few of her activities. She likes school, and she always keeps doing her best and pushing ahead. But as she added more and more activities and responsibilities to her plate, her grades started to slip. She had been an *A* student in the past, but she wasn't ready to drop everything else just to get her schoolwork back on track. One evening, during a session, Hunter and Aaliyah sat down and she opened her honors chemistry book. It was already clear from the look on her face that her mind was elsewhere. Hunter asked what she was thinking about...and out it came. "Oh! Sorry. I was just thinking about when I can finish the posters for our volleyball tournament. I volunteered to do that today." He explained that now wasn't poster time, and that it would be best to finish her chem homework first. "So, is the reaction between...Aaliyah? He-lloooooo?" This time, her answer said it all. "How long do you think it will take me to study for that English test? I also promised my mom that I'd wash the dog. I just have *so much* to do tonight." Aaliyah's attention was all over the place.

The easiest way to think of your attention is that it's like a box in your brain that holds your thoughts. At that moment in time, Aaliyah's attention would have looked something like this:

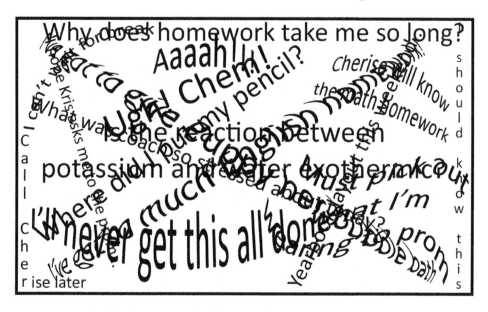

Whoa. Based on this, it's no wonder that it took Aaliyah forever to complete her homework. When you try to put your attention on multiple things, what you end up doing is constantly switching back and forth among them. All that switching makes progress impossible, because you don't focus on *anything* long enough to see it through. And since nothing is getting done, you can stay in this mode for hours. You repeatedly think about— or worry about—each of these things in succession, but you don't make any real headway. For Aaliyah, the result

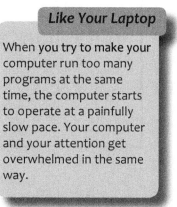

Like Your Laptop

When you try to make your computer run too many programs at the same time, the computer starts to operate at a painfully slow pace. Your computer and your attention get overwhelmed in the same way.

was that she felt frenzied and worried and really stressed out. Aaliyah was totally overwhelmed.

Aaliyah definitely wasn't getting anywhere. Being overwhelmed kept her from moving forward with her work. What Aaliyah didn't realize was that she was putting herself in this stressed-out, overwhelmed state. And she didn't have to quit her activities in order to fix it. She just had to use her attention better.

It was true that Aaliyah did have a lot of things to do. But thinking about all of them at once was definitely not the best way to deal with them. It only made her feel worse, because the human brain doesn't work that way. Hunter helped her to take the mishmash of things in her attention and separate out the tasks. The reality was that if she was going to make progress with *any* of her tasks, Aaliyah had to set aside the English test and the volleyball posters and her Rottweiler's bubble bath and trust that she would get them all done once she finished her chemistry. She had to take charge and completely wipe her mind clear, so that she could have her attention on *just one thing*.

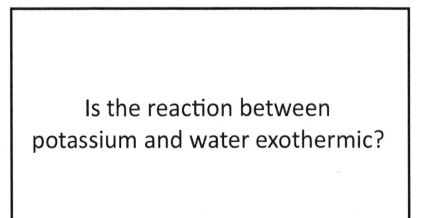

Is the reaction between potassium and water exothermic?

Aaliyah was able to put her other to-do's aside and finally get down to business with her chemistry homework so that she could make progress again. For her, it was about making a plan to deal with all of the things she *needed* to accomplish. But other students max out their attention by focusing on multiple things that *aren't* necessarily essential. Plenty of people pride themselves on being able to watch TV while they do homework. But if you're trying to do both at once, you're not getting the most out of either. The next day, you might find out that you made some pretty obvious mistakes on the math problems. *And* you didn't get to see who was eliminated from *Top Chef.* Just don't risk it. Attention can be on one unautomated thing, and only one. You may tell yourself that you "work best" when music is playing or the TV is on—or that you can text your friends while working—but your brain says that's not true. Homework, TV, music, and phone calls are *all* important. Give them all of your attention...separately.

Any time you feel overwhelmed, it just means that your attention is crowded. It's true—you can't handle this *all at once*. But you *can* handle it. Choose one thing that you need to accomplish and put your full attention on that. When you're done with that, you can deal with the next single piece. Talk to your friend and *then* read *Huckleberry Finn*. Finish chem and *then* study for English. And probably leave the Rottweiler's bubble bath for last.

Letting yourself get overwhelmed is the easiest mistake to fix. That's because one of the coolest things you can do with your attention is to clear it out. **You can only ever do one unautomated thing at a time if you're going to be productive.** By the way, that news should come as a huge relief. You don't have to try to think about ten things at once. To get the most out of your attention, sometimes you need to get rid of everything that's *in* your attention and start over with just one task.

Drawing a Blank: Why Having no Clue is the Only Clue You Need

Have you ever had this experience? You're in class and your teacher asks you a question or hands you a quiz and you don't have the slightest clue where to begin or even what the question means. You find yourself fixating on the problem, but you're making no progress. You're stuck in the mud. You're spinning your wheels. You just can't seem to move forward.

This feeling is awful. It's panic-inducing. It leaves you feeling uneasy. It's pretty much the worst. But, we have a little secret to share with you. You may think that drawing a blank is your brain's way of telling you that you've reached the limit of what you can do or what you know. But in reality, the feeling of drawing a blank is your attention giving you a signal that it wants to dig in and get its hands dirty. If you don't understand something, that doesn't mean you should just skip that section of the test or turn in a half-done homework. Instead, you have to work with the major clue that your attention has given you. So where does the clue lead? Well, to find out, let's go back to Aaliyah's chemistry homework.

Aaliyah did a great job of clearing out her attention so that it was just on her chemistry problem. Now, she was able to get to work. She picked up her pencil, looked at the problem on the worksheet—and looked...and looked...and kept looking at it. An uneasy expression crossed her face. When Hunter asked her what she needed to do, she got frustrated, threw up her hands, and said, "I have no idea! This is totally beyond me." Aaliyah really did feel like she had no idea. But was that the truth? Or, was this material just beyond Aaliyah *right now*?

Obviously, Aaliyah wasn't getting anywhere by reading the question over and over. Aaliyah wanted to abandon ship, but Hunter thought that first, she should take a closer look at the question that she was trying to answer.

Is the reaction between potassium and water exothermic?

In looking at the smaller aspects of this problem, it was clear to Aaliyah where the issue lay. Aaliyah had no idea what "exothermic" means or what the "reaction between potassium and water" was. She couldn't have her attention on the full question if all the individual pieces were not yet automatic for her.

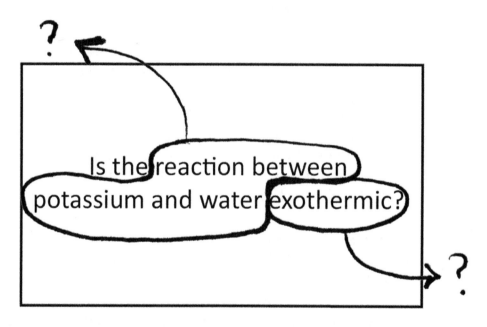

When you zoom in to deal with specific missing pieces of a problem, you can either clarify and refresh them, or you can look them up and learn them for the first time. The word "exothermic" definitely wasn't ringing any bells for Aaliyah, so she went to the textbook. By looking the word up, Aaliyah found out that "exothermic" is the word you use when a reaction gives out heat. Sweet. That's fixed. Aaliyah already was in much better shape because now she knew that what she was really trying to figure out was whether the reaction between potassium and water gives out heat.

So, in order to determine if that reaction gives out heat, Aaliyah just needed to figure out what happens during the reaction between potassium and water. Since she didn't think she knew anything about it, she looked up the reaction online and found tons of videos. Once she clicked on the first one, it became clear why so many people thought this reaction was YouTube-worthy. All of these videos started off with an innocent looking bowl full of water, but once a small piece of potassium was added, things got crazy. First, the potassium would whiz around on the water at a high speed. Then, it would get so hot that it would set itself on fire. Purple fire. Finally, if the piece was big enough, it would explode or even blow up the bowl it was in. That's when Aaliyah suddenly remembered that she had seen this reaction before. Her teacher had demonstrated it in class last Monday, only he'd done it with a much smaller piece of potassium. "Oh, wait! I saw that. Yeah...If exothermic means gives out heat...then that's definitely what it was. Is that it? Is that all it was asking?" Yep. Pretty straightforward, right?

Two minutes ago, Aaliyah panicked and felt totally lost when she read the question. But after learning one fact and reclarifying the other, she had no problem answering. That's because Aaliyah assumed that when she drew a blank and got stuck on this question, it was happening because she'd "maxed out" her intelligence; the question was just too hard for her. Her instinct told her to walk away. But by taking her attention off of the whole question and focusing it on the smaller pieces that were unautomated, Aaliyah was able to dig in and answer the question with no trouble at all.

Now, here's the best part. Whenever you focus your attention on learning or refreshing a particular word or fact, you are making it more and more automatic. Pretty soon, you'll never have to actively refresh it in the future; it will always be there for you. Your attention will be free to focus on the more complicated parts of that subject.

No question you encounter is actually "beyond" you; it's only beyond what you can do before you've looked up and refreshed the pieces. In other words, if you find yourself staring at the question over and over, that is a sign that it's time to retreat...to the back of your textbook. It's perfectly normal to encounter questions or problems that feel like you're trying to move a mountain. But there's no mountain that you can't chip away, one rock at a time. And there's no problem you can't solve if you break it down into small pieces. Your attention makes it possible for you to break down and solve even the most complicated problem; that's why it is so valuable. And you're in charge of it. Use it wisely, grasshopper.

What Does My Brain Need From Me? One Unautomated Piece At a Time

Frustration in school doesn't happen because school is frustrating; it happens because you're asking your attention to do something it's not supposed to be able to do. It's perfectly natural to get overwhelmed or to hit those moments when you have no idea; it happens to everyone—even to the best brain masters out there. But what do you do when you get to that place? Do you let yourself stay in a frenzy, or do you take control of your attention? Do you clear up what you don't understand, or do you stare at the question, hoping the answer will come?

We bet that for years, you've heard people give advice like, "One thing at a time!" and "With persistence, *anything* is possible!" Oh, and of course there's the good old, "Pay attention!" We understand—those wisdom wielders can be annoying. But guess what? *They're exactly right.* In fact, that advice is the work of some really sneaky conspiracy-fighters.

Your attention is an amazingly powerful tool. With your attention, you can focus your mind on the motion of a single atom or the vastness of the universe. You can focus on the fact that someone is professing their undying love for you, or on the fact that an angry warthog is charging at you from just behind them. The point is, you are in control of where your attention goes. And because your attention controls your automaticity, when you choose to put your attention on something, you are *choosing* to make your brain stronger in that subject. Do you know what that means??!! That means that you *control* what your brain becomes.

That's right. With the help of attention, you get to decide what's going to be easy for you. *You decide* what you want to become an expert in—whether you're going to be great at painting portraits or solving mathematical proofs or playing the accordion. Even on an everyday level, you get to decide what things you will consistently get right and how quickly you get them right. That's pretty amazing.

Edison could have spent years staring at that light bulb without knowing where to begin. That's why picking one piece— any piece that isn't working—is so important. Now think back to the list of students' theories from the first chapter. What happens when you are focused on the idea that you "don't have an ear for languages?" The problem is that your attention is on "languages," which is a huge piece. And you can't fix "languages." You *can* fix your Spanish vocab. You *can* fix present tense verbs in French. You can fix small pieces of any specific language until you're fluent. The only thing you need to remember is this: to make the most of your attention, you just need to deal with *one unautomated piece at a time*.

When you saw that the title of this section referred to "attention" as "your most valuable resource," you probably thought of about twenty other things that you would consider more valuable. But now that you know that your attention is the key to customizing your brain, perhaps you'll move it up the "Most Valuable Resources" list a bit. At least to the spot above "chapstick." And by the end of this book, we're sure it will be #1.

Chapter 4

Emotions

Why Feelings Aren't Facts

By controlling your attention, you get to control what you automate. But there's a third aspect of your brain that is happy to get in the way of that process. Your emotions play a *major* part in how you do in school. They can make your study time fly by, or they can actually shut down your ability to learn without you even realizing what has happened. That means you can't just let them run wild. But running wild is exactly what they want to do, because emotions come from the "animal" part of your brain.

The Purpose of Emotions

Most people don't stop to consider why we have emotions or what they really do. For the most part, things like anger, jealousy, and joy just seem like little whims that pop up from time to time, adding spice to the day. But that is far from true. Emotions are one of the oldest and most essential parts of the human brain, because they are specifically meant for dealing with serious stuff—like matters of life and death.

If you were a caveman, you didn't need to turn on the TV to get your daily dose of drama. All you had to do was walk outside. If you wanted a snack, then you couldn't just raid the fridge; you had to get the whole tribe together to kill a woolly mammoth. Once you got to that yummy, steaming beast carcass, you might have found a sabre-toothed tiger munching on your hard-earned mammoth, which was basically the stone age equivalent of someone stealing your tater tots. To top it off, your fellow tribespeople would have had less-than-stellar manners. After dinner, if one of them took a liking to your blanket...or your mate...you might have found yourself with a rock in your skull.

Cavemen had to be all about survival. They didn't have the time to analyze or philosophize because for prehistoric predators, dinnertime was all the time. Cavemen needed to react right away. These life and death situations were exactly when emotions saved the day. That's because emotions short-circuit the human brain and trigger the behaviors necessary for survival.

If a caveman saw a snake, instinct would take over; he was essentially programmed to freeze up and then back slowly away, trying not to attract the snake's attention. In that moment, that was the *only action* that the caveman could do—he could not think to do anything else. That's because a very specific part of his brain had taken over—a part of the brain that you still depend on today.

Inside your brain is a small region called the *amygdala* (uh-MIG-duh-luh). It's shaped just like an almond...and it makes you do pretty *nutty* things. (Ba-dum ching!) You can think of the amygdala as the gatekeeper to your attention. If your attention is the boss of the jungle, then the amygdala is the boss' bodyguard. And nobody gets to see the boss without the amygdala's say-so. When

It's Greek to Me!

Amygdala actually comes from the Greek word for "almond." That's why scientists chose that peculiar-sounding name.

the amygdala senses danger, it puts your attention on lockdown. Your amygdala does this to your attention as a self-defense tactic so that you don't think. If you're encountering a snake or some other threat, you can't afford to waste your attention on anything that's not related to your survival. In other words, when your brain is in "fear mode," you literally cannot think straight. That means that if you told the caveman the snake wasn't poisonous, or asked him to think about a math problem, or any other piece of information, he wouldn't even hear it; the amygdala would block all that information from his attention, and he'd just continue running away or climbing a tree.

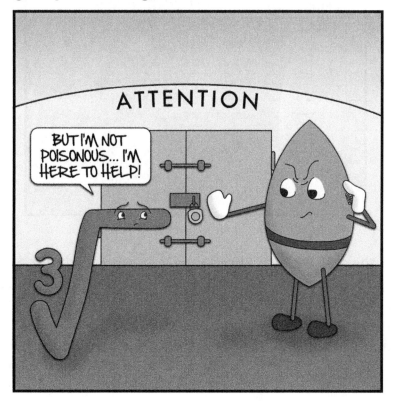

But the amygdala has good times too. The boss' bodyguard may be burly and scowl a lot, but underneath that tough exterior, he's a fun-loving guy. When your brain is in "joy mode" and things are going well and there are no predators in sight, the amygdala switches from stone-faced bodyguard to gracious host.

Your attention is fully accessible; if you're in a good mood, then learning is like an open house party. In fact, scientists have shown that while fear prevents learning, feeling happy actually makes learning easier to do.

In the 21st century, the things you ask your brain to do on a daily basis have changed, but what hasn't changed is how much power your emotions wield over your brain as a whole. Structurally speaking, if you took your brain and peeled it like an onion (please don't try this at home), the outermost layer is the most uniquely "human." That layer is credited with being responsible for complex and abstract thinking, which in modern times includes all of your schoolwork. But as you go deeper and deeper toward the core, where your amygdala dwells, your brain is more and more like an animal's. The "animal"

Let's Get Physical

When you experience fear, blood rushes to your feet to prepare you to run away. When you experience anger, blood rushes to your hands to prepare you to fight.

parts of your brain deal with the most basic survival instincts—things like breathing, hunger, thirst...and emotions. Those needs are so essential that they can easily overpower the outer layers. It doesn't matter if you've done your ten thousand hours of practice. It doesn't matter if you're a genius. If you get hungry during class, then in an instant, your animal brain can shut that all down and make you as stupid as a caveman.

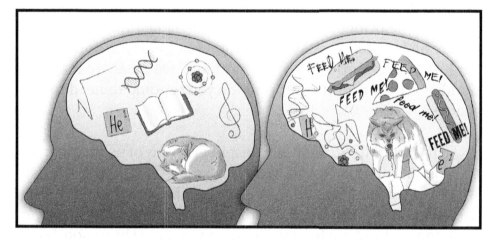

Your animal brain is really good at its job, and emotions can be extremely powerful—and extremely distracting. But there's good news. It's totally possible to discipline your emotions and train your brain's animal responses to certain situations. By doing that, you guarantee that information can get into your attention whenever you need it to. Basically, you beat cavemen any day, because you get to be in charge of your emotions. And, your snacks don't fight back. That's what we call progress.

There's a Time and Place for Emotions: Why Cavemen Fail Math Class

Today, the natural fear response is still beneficial in life-and-death situations. For instance, if your teacher went around the classroom placing a King Cobra on each student's desk, it would be perfectly reasonable for everyone to freeze up and stay as still as possible, hoping that the snake might just slither away. That animal-like response is really helpful. Thank you, amygdala.

While fear can be a good response for dealing with a snake, it is a terrible response for dealing with schoolwork. If your teacher goes around the classroom placing a math test on each student's desk, and you are afraid of math, what happens? You guessed it. You treat that math test like a King Cobra. Your brain goes into "fear mode" and then your amygdala has to respond. "We're on lockdown, people!!!!" From that point on, nothing can get into your attention. And by "nothing," we mean no math, no numbers...no *any* of the information you're going to need to take that test.

Thanks to the Straight-A Conspiracy, many of us have learned to be afraid of a particular subject, like math. And guess what? Anything you do over and over on a daily basis is practice—even dreading math. Automaticity makes it easier and faster for you to become afraid each time math comes up. (Do 10,000 hours of dreading, and you could be a math-fear genius!) No matter what subject it is, if you've trained your brain to think it's scary or intimidating, then you've trained your brain to close off your attention—the *exact* part of your brain that you need to use in order to learn.

This is exactly what happened to Meghan Walsh. Meghan was a senior who loved her government class and was running for Student Council. She was a conscientious student who enjoyed most of her classes. Math just had always been the subject that was harder than the rest. So, when it came time to decide whether to sign up for calculus, she got really nervous about what was to come. In Meghan's school, the calculus teacher had a reputation for being really tough; but Meghan also knew that colleges would like her better if she took on the challenge. So she signed up, and then she counted down the days until the dreaded class began.

Each day of senior fall, Meghan entered the calculus classroom full of worry that she wouldn't be able to handle the class. For the first week, things actually went okay—there was a lot of review from last year, and most of the new concepts were pretty easy. But by week three, it was all going just as she had feared it would. Meghan really had to force herself even to walk through the door of the classroom. Each day, freaked out that she'd get left behind or ruin her chance at attending a good college, she would try and try to understand the lesson. But somehow, it never seemed to have sunken in by the time she left. Her math homework took longer than the rest of her subjects combined, her quiz grades were terrible, and pretty soon, she just resigned herself to a terrible calculus fate. Obviously, what she'd always heard was true: calculus was totally impossible.

Is That a *Fact*?

There was a huge problem...and it wasn't Meghan's brain. By being afraid of calculus class, Meghan was doing the same thing to her brain that happened to the caveman. She thought calculus was scary, so before class even began, her amygdala had already put her attention on lockdown. New information absolutely could not get in! And each time she was faced with a math assignment, she froze up and then backed off, just as she would have done with a snake. As long as Meghan was afraid, her ability to learn stayed switched off, and she couldn't make any progress.

If she was ever going to conquer her fear, Meghan needed to separate the *feelings* she was having about calculus from the *facts* of the situation. That way, Meghan would really be able to see whether feelings were ruling her work.

Thought #1: Calculus is "flat-out impossible."
Is that a *fact*?
"Yeah."

Really? Interesting. So, have no humans *ever* been able to do calculus? What about high school humans, specifically? Can calculus just *not be done by anyone*? If that's not true, then the idea that calculus is "impossible" is only a *feeling*.

"OK, fine. Calculus is impossible for *me*. I can't do it!"

Thought #2: Calculus is impossible for *me*.

You haven't learned *any* calculus this year? Even the most basic pieces?

"Well, some."

OK, so then that's a feeling too.

Thought #3: It's not impossible, it's just too hard. I can't do well.

Have you, in life, automated things? Have you ever learned anything new?

"Yes."

So then it's a fact that your automaticity works. Can you use your attention to break down calculus?

"Ugh. Yes."

Great. So with fix-it-focused practice, you *could* do well.

Thought #4: Calculus is scary, like a poisonous snake or a tiger.

"I get it, I get it. Feeling."

Excellent. The picture is becoming clearer.

As Meghan separated the feelings from the facts, she realized that her feelings about calculus had been winning. She had treated them as facts, and in return, they had led her to a place where calculus was so scary that it really *was* impossible for her to learn it. But while Meghan thought it was impossible to learn because of *calculus*, it was actually impossible to learn because of her *emotions*.

Meghan's scared response to math had become a habit; she had automated her fear. When Meghan finally took time to separate the feelings from the facts, she was able to see how much that habit was hurting her. But habits take some time to fully break. What was Meghan supposed to do if her fear returned unexpectedly in the middle of math class? She couldn't say, "Wait! Stop the class! Hold everything! I need to take a few minutes to look at my feelings and facts right now!" She needed something that would bring her back to the work in an instant.

When Your Attention Is Being Hijacked, Just Hit RESET

When your emotions get going, they take over your attention and control how you feel, what you think, and even what you see. Thankfully, this is not a one-way process. Just as your emotions trigger certain perspectives, a switch in perspective can trigger a switch in your emotions. For example, imagine that you're in a car. Traffic has slowed to a crawl and the car in front of you is recklessly weaving in and out of different lanes, honking his horn annoyingly, and maneuvering as if he's the only person with somewhere to be. He must be a horrible driver—and a horrible person. You decide to pull up alongside of that car to give the driver a piece of your mind, but when you do, you see that it's a terrified man whose wife is in the passenger seat, clearly pregnant...and clearly in labor. In an instant, you're moving out of the way, honking your horn at the other cars too, helping him to get to the hospital. The blame and anger you felt is gone. With one new piece of information, your perspective changed, and your emotion went away.

Fortunately, the joy of a new baby isn't the only thing that can change your emotions. You already know how to do it yourself. You are actually able to reset your emotional mode to one that is neutral enough that you can think clearly. That's what happens anytime that you are furious at your friend but then decide that getting into a screaming match isn't worth it. That's what happens when you feel really disappointed about not making the soccer team, but then decide it's for the best. That's what happens when you get cast in the school play, but then decide not to triumphantly celebrate all day, because your best friend didn't get cast and you don't want to make her feel bad. In other words, you choose a new perspective that you know will lead to the best outcome.

Those choices happen so instantaneously that often, you're not even aware that they are *choices*. But what you're really doing in that momentary flash is recognizing the emotion that has come up, evaluating it, and then overriding it with reason.

It's great that you've already trained your brain to make these split-second emotional changes. But you can't *always* rely on what's currently automatic for you. You've trained your brain not to start unnecessary fights, but you may also have trained it to be scared of math tests. Sometimes, changing your emotion has to take some time and feel much more deliberate. You've got to talk yourself into moving forward. Essentially, you need to do fix-it-focused practice on your emotions, gradually improving how quickly you can reset your emotion until eventually, your new perspective is automatic.

Once Meghan really understood what her fear was doing, she could finally see that her emotions had tricked her into believing that she would "never get calculus." It was time to take down her fear.

Meghan needed to be on the lookout whenever she was working on math. Every time her fear popped up, she needed to override that emotion by changing her perspective on the math; she needed to hit RESET. A RESET is a statement you tell yourself that helps you to clear away an unhelpful emotion, so that you can take back control of your attention.

Whenever she started to feel afraid, Meghan would tell herself exactly what she needed to hear in order to RESET that emotional state: "What's there to be afraid of? It's just math. I've got this." In the beginning, Meghan could tell that her words didn't exactly match how she felt; the fear was still there, and she had to fake that cool confidence a bit in order to get her mind off of being afraid. Sometimes, she'd even take it further: "I looooove doing this math! It's just the *best.*" Meghan didn't necessarily believe it, but she faked it enough to bring her attention back to the work. Over time, the better she came to understand the material, the less frequently that fear would pop up, and the less she had to "fake" feeling ready to do the math. Just like learning 2+2 or reading, Meghan trained her brain to jump straight to her new "math-friendly" attitude. Eventually, it seemed ridiculous to her that she'd ever been afraid of math. After all, math was just math. Squiggles on a paper. Not a cobra.

Bad Feelings in the Classroom: How Students Get Tricked Into Hating School

If left unchecked, emotions start to do something far more dangerous than just hijacking your attention. Your emotions start to affect your entire view of reality. Think about this. You're going along with your day, and you're in a fantastic mood. Then, all of a sudden, you realize that you left the giant English essay that you've been working on all week at home—and it's due next period. Ugh! Everything that happens for the rest of the day gets on your nerves. "Oh! That's *real great* that you got a new jacket, *Steve*!" "No, mom! I *don't* want a delicious cookie!" "What the !@%$#%@ are you looking at?" You forgot your homework, which annoyed you, and your emotion has twisted your view of reality so that you experience everything as being annoying—even though it's all perfectly normal. Cookies are just cookies, and Steve's jacket is neither annoying nor exciting; in reality, it's just outerwear. But when you're blinded by your emotion, it changes the way you feel about those cookies and that jacket and everything else that happens to you.

A few hours after snapping at your mom for offering you cookies, it's likely that you could recognize that you were just being emotional. In retrospect, being angry about cookies is clearly unreasonable. We can all generally tell (whether or not we like to admit it) when something we did was motivated by jealousy or anger or excitement or fear. But there is one secret emotion that doesn't feel like an emotion at all. This feeling is poison for school, because it seems more like a fact than any other. It does a frighteningly good job of altering your view of reality, and many people go their whole lives unknowingly letting this emotion dictate the choices that they make. All of the tricks of the conspiracy work together to create one specific emotional experience in you: the experience of feeling stupid.

Here's where it *all* comes together. Unfair comparisons, unrealistic expectations, getting overwhelmed—these are all ways that the conspiracy tricks you into viewing perfectly ordinary experiences as a sign that there may be something wrong with your brain. You don't know the answer as quickly as some other kid so, because you're not thinking about automaticity and unseen work, you feel stupid. And that feeling is the absolute worst feeling to have in response to your mistakes, because what most of us call "feeling stupid" is really the emotion of shame.

Shame is the feeling that comes from thinking that there is something wrong with you, and that makes it just about the most unpleasant feeling in the world. And when something causes a feeling that is that un-fun, the obvious

> **Sound Familiar?**
>
> Here are some of the things people do to keep from being wrong in front of others: not speaking up in class, acting as if they already know the answer, making excuses for why they didn't get it right, hiding tests that have bad grades. These are ways of trying to avoid the experience of feeling stupid.

choice is to go to great lengths to avoid it. Well, guess what? Your brain is wired to support that. Every emotion motivates specific behaviors, and in the case of shame, you naturally cover up and avoid. When you get ashamed or embarrassed, you want to cover your face. You want to avoid your mistakes, or whatever else may be the source of your embarrassment.

Here's why that's a major problem. Fix-it-focused practice is about bringing your mistakes into the open, facing them in an unemotional way, and taking action to make them better. If you feel "stupid," then your natural reaction will be the exact opposite: you *won't* fix your mistakes, your attention *won't* be available, and in the end, you actually *won't* improve.

Those behaviors will obviously lead to less-than-stellar grades. But the crazy part of this is that when that grade is sitting on your desk, it's hard to realize that shame is responsible for what happened. Instead, the conspiracy has trained you to take it as a "sign" that you really *aren't* that smart. And thinking that way is only going to fire up that shame all over again. You tell yourself that you have "proof" of your lack of intelligence.

This cycle can go on for years, because even though we all talk about "feeling" stupid, almost no one thinks of it as a RESET-able emotion; we don't treat "feeling stupid" like a *feeling* at all. Instead, we take the experience of *feeling* stupid and mistakenly conclude that we actually *are* stupid.

Students who have been coming to that conclusion for a

while often reach a place where they seem pretty *un*-emotional about the whole thing. They've seen the evidence, they "know" they're not good at this particular subject, and they've accepted their fate. Thanks to the conspiracy, "stupid" doesn't feel like a temporary emotion; "stupid" feels permanent. But the students who have accepted that feeling without challenging it are totally missing out! Feeling "stupid" is not a lifelong diagnosis; it's just an emotion, and it just needs a RESET.

Kyle Kaminski: The Most Stressed-Out Kid on the Block

Kyle Kaminski was a stocky kid with a wild mop of brown hair and an even wilder imagination. Everything Kyle did, he did with extreme intensity, and school was no exception. Every day, he would go to his room, spend hours on his homework, and emerge looking like he'd just lost a fist fight with Chuck Norris. Clearly, school was stressful for Kyle, and anyone who met him could see that he had a whole mess of emotions going on with anything related to school. Often, Hunter would ask Kyle, "*Why is your schoolwork going like that?*" Each time, Kyle would snap out of his frenzy and with sudden clarity say, "Because I'm stupid."

Whenever Kyle couldn't take the stress and panic anymore, he would put the work down and turn to something that was always fun. Kyle loved all things fantasy. He was an expert in several sub-fields, including but not limited to orks, goblins, elves, dragons and magic spells. He had read every word of every book of J.R.R. Tolkien's at least ten times. He owned not one but two cloaks, although he reserved them for special occasions, like when he was leading a game of Dungeons and Dragons. Kyle could spend hours spewing little known facts about Middle Earth or the Seven Kingdoms of Westeros, and he had taught himself to speak Elvish.

Kyle's greatest ambition was to be the next Tolkien—to create a fantasy world as rich and full as the one in *The Lord of the Rings*. What he didn't realize was that he already had. In his efforts to understand why his work took so long and why his grades were low, Kyle had created a fantasy world in which he had completely convinced himself that his brain was defective, and that there was nothing he could do about it. Kyle was what we call a *stupichondriac*.

A hypochondriac is a person who spends way too much time worrying about his or her health. When a hypochondriac gets a stomachache, he thinks it's a sure sign that he has contracted some exotic disease. It doesn't even occur to him that the real cause of his pain might be the three chili dogs that he inhaled for lunch. Stupichondria works in the same way. When a stupichondriac makes a mistake, he doesn't think that it's a small thing that he can fix—he thinks it's a sure sign that he's just not smart. Kyle spent every minute of his study time looking for "evidence" of his stupidity in everything that happened, and there was barely any room in his attention for the work.

After years of this behavior, Kyle had spent so much time automating those emotional responses that once he was in that mess, it was like he couldn't escape. When Hunter talked to Kyle about this inescapable mental place, Kyle had an idea. "It's just like the Demiplane of Dread. In Dungeons and Dragons, the Demiplane of Dread is where the dark lords rule over their domains. You get pulled *into* the Demiplane of Dread by the Mists...which are like your emotions, pulling you into this inescapable domain. Many times, I've been with my adventuring party when our fires have been blotted out by the mists. But I love when that happens, because Ravenloft is my *favorite*! Did you know..."

"Okay! Okay! That works; you totally get this." Hunter had to interrupt. The session was only so long.

"It's alright," Kyle retorted. "This is pretty advanced stuff."

So, if Kyle's D&D character, Kavendithas Lorearthen, the dwarf cleric, had to be afraid of the Demiplane of Dread, then in school, Kyle had to be wary of entering what we started to call the Demiplane of Doubt. The second that Kyle heard that name, he instantly understood why going to that place was a problem. The Demiplane of Doubt was Kyle's personal place of no return; he was pulled in by his emotions and his stupichondria, and he could wander around in there indefinitely. If you could actually see Kyle's Demiplane of Doubt, it would look something like this:

It's pretty obvious that after going through the Demiplane of Doubt, Kyle's process would be unpleasant and would take forever, and the work that Kyle actually did wouldn't be *A* material. After all, each time Kyle made a mistake or got confused, he would go through this enormous loop of shame, self-doubt, fear, and lots of other unhelpful emotions. Of course, the alternative would have been just to look something up, learn it, and move on. But Kyle's attention was completely hijacked by his emotions— especially shame. What he could have completely accomplished in one hour, he partially accomplished in three. And at the end, when he still didn't understand it, well, that just became more evidence that he was "stupid." The stronger that evidence seemed to be, the more helpless Kyle felt to do anything about it. It didn't even matter that countless people, from teachers to his parents to his friends, had tried to give Kyle advice and encouragement. Kyle's emotions were blocking *everything* from getting into his attention.

Because Kyle loved fantasy so much, whenever he started a new series, he was happy to dig in. His attention was totally available for learning. That's why he was able to remember all of those facts. Kyle had spent months perfecting his Elvish accent—a sign that he was perfectly capable of fix-it-focused practice. But when it came to school, he felt "stupid" and there was no attention available to perfect anything.

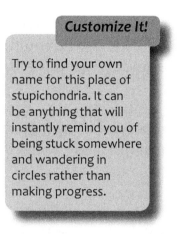

Customize It!

Try to find your own name for this place of stupichondria. It can be anything that will instantly remind you of being stuck somewhere and wandering in circles rather than making progress.

Kyle felt as if he was spending a ton of time on schoolwork. He was. But when you got right down to the facts, the reason why Kyle wasn't doing well in school was because he didn't fix his mistakes. Instead, he spent his time feeling bad about them. The solution was very straightforward.

Kyle needed to separate the feelings from the facts if he was ever going to break this cycle. Kyle thought it was a *fact* that he was stupid, but he'd reached his "fact" through a mess of unfair comparisons and unrealistic expectation. Those weren't scientific conclusions; they were *emotional* conclusions, and there was no place for them in Kyle's school day. But while his attention was on all of those feelings, Kyle was totally ignoring something that *was* a fact: his automaticity and attention worked fine. You may think that being fluent in Elvish is "not practical for everyday life." It isn't. But the important thing to note was that Kyle had taught himself a foreign language. Flawlessly. And if he could make Elvish automatic, he should be fine with sophomore English and math classes.

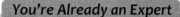

You're Already an Expert

Remembering celebrity trivia, the stats of your favorite sports team, or the ins and outs of video games means that your brain is ready to automate any school subject too.

If Kyle was going to clear his attention of stupichondriac thoughts, he would need something to serve as a substitute—a thought that would be more productive. With the right RESET, he could skip right over the automated doubt and shame and get down to the work.

RESETs often work best when they're personal; the most important thing is that it means something clear to *you*. Perhaps unsurprisingly, Kyle's RESET was the following:

Apparently, that was the Dwarf phrase for, "Axes of the Dwarves! The Dwarves are upon you!" (Hey, you get to decide on whatever phrase works for you.) What is great about the RESET Kyle chose is that it was really specific and personal to *him*, so he would always know how to muster up the courage to charge his way out of the Demiplane of Doubt.

With his RESET as a touchstone, Kyle was unstoppable. As soon as he started to feel bad about a mistake, he could stop what he was doing and shout (or whisper), "Axes of the Dwarves! The dwarves are upon you!" to cut off that unhelpful emotion before he entered the Demiplane of Doubt. By saying that phrase to himself, he forced himself to take charge of his emotion. He used the RESET over and over again, and in time, his thought process became entirely different. After fixing enough of his mistakes, Kyle realized his brain could handle anything, and feeling stupid became a thing of Kyle's past.

RIVER OF ABUNDANCE
FRUITS OF LABOR
Knowalot
YOU SHALL PASS!
Mountains of Knowledge
MATH WIZARD
THE HILLS ARRALYVE
AWESOMES CREEK
Wisdom Woods
FRUITS OF LABOR
THE DISCUV FAIRIES
Sea of Opportunity
Mountains of Dread
THE AWESOMENESS MONSTER

Zack McManus: The Kid Who Couldn't Care Less

Stress attacks, Demiplanes of Doubt, and hair that looks as if you fought with Chuck Norris are not the only indicators that your emotions have interfered with how you're doing in school. We've got someone else for you to meet.

Zack McManus was the anti-Kyle Kaminski. While Kyle was high-strung, Zack McManus lived his life at a consistently chill pace. His voice had the low, mellow quality of a surfer dude. He wore baggy pants, and every day for breakfast he ate a fully-loaded meatball sub. Zack had a great sense of humor. And it was basically impossible to get him worked up. If Kyle's school day was about total emotion, then Zack's was about no emotion.

Zack had perfected the art of switching off his brain the moment he walked through the doors of his high school. He thought everything that his school expected him to learn was a waste of time. So, he didn't do any work, and he didn't try. It was annoying when his parents nagged him, but, by and large, he just did his thing. Mostly, that consisted of spacing out and then nodding thoughtfully whenever the teacher looked in his general direction.

Upon meeting Zack, one could easily have concluded that he was just one of those kids who doesn't care about school. He didn't seem bothered by his bad grades. In fact, unlike Kyle, he seemed to have no emotion about school whatsoever. But we knew enough kids just like Zack to know what was behind his seemingly indifferent exterior.

It's a Feel-Good Activity

Eating tasty food or laughing at a joke is pleasurable because your brain releases a "feel-good" chemical called dopamine. Guess what else is a major dopamine trigger? Learning. That's right, your brain is wired to love learning.

Zack was pretty convinced that "not caring" was just his personality and that getting excited about school just wasn't him. That was no big surprise. People misinterpret the "whatever" attitude all the time. They think it means that the student has never cared about school, but they couldn't be more wrong. In reality, human beings are all hardwired to love learning. But the messages of the Straight-A Conspiracy are so subtly powerful that they attack that love of learning until students come to believe that school is pointless. Kyle's trouble in school was that he was stuck feeling stupid. Students like Zack are usually one step past that. They've experienced those feelings of doubt and shame and fear early on, and they have found a way to avoid feeling them ever again.

| STUDENTIS EXCITICUS | STUDENTIS INSECURUS | STUDENTIS AFRAIDICUS | MISTAKUS AVOIDICUS | ATTENTIS MINIMUS |

You know how when your parents are complaining that you didn't do something they asked you to do, you say, "Whatever"? That "whatever" is a brilliant emotional strategy. By deciding that what they're saying doesn't *really* matter, you don't have to feel bad about not doing it. In terms of avoiding unpleasant feelings, **Whatever is Clever**. If you really think about it, "whatever" doesn't start from a place of not caring; it's a way that you choose to *get* you to a place of not caring. That place of not caring is really the emotion of apathy—having no feelings about anything. If you're apathetic about school, then it won't excite you, but it also won't upset you. If your only goal is to protect yourself from feeling guilty or bad or bummed out, then getting to a state of apathy is a neat, smart solution.

As it turned out, Zack wasn't just a kid who didn't care about school; he was a kid who had *trained himself* to not care about school. The more Zack opened up to us about his history as a student, the clearer it became that he had reached the point of apathy for a reason. As early as elementary school, he had felt as if he wasn't as smart as he should be in math and writing. Whenever he didn't understand the material, he would start to feel stupid. He'd guess at the answer or stress himself out. Early on, Zack had become a huge stupichondriac. But rather than dwelling on it, like Kyle did, Zack had decided that the easiest thing to do was to step back and stop paying attention. Feeling stupid, especially in front of his friends, felt awful. It makes total sense that as a little kid, Zack would have done anything he could to avoid having that experience again. And Zack realized pretty quickly that if he told himself that school didn't matter, then he didn't have to care that he wasn't doing well in it.

While avoiding his schoolwork altogether had dampened some of those negative feelings, being apathetic about school had come with some pretty heavy consequences. Zack felt as if he had been avoiding the work for so long that he had no chance of ever catching up, so he shouldn't even bother trying. He had so thoroughly switched off his emotions that even asking him to do a tiny fix was like asking him to move a mountain. Those feelings were keeping him

Why You Procrastinate

People don't procrastinate because they're lazy. People procrastinate because they're emotional. Shame, fear, and self-doubt trigger that desire to put off getting started on your work.

stuck in a cycle just as strong as Kyle's Demiplane of Doubt. If Zack was going to find a way to move forward, he would clearly have to look to the facts.

Zack may have felt like school was a waste of time. He may have felt like he'd never use any of the stuff his teachers taught anyway. But there was one fact that he couldn't avoid: Zack's dad had said that until Zack improved his grades, he couldn't use the car. Zack wasn't in a place yet where the "love of learning" or the "importance of preparing for your future" was going to push him past this emotional hurdle. (In fact, when people said those things, it made him want to vomit.) But what he *did* care about was his social life. So he started simply, with a RESET that worked with how he felt at that moment: "If I want to use the car, I have to get this done." It wasn't inspirational, but it did the job. It made his attention available for fix-it-focused practice. Moment by moment, whenever he needed a push, he reminded himself to keep going by repeating that sentence.

By the end of the semester, Zack's fix-it-focused practice wasn't just getting him car usage—it was actually paying off. Zack was kind of enjoying getting *B*'s instead of *F*'s. By that point, the car was old news, and his RESET had evolved. Now, if he felt like skipping his homework, he'd remind himself that—although he'd never admit it to anyone—he always felt better when he got an *A*. Zack wasn't a kid who "didn't care about school," because kids like that don't occur in nature. Often the kids who claim to care about school the least are the ones who have been affected the most by their grades. Zack was a kid who forced himself to stop caring about school, because he had the wrong idea about his intelligence. Once Zack separated the feelings from the facts and started to do the work again, his natural love of learning— which had been squashed for ten years—returned in no time. You can squash it. You can strangle it. You can ignore it. You can try every way you can think of to kill it. But your love of learning is such a fundamental part of how your brain works that no matter what you do, it will never go away.

What Meghan, Kyle, and Zack learned to do is exactly what you need to learn to do. They all became masters of their emotions, recognizing when they were in an emotional mode that was hijacking their attention, and learning to RESET it. Then, they took that RESET and used it so often that it became automatic, until eventually, the fear, shame, and apathy went away completely. Here's a quick guide to which emotions are helpful— and harmful—when it comes to learning. You can use this as you learn to become (dungeon) master of your own emotions and be the boss of your attention!

Emotions that Help Your Attention	Emotions that Hijack Your Attention
Confidence	Discouragement/Helplessness
Joy/Happiness	Intimidation/Anxiety/Fear
Value/Pride	Embarrassment/Feeling Stupid
Curiosity/Wonder/Interest	Boredom/Apathy
Love of the Subject or Class	Jealousy of Peers
Desire (Your goals)	Frustration/Anger
Neutral (No Opinion)	Contempt/Hatred/Annoyance

What Does My Brain Need From Me? Catch the Emotion and RESET

Emotions are supposed to be temporary states, but if you don't RESET the unhelpful ones, they can last for a really long time. The reason why people reach the point of stupichondria is because emotions cause people to reject any information that doesn't agree with what they're feeling; the emotion is so strong that it feels truer than any logic that people might hear. Students like Kyle and Zack hold on to their negative feelings for years, but the crazy part is that it takes almost no time to get rid of them.

Meghan said she would "never get calculus." Kyle thought that "being good at fantasy stuff doesn't count." Zack thought he just wasn't a "school" person. Sound familiar? Think back to the theories about lacking "an ear for languages" and being "a bad test taker" that we showed you in Chapter 1.

What's really behind all of these theories? Emotions. Sure, these students made unfair comparisons and had unrealistic expectations. And it's true that once those things had gotten them off track, they asked too much of their attention and didn't fix their mistakes. But *none of that would have happened* if it weren't for emotions. In fact, this list of theories is the end product of a long, complex sequence of attention-hijacking emotions that consistently sabotage our learning process. The Straight-A Conspiracy trains people to have unhelpful emotional responses that make them doubt their brains—and ruin their grades. All of those emotional thoughts, from "I'm just bad at this" to "This doesn't matter" shut down your attention and *actually make you dumber*, which makes other people look smarter in your eyes.

There is no one who "doesn't care about school" from the getgo. We all care *so deeply* about school, and about doing well in life and being smart, that these emotions run wild and pull us off track. If we didn't care about how quickly or easily we could get something right, then we'd all just plug away at those mistakes with no stress at all. If we didn't feel frustrated or ashamed, then we'd have no reason to give up. So now you know, it's not just that the conspiracy spread these lies; it's that these lies took over the deepest, most animal part of your brain...and then they turned it against you. And the result of that is that you just live your life, thinking that your emotions are telling you the truth about who you are and what you can be.

You can't let your emotions determine who you think you are. You have to *manage* your emotions based on who you want to be. After all, who's in charge here? As Meghan, Kyle, and Zack all found out, the life you want doesn't just happen. You need to take charge and make sure that it's going the way you want it to go right now. What fix-it-focused practice will do for your neurons, a RESET will do for your emotions. With these two tools, you can take total control of your experience of school—and ultimately your experience of life—on a day-to-day basis. You now have all of the essential tools you need to be the master of your brain.

Chapter 5

The Easiest Decision You'll Ever Make

Now that you've come *this* far...we have one final bomb-drop. Make sure you're sitting down. This isn't going to be easy to hear. (deep breath...)

For a teenager who's supposed to be all rebellious, you sure are a sheep.

Seriously. Not necessarily the woolly kind that leads to sweaters, but the conformist kind that goes where he or she is told to go and does what he or she is told to do. Sheep follow the flock. They don't question the shepherd, or where the shepherd is leading them. Whatever the shepherd makes them do, that's what their life is. That's you. Baa-aa-aa-aah.

Think about it. For your entire life, you were consistently fed messages about people being born geniuses, and you swallowed them. All around you, you saw what you thought was evidence of some people "just getting it" and you treated it as truth. You felt what the conspiracy wanted you to feel. You did what the conspiracy wanted you to do. You never questioned it; you just went along with it.

Worst of all, you turned against yourself. You became your own worst enemy. You attacked yourself when your classes didn't go well and learned to take every mistake as a reflection of your lack of intelligence. In other words, you thought there was something wrong with you, when, in reality, there never was.

But everything has changed. Now you know the truth about your brain. You understand how automaticity works. You know what your attention can do. You know how to RESET your emotions. The fact that you can rely on your automaticity, attention, and emotions means that your intelligence is never in question. And that means that your eyes can now be open. Everywhere you look, you'll be able to catch people in the act of promoting the conspiracy's ideas. You'll see your classmates, parents, and even teachers falling victim to that old-school thinking, blindly following the flock.

It's time to make a decision. Up until now, you have had a set of beliefs about what your brain could and could not do, and that set of beliefs led you to a place where you only *wished* that you were the kind of person who could get better grades. What's worse, the dreams you have had for your future are not *your* dreams. They're the dreams you've settled for, because your beliefs have put a limit on what you think you can do. You're welcome to keep living in the warped reality where you think that your comparisons are fair, and that your expectations are realistic, and that you've seen everything that your brain can do. You can hold on to your old ideas, stay a stupichondriac, and be a pawn of the conspiracy for the rest of your life.

That's your choice. But, you also have a huge opportunity in front of you right now. You can stop conforming. You can wipe the slate clean. You can commit to throwing out everything you've believed about your own brainpower in the past, and you can decide that you *are* the kind of person who can get better grades. You can choose to finally be *in control*.

Now, we understand—your old beliefs are comfortable. After all, you've been working in the same way for a LONG time. Life as a sheep is familiar. It's safe. Well, no one ever rose to the top by playing it safe. You may have friends who don't yet understand the full potential of their brains, and they won't see what a majorly exciting change you're trying to make. You may have parents or teachers who unknowingly talk about your "natural ability" in some area. Stay strong. Going out on your own—going against what most people believe—isn't always easy. But it's important. It will be thanks to leaders like you that the Straight-A Conspiracy will fall apart and the flock mentality about "born genius" will be destroyed. In the meantime, you'll be living the life of the twenty-first century genius...while everyone else sits back, complacently chewing their grass.

So, you have two options. On one side, you have continued sheepdom. On the other side, you have a fresh start, a new understanding of your brain, and the power to achieve anything you've ever dreamed of doing. It's totally up to you. Maybe you're not interested in taking charge of your life and taking advantage of your limitless potential. It's your brain, and only you can decide what to do with it. But we can tell you—as people who have already left the flock—this should be the easiest decision you'll ever make.

PART THREE

SCHOOL MADE SIMPLE

Apparently, you've decided that the best way to take down the conspiracy is to stop being a sheep and start getting great grades yourself. We agree! Get ready to see school in a totally different way than you ever imagined was possible. For example, we bet you had no idea that the secret to never making a mistake is contained within every box of cake mix, or that the key to acing any exam can be found a few short paces from the Savoy Hotel in London. This is where things get really fun.

We're going to show you the six study techniques that will allow you to get an *A* in any class. Just as you had previously automated those doubts and insecurities about your brain, you now need to automate these six ways of tackling your work. The result will be that school is far, far simpler than you ever thought it could be.

In the rest of this book, you'll find sample problems from a smattering of topics across all typical high school subjects. Since we have no idea what you've already studied, we're assuming that you are seeing these topics for the first time. If you've seen any of these topics before, then that's great! You will be able to put all of your attention on the *way of working*. That's what really matters.

In reality, these six study techniques are just six different kinds of fix-it-focused practice, each of which helps you to improve a different aspect of your performance. Anybody who wants to get ahead in any career uses fix-it-focused practice on a daily basis. How do you think a screenwriter writes a screenplay? How do you think an athlete improves his game? The place where you train yourself to become a fix-it-focused practice champion is school. Great grades are just around the corner. Go and get 'em.

Chapter 6

Make It Cake-Mix Clear

You, your parents, your teachers, your friends...almost everyone has both fallen victim to *and* unknowingly perpetuated the Straight-A Conspiracy. But there is one lady who has never, ever succumbed to the lies and deceptions. This lady holds strong and will never cave, no matter what. This lady has played host to Presidents, she has sold more books than Hemingway at the height of his career, and she has long served as the figurehead of a billion-dollar empire...all while teaching people that they were capable of much more than they'd ever imagined. This lady is Betty Crocker®.

OK, so Betty's technically not a *real* lady, she's more like a corporate mascot. But that's beside the point. Betty Crocker is a conspiracy-fighting genius. Seriously! Do you even *know* what she did for bakers everywhere??!! Before Betty Crocker, making a cake was a *huge* ordeal. It was a really intricate process that involved lots of ingredients and could take hours to pull off. You would have flour on your face, chocolate smeared on your clothing, and the counter would be a mess. Worst of all, you might go through *all* of that work, and then if one tiny thing wasn't done perfectly, your cake could be a flop when you took it out of the oven. What a pain in the bundt.

Fortunately, in the 1950's, kitchens across America catapulted into the future. They had to. Between keeping the kids from listening to that demonic rock-and-roll music, figuring out that newfangled television set, and deciding whether to vote for Dwight Eisenhower or Adlai Stevenson, what sensible adult had time to fuss with meals all day? Appliances like refrigerators, hand mixers and automatic coffeemakers became commonplace. There was the Drink-o-Matic, the Drip-o-Matic, and the Chop-o-Matic. Ease was the name of the game. When you opened the door to your guests for your dinner party, you wanted the food to look divine, the countertop to be sparkling, and every hair on your head to be in place without a bead of sweat showing. "Oh... this triple-layered Bavarian chocolate chiffon cake? It was no effort at all!"

Betty Crocker understood just what the bakers of the 1950's needed, and so she gave dessert a major makeover. Boxed cake mixes had been around for a few years, but Betty Crocker took that quick-and-easy approach and expanded it to *everything*, from cupcakes to cookies to brownies. No matter how hard the original recipe was, by the time Betty was done with it, she had transformed it using her signature 1-2-3 simplicity. Betty brought stress-free success to bakers everywhere. Best of all, by making baking easy, she also made it fun.

America has been obsessed with Betty Crocker ever since. (I mean, seriously, have you *tried* that carrot cake? Out of this world!) But we've all been so distracted by the deliciousness of her cakes, brownies, and frostings that for decades, none of us saw the truth: **in every scrumptious bite lies the secret to making school easy and error-free**.

The reason why Betty Crocker products are so amazing is that the food scientists at General Mills have made the process of baking totally clear and 100% reliable. Betty would **never** buy into the idea that anything was too difficult to understand,

and that's why her name represents the gold standard for clear instructions and reliable results. Imagine that you are in the kitchen and you decide that you're going to make one of Betty's super-moist Chocolate Fudge cakes. Here's an example from the actual instructions on the back of Betty's cake mix box:

You will need:
1 ⅓ **Cups of Water**
½ **Cup of Vegetable Oil**
3 **Eggs**

2. Beat cake mix, water, oil and eggs in large bowl on low speed 30 seconds, then on medium speed 2 minutes, scraping bowl occasionally. Pour into pan.

It's like the Sistine Chapel of instructions! If you're failing to see the masterpiece that lies on that cardboard package, then think about it this way. These directions are so specific and clear that you, the at-home baker, *can't go wrong.* If your goal is to eat this cake, you are not going to use eight eggs. You are not going to use a full cup of vegetable oil. And you are (hopefully) not going to add fish sauce. Amateur bakers run into trouble for one simple reason: they don't have a 100% solid understanding of the instructions. Betty understood that, and so she made those instructions so clear and easy that any baker could follow them. She even takes about fifteen ingredients, from cocoa to leavening, and combines them so that all you have to worry about is "cake mix." Betty saves you time and saves you from having to buy dozens of ingredients. But the biggest benefit of all is that she saves you stress. It's *very* unlikely that making this cake will feel confusing or frustrating. Instead, you'll probably enjoy it, because you know that if you follow the rules, you're 100% guaranteed to eat a delicious slice (or three) of cake.

If your cake tastes really dry or seems too gloopy, then you just didn't follow one of Betty's rules. In the same way, if you get something wrong in school, then you just didn't follow one of the subject's rules. Although subjects like math and English can seem very different from each other, every subject that you take is based on a set of well-established rules. Your job is to make sure that you break down the rules of each subject until they are as clear and easy to follow as Betty's instructions are.

It's that straightforward. That should be awesome news to you. There's nothing vague, unclear, or personal about it. If there's a red X on your page, then it's marking the spot of the exact place where you need to clear up your rules. Preventing future red X's is as easy as making that rule Cake-Mix Clear.

To understand how fuzzy rules cause mistakes, imagine that you picked up the box of cake mix and it looked like the following:

You will need:
Water
Some Kind of Oil
Eggs???
Whatever other stuff you think might work

2. Put 'em together.

Suddenly we're not so confident about how this cake will turn out. There's a big difference between no eggs and eight eggs, but in this case, either one satisfies these vague directions. And "whatever other stuff you think might work" is frighteningly open-ended. In fact, you've got a better chance of beating Thor at Whack-a-Mole than you do of making a perfect cake with this recipe. And even if you find some fluke success, you probably won't be able to repeat it.

Betty made her recipe so clear that it guarantees a yummy cake every time. And **what Betty has done for the rules of baking, you can do for the rules of any subject**. Lots of students know how to memorize a bunch of rules. But Betty will show you that being familiar with the rules is not the same as turning those rules into a sure-fire recipe for action. Your very first move with any new material should be to make the rules Cake-Mix Clear.

There's a Recipe for Algebra

Charlie Wexell was a little lanky. Actually, he was a lot lanky. If awkwardness was an Olympic sport, then Charlie Wexell would be the new Michael Phelps. Fortunately for his social life, His Wexcellence had learned to use his physique to his advantage. He'd become the ultimate class clown. He joked about school, did spot-on impressions of his teachers, and even found ways to laugh off his disastrous math grade. In fact, his jokester persona fooled a lot of Charlie's classmates into thinking that he never worried at all about how school was going.

But, behind all the jokes, Charlie actually felt pretty bad about his math grade, and when his progress report came home, his parents threw a fit. From that moment on, they were constantly on his case, saying that he could bring up his math grade if he only tried harder. Charlie found this really annoying, and the conversation always turned into a huge argument. Charlie tried to make his parents understand that he wasn't lazy—he just didn't "get" math at all—but his parents just wouldn't let it drop. In reality, none of this drama needed to happen. Charlie simply needed to bring some dessert-based thinking to his academic life.

For starters, if you're going to make your rules Cake-Mix Clear, you need to know *which* rules are giving you problems. When Katie asked His Wexcellence what was giving him trouble, he answered without hesitation: "math." That assessment was overly harsh. Although it *felt* to Charlie like he had nothing going for him in math class, he actually knew plenty of math, like working with exponents, fractions, and graphing. In reality, it was Charlie's lack of specificity about what was causing him problems that kept him from saving his grade.

Because Charlie didn't have a solid grasp of what had gone wrong, Katie suggested looking in the most obvious place: the first question of the first algebra quiz of the semester.

Charlie Wexell

Composite Functions Quiz

1. Find $f(g(x))$ where $f(x) = x^2 + 3x - 2$ and $g(x) = \sqrt{x}$

$f(g(x)) = (x^2 + 3x - 2)(\sqrt{x})$
$f(g(x)) = x^2\sqrt{x} + 3x\sqrt{x} - 2\sqrt{x}$ -5

$f(g(x)) = (\sqrt{x})^2 + 3\sqrt{x} - 2$
Simplify from here...

Katie: Okay, Charlie. So, you're doing composite functions. Why did you give the answer you gave in question 1?

Charlie: Seriously, I had no idea what to do. I just sort of combined them. I've never really gotten functions.

Katie: Great! Well, in that case, let's go to the root of the issue and make sure that functions are Cake-Mix Clear for you. Functions show up a lot in high school math, so it's worth refreshing this concept and making sure you have it down.

Making a Recipe for Action

Within the first minute of reading a Betty Crocker cake recipe, you feel ready for action. Thanks to the extremely user-friendly instructions, you are able to answer the only two questions that matter:

What do I do? When do I do it?

For example:
What do I do? *Beat the cake mix, water, oil, and eggs in a large bowl.*
When do I do it? *After I've pre-heated the oven.*

Answering those two questions is the key to making any rule Cake-Mix Clear, no matter what assignment you're tackling. In your textbook, rules can show up in many different forms. You need to take the information that is given to you, break it down, and translate it into a recipe for action until it's as straightforward, reliable, and easy to use as Betty's recipes are. To see this in action, let's take a look at the definition of a function that Katie found in Charlie's textbook:

24   ALGEBRA: FROM PRINCIPLES TO PRACTICE

Quick Review

Using Function Notation

f(x) represents the value assigned to the variable x by the function f. When x is the input, the output is f(x).

Example: $f(x) = x^2 + 4x - 6$

When x = 3, $f(3) = 3^2 + 4(3) - 6$

$f(3) = 9 + 12 - 6 = 15$

Practice Problems

You Can Make it Happen

We know that not all teachers give back quizzes and tests. If that's the case, don't be afraid to ask your teacher if you can make a photocopy or even just copy down the problems that you got wrong. If that doesn't work, then maybe you can schedule a time with your teacher to go through the problems that you got wrong. You can always find a way to play by the rules and still succeed.

Katie: Alright, Charlie. What does that rule mean?

Charlie: It means that...f(x)... represents the value assigned to the variable *x*...

Katie: OK, stop. That's a great job of repeating, Charlie. 10 points for Gryffindor. But you need to *think about each piece of* this rule and break it down until it's something that you actually can *do*. Now, you can start by digging into the written-out rule or the example. But wherever you start, the question you need to answer is, "What do I do?" In other words, what action is being taken, or what steps are being followed?

To Charlie, the written-out definition seemed like gibberish, so he started with the example. After looking at it for a bit, he recognized a pattern in the first two lines of the example.

Example: $f(x) = (x^2) + (4x) - 6$

When x = 3, $f(3) = 3^2 + 4(3) - 6$

Charlie: They just changed all the *x*'s to *3*'s.

Katie: Yes, Charlie! That's excellent!

Charlie gave Katie a wry smile. "Don't you mean *Wexcellent*?"

Right. Sure, Charlie. Anyway, the answer to, "What do I do?" is to take whatever value is replacing the x in f(x), and then use that to replace *all* of the *x*'s in the equation.

I Swear It's Not There!

When they're looking something up, a lot of students will randomly flip pages. Then when they can't find what they want, they say "It's not there!" Look it up in the index first! That way, you'll find the right page as quickly as possible.

By taking these steps, Charlie had made the rule clear—certainly clearer than the book's definition. But "clear" isn't good enough. That rule needs to be "put-it-on-the-back-of-a-box, sell-it-in-stores-nationwide, so-easy-a-three-year-old-can-do-it clear." It needs to be like cake. So, what is another way that you can phrase this or set it up so that anyone could understand this rule?

Charlie was quick to respond. "Well, it's not even really about math…it's kind of just plugging things into the right spots."

Exactly! So for this rule, maybe a visual is the clearest option:

$$f(x) = x^2 + 4x - 6$$

$$f\underline{\quad} = \underline{\quad}^2 + 4\underline{\quad} - 6$$

$$f(3) = (3)^2 + 4(3) - 6$$

Now *that's Cake-Mix Clear*. It certainly doesn't require any puzzling out. Take the whole expression, parentheses and all, and drop it into each box. If that's the case, then what would f(4) look like? What about f(10)? What about f(pigeon)?

$$f(x) = x^2 + 4x - 6$$

$$f(\underline{4}) = (\underline{4})^2 + 4(\underline{4}) - 6$$

$$f(\underline{10}) = (\underline{10})^2 + 4(\underline{10}) - 6$$

$$f(\underline{pigeon}) = (\underline{pigeon})^2 + 4(\underline{pigeon}) - 6$$

Sweet. So with this level of clarity, your new recipe is the following:

For First-Time Flawless Functions...

YOU WILL NEED: A Function

f(x) = x² + 6x
Find f(3)

f_ =

1. Make Every "X" a Slot. Rewrite the equation with slots where the x's are.

(3)

f(3)= __² + 6__

2. Fill in Every Slot. Take the number next to f and insert it into every slot.

What Charlie had done with his recipe was the key—restating the rule in a way that made it easy to use every time. "That's so easy! Now it makes sense why the textbook talks about 'input' and 'output.' You plug the same value in everywhere, and then the output is what you get!" Just a few minutes earlier, Charlie was feeling totally confused and hating math, and after this process, he thought it was a breeze. There's a very simple reason for this. Everything is easy when you know what you're doing. **If something is hard, you just haven't made it Cake-Mix Clear.**

"But wait—if I'm just plugging in a number and solving, then isn't that the same thing as an equation like y=x+2? You just plug in a number and solve. So, why do they have to use 'f' and make it look a million times harder than it actually is?" It was great that Charlie recognized that in this case, the function problem was just as easy as solving an equation with two variables, like *x* and *y*. That was a good way to think of it at Charlie's level, because he was right—it's no harder than that. But since Charlie was working on composite functions, he was actually about to see why in some cases, it's more helpful to use f(x). It was time to make the rule for composite functions Cake-Mix Clear.

Charlie went back to the textbook and found the rule for composite functions, which was the following:

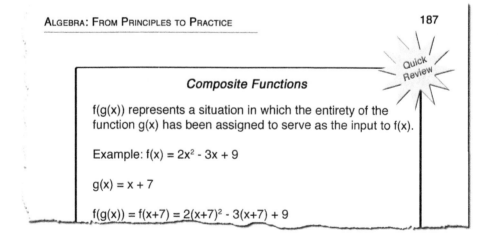

ALGEBRA: FROM PRINCIPLES TO PRACTICE   187

Composite Functions   Quick Review

f(g(x)) represents a situation in which the entirety of the function g(x) has been assigned to serve as the input to f(x).

Example: $f(x) = 2x^2 - 3x + 9$

$g(x) = x + 7$

$f(g(x)) = f(x+7) = 2(x+7)^2 - 3(x+7) + 9$

Charlie looked at the new example and realized that the same sort of fill-in-the-blank action was happening. "This is exactly the same thing as before, it's just that instead of having one number as the input, they're using a whole function as the input every single time. It's like—a mathematical turducken."

What the... Oh, wait! That's exactly right. Weird example, but nice work, Charlie! Just like a turducken is a turkey stuffed with a duck...stuffed with a chicken, a composite function is one function stuffed with another. It's still about filling slots. You're just filling in another function instead of a single number...or a single duck. The rule was essentially still the same:

For Mathematical Turducken (Composite Functions)...

YOU WILL NEED: Two Functions

$f(x) = x^2 + 6x$
$g(x) = x - 2$
Find $f(g(x))$

1. Make Every "X" a Slot. Rewrite the outermost equation with slots where the x's are.

2. Stuff Every Slot. Take the whole inner function and stuff it into every slot.

And in that case, the following worked perfectly:

$$f(x) = 2x^2 + 3x + 9$$

$$g(x) = x + 7$$

Find $f(g(x))$

$$f\underline{\quad} = 2\underline{\quad}^2 + 3\underline{\quad} + 9$$

$$f(g(x)) = 2(g(x))^2 + 3(g(x)) + 9$$

But since $g(x) = x + 7$, we can go further:

$$f(x + 7) = 2(x + 7)^2 + 3(x + 7) + 9$$

Every time that Charlie ever dealt with a function, this rule of replacing the letter in the equation with slots and then filling them in would be true. The specific variables used could change. The equations themselves might get longer and more complicated as the levels of math went on. But the rule would *always stay the same.* Now that Charlie was Cake-Mix Clear on this rule, dealing with any function would be easy *for life.*

> **You Just Never Know...**
>
> When the internet first started up, many non-computery people called it a "fad." They could never imagine that it would end up becoming an essential part of people's everyday lives. In the same way, when you first start learning something in school, it's hard to fully appreciate how useful it might be. The better you understand something, the more you'll wonder how you ever lived without it.

As a bonus, Charlie could now understand why functions were necessary. *Y* worked well in a simple equation such as $y = x + 2$, but you could never make this equation-in-an-equation work using only *x* and *y*. Functions are set up specifically to make this kind of multi-layered computation possible.

Now that Charlie's rule was Cake-Mix Clear, it was time to go back to the original test question.

Charlie Wexell   **Composite Functions Quiz**

1. Find $f(g(x))$ where $f(x) = x^2 + 3x - 2$ and $g(x) = \sqrt{x}$

$f(g(x)) = (x^2 + 3x - 2)(\sqrt{x})$
$f(g(x)) = x^2\sqrt{x} + 3x\sqrt{x} - 2\sqrt{x}$ -5

$f(g(x)) = (\sqrt{x})^2 + 3\sqrt{x} - 2$
Simplify from here...

Charlie Gets the Same Answer as His Teacher!

$f(g(x)) = f(\sqrt{x}) = (\sqrt{x})^2 + 3(\sqrt{x}) - 2$

By using his recipe, Charlie set the problem up in a way that was easy to solve. To finish the problem, there were more rules that he needed to know, beyond the rule of functions, such as how to deal with radicals and how to deal with exponents. Because he *was* already pretty solid on these other rules, he was now set to work his way to the right answer! You may or may not have learned those other rules already, depending on where you are in math, but what you *can* see is that fully understanding the function rule means that Charlie could now set up function problems correctly every single time.

That's all that math is—a bunch of rules that you follow. If the rules are clear to you, then the math will be easy. And the best part is, you use a *lot* of the same rules over and over again. That means that making one rule solid can make a difference in a lot of problems. Not knowing the basic rule of functions had been messing Charlie up for most of the semester and making him think that he would "never get it." Often, months of mistakes are actually the result of a few small rules not being Cake-Mix Clear.

Of course, the only way that you can really know if a recipe has been perfected is by eating the cake. You need to assess the final product. In that same way, once you get a recipe for action in any class, you need to test it out by doing some sample problems and checking your results against answers that you *know* are correct.

Charlie went through the rest of his quiz, using his Cake-Mix-Clear rule and checking the answers that he got against his teacher's corrections. Once he had tested this rule enough to know that it would make a great cake every time, Charlie knew it for good. Over time, as he gave the cake-mix treatment to more and more of his math, he added to his recipe box of rules until he was ready for pretty much anything he faced in algebra class.

HOW DO YOU KNOW WHEN IT'S CAKE-MIX CLEAR?
You know exactly what to do, and you get it exactly right, every time. If you're following rules that are Cake-Mix Clear, you never have to get a problem wrong.

THE SIGN SAYS, "NO SHIRT, NO SHOES, NO SERVICE."

When you walk into restaurants, there is often a sign posted somewhere on the door that says, "No Shirt, No Shoes, No Service." That's a rule that is in place in order to keep the food establishment sanitary… and appetizing. If you walked into a fast food restaurant with no shoes on and asked for a burger, you would be refused service. You broke the rule. And when that happened, and the person at the counter stood angrily pointing at the sign, you probably wouldn't say, "No fair! I'm just naturally bad at wearing shoes!" Likewise, if you try to tell a judge that you just didn't get the "parking-sign-reading gene," then he's not going to dismiss your $60 ticket. The rule was posted, and it was your job to figure it out. But you broke it. It's as simple as that.

In this chapter, we've already told you that *every subject in school* is essentially about learning rules and then following them. When you break a rule, you get something wrong. That seems as straightforward as getting no hamburger for being shoeless or getting a ticket for parking in a loading zone. But instead, the conspiracy has twisted our idea of what that red "X" means on our homework and tests. Rather than seeing it as a simple cause-and-effect relationship that we can easily fix, we see it as a reflection of who we are and what we're capable of achieving.

Here's the bottom line. If you want a burger, wear shoes next time. If you don't want a ticket, don't park in that spot during the wrong hours. And if you don't want to get a problem wrong, *clear up the rule.* It makes no sense to give up on yourself, your brain, or this subject just because you got something wrong. If you want to combat the conspiracy, treat your X's like you've been denied a juicy burger and *do something about it* for next time!

There's a Recipe for Grammar

Betty Crocker's approach to cake doesn't just work for math. It applies to anything that you ever want to learn. Time to find the easy recipes for some other high school subjects.

Figuring out grammar and punctuation can seem kind of like a guessing game. Beyond the obvious stuff like capitalization and periods, it often seems sort of arbitrary—you just toss in commas wherever they look good, avoid semi-colons altogether, and hope for the best when you turn in your papers. This is exactly the approach that Hunter took to punctuation and grammar when he was in high school. His assumption was that with all things grammar, sometimes you luck out, and sometimes your teacher just marks it wrong for no reason.

That viewpoint, of course, was crazypants.

There's nothing fuzzy about it. Grammar and punctuation—and really, *all subjects in high school*—are based on very clear, straightforward rules. And if you make those rules Cake-Mix Clear, you can be 100% sure that you'll never lose points for those seemingly little things again. We're going to start with just one of the punctuation rules—but one that particularly tends to confuse people. Certainly, it was the thing high-school Hunter thought he had the least hope of mastering. Today's lesson? The colon.

For most people, the colon is like the weird crazy ingredient that only TV-competition chefs use when they're making cakes. It's the key ingredient in apricot-filled pumpkin cake with brown butter frosting. It's unpredictable, it's not to everyone's taste, and you're really not sure what to make of it. If you saw it in your cupboard, among the other baking supplies, you'd make an effort to avoid it. It's not worth the risk. Yet an experienced, confident chef *loves* that ingredient and knows *exactly* how to use it to make a dessert worthy of the grand prize.

It's all about giving yourself lots of options—and knowing how to use them. If you've been like high-school Hunter, then you've been safely sticking to commas and periods to punctuate all of your writing. *HOW BORING!!!* That's like vanilla cake, all the time. Vanilla. Vanilla. Vanillllllllllllllla. Aren't you sick of vanilla? The colon isn't dangerous or unpredictable or intimidating; it's just as handy as vanilla extract. The bottom line is that it's always great to have more flavors from which to choose. If we're going to benefit from the wide variety of flavors that come from all the pieces of punctuation, then we need to understand each of them better. Let's start by looking up the rules for the uses of colons and breaking them down, until we have a recipe for action.

If you check in your English textbook, you will likely find a few different rules that involve colons. Some of those rules are instantly easy to follow. Just by reading them, you can make them Cake-Mix Clear. For example, read the following:

Grenfell's Comprehensive Grammar: A Course Reader, 1912 ed.   **63**

Use a colon to follow the salutation of a business letter even when addressing someone by his/her first name.

ex) Dear Jean Perwin:

When expressing the time numerically, use a colon between the hours and the minutes.

ex) At 8:10 p.m., President Roosevelt was shot in the chest. In spite of this inconvenience, he proceeded to deliver a ninety-minute speech to the people of Milwaukee.

Use a colon to divide the title of a book from the subtitle.

ex) I am reading Grenfell's Comprehensive Grammar: A Course Reader. I don't recommend it.

In each of these cases, the wording of the rule and the related example make it easy to understand that particular use of the colon (even if this grammar book is super-old and unrelatable).

All you have to do is memorize the rules. Now, beyond vanilla, it's like you have chocolate, toffee, and carrot. That's a great start, but there are more flavors out there to be enjoyed. And there are other uses of the colon. Those ones require a bit more clarification; the recipe for action is not immediately obvious from your textbook.

This next colon rule teaches you how to make the written equivalent of chocolate fudge cake with salted caramel buttercream frosting. Punctuation has never been this intense! (Or this appetizing, frankly.) But you might need to clear things up in order to get a recipe you can use.

---

64   Grenfell's Comprehensive Grammar: A Course Reader, 1912 ed.

Use the colon at the end of a complete sentence to introduce a list of items that specify or give examples of what the sentence is discussing. (Note: do not use a colon if introductory phrases like "including" or "such as" appear.)

ex) For her vacation, Laura brought the absolute essentials: her wool bathing costume, a parasol, and her best modeling poses.

ex) I would trust only three people with my penny-farthing bicycle: my cousin, my best friend, and New Jersey Governor Woodrow Wilson.

The colon is *incorrectly used* in the following sentences:

ex) Claire was desperate to get autographs from: Mary Pickford, Charlie Chaplin, and the great Irish-American singer Chauncey Olcott.

ex) Bud has many hobbies and interests such as: beekeeping, moustache cultivation, and bare-knuckle boxing alone in the woods.

At about this point, Hunter would've "accidentally" dropped his textbook into a murky lake and run for the hills. Sheesh! (That's mostly because Hunter is intimidated by well-groomed beekeepers.) But once you understand it, this rule is no more difficult than using a colon in "8:10 p.m." Now that you have the rule in front of you, you can break it down to figure out what the textbook's explanation really means.

Is Everything As Obvious As "Eggs"?

Here's some extra insight into the brilliance of Betty Crocker. Think about the words she uses in her recipe: water, vegetable oil, cake mix, eggs. No single piece of a Betty recipe needs any further clarification...even for the most inexperienced cake-creator. This may be the first time you've ever made a cake before, but that's no problem, because when you see those instructions, you can certainly understand "eggs." Likewise, your job in school, when making a rule Cake-Mix Clear, is to keep clarifying that rule until every piece is as obvious as "eggs." We call that the Eggs Test, and it's the one way to make sure that you've made your rule as Cake-Mix Clear as it can possibly be.

Now, when you're using the Eggs Test, you can't take *anything* that you've seen before for granted. You need to be 100% certain that you know exactly what each term means. The rule says that you can only use a colon after a complete sentence. It's easy to think, "I understand what 'complete sentence' means! It's a sentence! That's complete!" This is when the Eggs Test is the most useful. Could you pick out a complete sentence in a crowd of almost-sentences? Or even...in a fridge?

Did you find the eggs? What about the complete sentence? If you aren't totally positive which one is the complete sentence within the first read, then "complete sentence" is one thing that doesn't pass the Eggs Test yet. That means the definition needs some work before it's Cake-Mix Clear. Check out the following breakdown:

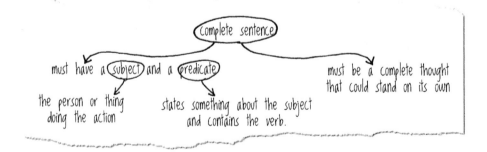

With a better idea of *exactly* which components a complete

sentence requires, it becomes easier to identify the complete sentence in the refrigerator. In order to qualify, it's going to need a subject and a predicate...*and* it has to be a complete thought that could stand on its own. Let's test those examples.

"Although it was raining outside." Not a complete thought.

"Doing everything at once!" No subject. Who or What is doing everything at once?

"This cheese smells like." "...Like what?" Not a complete thought. If you said this to your friend, they'd lean in to hear the rest.

"The gnomes live under the street." Subject ☑ Predicate ☑ Complete Thought ☑

Bear in mind, until this becomes more automatic to you, it will still require a bit of thinking to check for those components. Eventually, you'll recognize what a full sentence looks like just as quickly as you can recognize the eggs.

Now, let's look at this in terms of the larger colon rule that you're working to clarify. If you were to come across this rule, breaking down "complete sentence" would be *one part* of your job. But even the parts of the rule that seem to be clear already still deserve some attention. For instance, "list of items" is not confusing, because you know what a list is and what items are. But you do need to take a quick moment to *THINK ABOUT* what those parts really mean in the context of this particular rule, so that your recipe is ready to go.

Use the colon at the end of a complete sentence to introduce a list of items that specify or give examples of what the sentence is discussing.

must have a subject and a predicate

must be a complete thought that could stand on its own

the person or thing doing the action

states something about the subject and contains the verb.

items for vacation = wool bathing costume, parasol, and best modeling poses

Now that every individual part of this rule passes the Eggs Test, you're ready to make yourself a new recipe for action!

Making a Recipe for Action

As is always the case in grammar and punctuation rules, the answer to "What do I do?" is very easy. What do you do? Use a colon.

(Phew! That was exhausting. Oh man...we need a break. Alright, we're back.) Knowing what you do is half the battle. But the real issue for grammar—the one that is least clear to students like high-school Hunter—is *when* you do it. *When* do you use this particular colon? To figure this out, just think through that breakdown.

Based on the breakdown, it seems that the "when" for this rule requires the following conditions:

1) Complete sentence (subject, predicate, complete thought) before the colon
2) List of items that give examples or clarification
3) No words like "including" or "such as"

With this clearer understanding, let's go back to the examples for the grammar book and make sure we know why they were correct or incorrect. This means we need to check for the required conditions.

S = Subject P = Predicate

For her vacation, Laura brought the absolute essentials: All set! Use a colon!

I would trust only three people with my penny-farthing bicycle: Use a colon!

Claire was desperate to get autographs from: No complete thought. No colon!

Buck has many hobbies and interests such as: "Such as" = introductory words! No colon!

Breaking down the definition brought us a good degree of clarity. But by using the examples to test that clarity, we can make our understanding 100% solid. It always helps to see something in action. Here, the final two examples were incorrect because they did not satisfy *all* of the required "When do I do it?" conditions.

With your new Cake Mix Clarity, it's time to write a recipe.

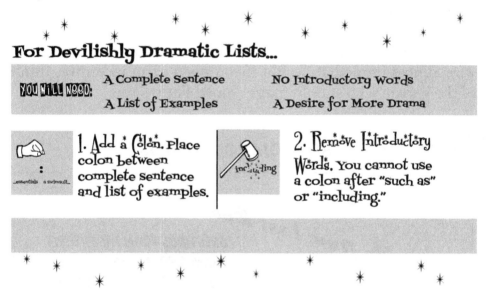

For Devilishly Dramatic Lists...

YOU WILL NEED: A Complete Sentence · No Introductory Words · A List of Examples · A Desire for More Drama

1. Add a Colon. Place colon between complete sentence and list of examples.

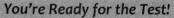

2. Remove Introductory Words. You cannot use a colon after "such as" or "including."

It's as straightforward as following this recipe. If you don't have all of the ingredients, then it's not time for a colon. Of course, the first few times that you use this recipe, you'll probably have to really think through the ingredients, what you do, and when you do it. If you're writing essays or doing English homework, it's possible that there won't be answers in a textbook against which to check

You're Ready for the Test!

The process of making things Cake-Mix Clear is the best way to study. Your attention is so fully engaged in unraveling the material that you're actually doing some major automating. Clear it up now, and when it's time for the test, you'll probably find that you barely need to study!

your colon usage. But as you turn work in and get feedback from your teacher, you can keep refining your rule until it's tighter, faster, and more reliable.

With practice, this rule will become automatic—as automatic as spelling "dog" or capitalizing the first word of a sentence. And eventually, you'll be using all punctuation correctly, from colons to hyphens to semi-colons, without even thinking about it, the same way that your English teacher does.

Making your grammar rules automatic pays off in a major way, almost immediately. But if you need extra incentive, think of the person who should matter most: Future You.

A THANK YOU CARD FROM YOUR FUTURE SELF

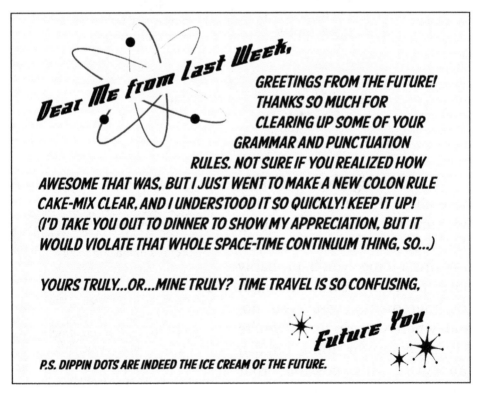

Dear Me from Last Week,

GREETINGS FROM THE FUTURE! THANKS SO MUCH FOR CLEARING UP SOME OF YOUR GRAMMAR AND PUNCTUATION RULES. NOT SURE IF YOU REALIZED HOW AWESOME THAT WAS, BUT I JUST WENT TO MAKE A NEW COLON RULE CAKE-MIX CLEAR, AND I UNDERSTOOD IT SO QUICKLY! KEEP IT UP! (I'D TAKE YOU OUT TO DINNER TO SHOW MY APPRECIATION, BUT IT WOULD VIOLATE THAT WHOLE SPACE-TIME CONTINUUM THING, SO...)

YOURS TRULY...OR...MINE TRULY? TIME TRAVEL IS SO CONFUSING,

Future You

P.S. DIPPIN DOTS ARE INDEED THE ICE CREAM OF THE FUTURE.

Future You is right. It takes a bit of effort at first to make a rule Cake-Mix Clear. But the more things that you clear up, the easier you are making it for yourself to learn every new thing in the future. For one thing, you're giving yourself a more helpful vocabulary with which to work. By knowing words like "predicate" and "exponent," you'll be able to quickly identify a very specific idea. There's a reason that experts in every subject, from grammar to math to science, have a set of special terminology. In the long run, knowing the special vocabulary of each subject will save you a ton of time.

But wait! There's more. Just like clearing up one rule about colons would help you learn the next, understanding regular functions made it a breeze to understand composite functions. The more things you learn, the more you'll see that new things *build upon* those earlier ideas. If you've got a Cake-Mix Clear base to work from, you'll be getting new rules down in no time.

And as you get more and more practice with your rules, you'll be able to make them even shorter—or combine them even further. For instance, when middle-school Katie was learning the colon rules, she figured them out individually at first. But by high school, she had used those rules enough times to notice something about colons: they always seemed to introduce something important. It was like a game show answer...or a dramatic result. Instead of worrying about all the parts of the rule, she realized that she could just think of the colon as one thing: a fanfare. Bum-ba-da-baaaahhhh! If that sentence deserved a fanfare, then it was time for a colon. "*For her vacation, Laura brought the absolute essentials...Bum-ba-da-baaaahhhh!...her wool bathing costume, a parasol, and her best modeling poses.*" (Talk about bringing the drama. I bet her wool bathing costume is even...gasp...sleeveless.) This made colons much more fun, and with this understanding, Katie wasn't afraid to use them. All the time. Like in this paragraph. And throughout this whole book. Check 'em out.

Punctuation: Every Piece Counts

Missing just one piece of punctuation can completely change the meaning of your sentence. Perhaps the most well-known example of this is the following set of sentences. Read them, and see if having the comma makes a difference.

Let's eat, Grandpa!
Let's eat Grandpa!

Clearly, those two sentences do not mean the same thing—especially to Grandpa. In the first, you want Grandpa to join you for a meal, and in the second, Grandpa is the meal. Punctuation shows your reader exactly how you want your words to be read. You have to provide those signposts so that someone doesn't take your words the wrong way... and start marinating your loved ones.

In making your grammar and punctuation rules Cake-Mix Clear, you're working to learn about all the different situations that can arise when you're writing...and what each situation requires. When you're addressing someone directly, use a comma. Showing that someone is talking? Add quotes. Asking a question? Then you need to use a question mark. It's not about being able to list the uses for each bit of grammar and punctuation as much as it's about knowing what punctuation can *help you express yourself most clearly* in any given situation. This way, you have options. For example, you could write the following sentence using commas:

John had only one rule in life, and it was that you can never trust anyone from Vermont.

That works perfectly fine. We get the point. But now, we know how to use more than just commas! We have *options*! And, if given the choice, we prefer to *bring the DRAMA!!!!* We all know what that means...

John had only one rule in life: never trust anyone from Vermont.

Whoa! Soap-opera face-slap fainting-spell evil-twin *DRAMA!* See that pause? Hear that finality? Oh MAN! That colon made the sentence so much more exciting! Do *not* put John in the same room as Ben, Jerry, or anyone who bottles their own maple syrup! He will *go off* on them! Using the colon lets you cut right to the chase. We don't want to hear "and it was that you can..." We just want the juicy answer! Now! BAM!

> **Mezcla de Tortas**
>
> Every language is entirely built on rules. You name it: Japanese, French, Chinese, Spanish, English, and probably even Elvish. All it takes to master any language is to automate those rules one by one.

So, you see, having the colon in your arsenal of punctuation is super-helpful. In fact, as you become more and more comfortable with it, you're going to start to see its addictive powers. Colons, colons, everywhere! And that's true for each new rule that you learn. The more punctuation you know, the more exciting *all* of your writing is going to become. Why keep settling for vanilla cake every day? Now you can feel totally confident making *any* flavor, from Candied Nut-Top Texas Sheet Cake to Rainbow Angel Birthday Cake.

And now, for the most important point: **grammar is not arbitrary**. It's not based on what "sounds right to you" or what "looks good." It's as clearly-defined as anything you do in math, science, or any other subject. It took Hunter way too many years to realize that. During high school, Hunter's stupichondria reared its ugly head any time there was writing to be done. Any kind of writing assignment was enough to send him into a sarcastic rant about how illogical and useless grammar and punctuation were. ("I'm learning science! The mysteries of the universe! I don't have time for something as petty as the comma!") The result of his refusal to acknowledge that a) he didn't know how punctuation worked, b) he was totally resistant to learning it, and c) frankly, he didn't think he *could* learn this, was years of unnecessary frustration and lost points on every essay. Years later, in fact relatively recently, Hunter realized the annoying irony of that whole period of his life. All that stuff he had avoided learning—predicates, appositives, and all the rest of it—were *exactly* what made up the logic of grammar and punctuation. English class was just as logical as math and science classes all along. Thank goodness this realization happened before Hunter started his career as a writer. Otherwise/:this book! would? be,,, a lot-harder: for" "you--to (un,derstand).

If you pick apart the rules, you can make any grammar or punctuation rule 100% dependable. As you automate the right way of doing each grammar rule, you're getting closer to knowing them all at lightning speed. Best of all, learning these small rules is the easiest way to massively improve your English grade.

Cake Mix To The Max

For Charlie, going through past tests and quizzes was a good way to figure out which rules he needed to make Cake-Mix Clear. With that process, he was able to prevent the same mistakes on future assignments. But in reality, you don't have to wait until after the test to make your rules Cake-Mix Clear; they should *all* be that clear from the start. No matter how difficult the material seems to be, it is based on rules, and you can find those rules and clear them up. That's what Danielle discovered in her toughest class of all.

Danielle was a sweet, softspoken high school junior who had spent the last year reading about and hearing about the amazing writing program at Duke University. She was convinced that it would be the perfect place for her; now, she just had to make sure she was the best applicant possible. When Hunter met her, Danielle had just started taking statistics, and she was afraid of getting a bad grade and hurting her chances of getting into Duke. But Danielle also never asked the teacher to re-explain the parts of statistics that were confusing to her, because she didn't want to look stupid in front of the other students in her class. Danielle felt as if she couldn't figure statistics out on her own. Statistics had all these weird symbols and strange terms and it was so hard to know where to start. Danielle was really hoping that Hunter could help her to get through it. Hunter had a better idea: offer her absolutely no help at all.

Danielle: So...I...um...we have homework and I'm supposed to find the standard deviation. (*Danielle looked at Hunter expectantly.*)

Hunter: And?

Danielle: Well, I was wondering...could you tell me what...I don't really know what the standard deviation is."

Hunter: Have you looked it up?

Danielle: No.

Hunter: Try that first.

Danielle: Okay. (*Danielle looked up what standard deviation meant and read out the definition. Again, she looked to Hunter. He didn't budge.*) I don't really understand that. Could you explain it?

Hunter: What don't you get?

Danielle: It says the standard deviation is the variation in a distribution. I don't know what the variation in a distribution is.

Hunter: What's a distribution?

Danielle: I'm not really sure.

Hunter: Mmmm.

Danielle: Should I look it up?

You get the point. It was time for some tough love. It was clear that it wouldn't help to tell Danielle the answers; she would benefit most from leading herself, piece by piece, to understanding... with the occasional push from Hunter. By the end of the session, Danielle had asked and answered so many of her own questions that she knew exactly what the standard deviation was and when to use it. To give you a feel for what she had to do, take a look at what the standard deviation equation looked like after she had made all the pieces as obvious as "eggs."

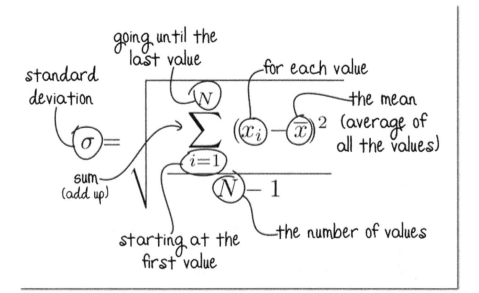

Obviously, if you don't know that "Σ" means "add up," then you've got zero hope of doing what this equation tells you to do. We're not going to explain to you all the parts of this equation here. What's important to realize is that Danielle had to first go to the smallest piece of the equation that she did not understand and look it up. As she cleared up the smallest pieces, she could then start to work on clearing up larger and larger concepts until she understood how the whole equation fit together. She made sure that every piece passed the Eggs Test before she moved to the next level. And how did she make sure her recipe was not only Cake-Mix Clear, but also reliable? She kept working through the sample problems in her textbook and checking her answers until she knew exactly what to do, and she got it right every single time. When she finished her homework, Danielle was totally shocked that she'd made it through. She also felt pretty awesome once Hunter pointed out that she really did figure this out all by herself.

With this technique, you don't need a tutor or a teacher or anyone else to help you. All you need is a book. Danielle figured out the ins-and-outs of her scariest class entirely on her own. Now that she knew she could look things up until she understood anything, there was

But Wait! There's More!

How do you take the Eggs Test to the max? Imagine that you're studying for a biology test on genetics. If you need to learn what "DNA" is, you can look up the fact that "DNA" stands for "deoxyribonucleic acid." That *is* what DNA is, but your *understanding* of DNA is no clearer. Your new term is not as obvious as eggs. Keep gathering more information. The Eggs Test may require you to look up *what something does, what it looks like,* or *how it's related to the rest of what you're learning.* Looking up a definition is not always a guarantee that you've made something as obvious as "eggs."

Clear Up the Medical Field

Doctors often seem amazing. It's like they have this special gift, but really what makes them remarkable is that they have learned all those little pieces one by one. For example, "myocardial infarction" is a medical way of saying "heart attack." You just earned a ten millionth of a medical degree.

World's Best Studying

Does making a Betty Crocker cake count as studying? Yes! Next time that you pick up a Betty Crocker cake mix... or brownie mix... or cookie mix... really pay attention to the simple, foolproof process that you're following. And then pay attention to how awesome your final product tastes. Best study session ever.

no stopping her. She lost her fear of statistics and started to get great grades. Best of all, when Hunter saw her a few months later, she had straight *A*'s and her confidence had skyrocketed. As she put it, "Looking things up seems super-obvious now, but back when I didn't feel so smart, it didn't even occur to me."

FIGURING IT OUT ON YOUR OWN COMES WITH A HUGE REWARD: A BOOST OF CONFIDENCE IN YOUR INTELLIGENCE.

Bake It 'Til You Make It

1) The only reason that you can ever get something wrong in school is because you broke a rule or messed up a fact.

2) You can make any rule or any fact Cake Mix Clear.

This is what you have to remind yourself whenever you see a mistake. Think about Charlie. He spent *years* getting things wrong on tests and homework assignments and feeling horrible about it. And in reality, he was making the same simple mistakes over and over again! As soon as he cleared up the rules that he didn't know, he was guaranteed to never see those *X*'s again.

Once he started to make things Cake-Mix Clear, Charlie became a homework-doing machine. He didn't have to think twice about any problems, and he wasn't stressed at all. Best of all, his parents got off his back. His grades improved, because he wasn't leaving anything fuzzy anymore. And Danielle won big-time, because in taking the time to really clear up rules *as she first learned them*, she was already doing a lot of the work needed to automate those rules. After one or two times using them, they were already automatic, and she barely needed any practice.

Actually, forget about Charlie and Danielle. What about YOU? We bet that you've had certain things that have brought you red *X*'s over and over again...and we know that that's no fun. But don't forget that red *X*'s can only mean one thing: you didn't follow the rule. All this time, the answer has been super straightforward. If you got those problems wrong, it's just because your rules are fuzzy. Starting today, making things Cake-Mix Clear can guarantee that you start to get everything right.

As you make more and more rules Cake-Mix Clear, you'll reach the stage where any time you want to learn something new, you already have many of the recipes you need right there, ready to use. That becomes an *enormous* advantage as school goes on. The clearer you make things now, the less work—and the less confusion—Future You will have to endure.

The students who do best in school are the ones who are always re-clarifying their rules. They don't confuse being *somewhat familiar* with a concept with being *totally clear* on a concept. Instead, they use their mistakes to their advantage when they're practicing, so that the mistake will never happen when it counts. These students get frustrated like anyone else does. But they also understand that if something is easy, it's because they understand the rules, and if something feels hard, it's because the rules aren't Cake-Mix Clear yet. Best of all, once every rule is Cake-Mix Clear, something great happens: the work becomes fun and stress-free...just like making Betty's cake.

You can make any rule in any subject Cake-Mix Clear. All you have to do is ask yourself these questions:

1) IS EVERYTHING AS OBVIOUS AS "EGGS"?
2) WHAT DO I DO? WHEN DO I DO IT?
3) DOES IT WORK? (CHECK IT AGAINST ANSWERS THAT
    YOU KNOW ARE CORRECT.)

Getting the Ball Rolling

There are tons and tons of rules that you will encounter during your school career, and we know that some of them seem like they would take forever to pick apart until they're Cake-Mix Clear. With all of that in front of you, where is the best place to begin? It's easy. Just commit to looking up words that you don't know. Once the words are all as obvious as "eggs," it will be easy to make the rules Cake-Mix Clear. Pretty soon, you'll be in the habit of breaking down every new thing that you learn!

Chapter 7

Take the Mystery Out of Your Reading

The Hardy Boys, Nancy Drew, Miss Marple, Hercule Poirot, and every character on every version of *CSI* combined can't compete with the crime-solving brilliance of one man: Mr. Sherlock Holmes. Sherlock Holmes is the most famous detective the world has ever known. If you can't picture him, he looks like this:

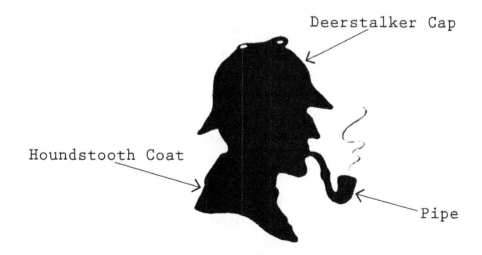

Deerstalker Cap

Houndstooth Coat

Pipe

But it's not just the snazzy getup that makes Sherlock so famous. It's that he takes cases that everyone else thinks are impossible to crack, and he works with the clues until he has solved them—every time. With Sherlock, no clue gets left unnoticed, no fact is insignificant, and everyone is a suspect until he or she can be definitively ruled out. Unlike the more run-of-the-mill investigators that he encounters, Sherlock never comes to a conclusion about what happened in a case or how exciting or interesting that case may be until he has rigorously examined all of the facts.

"It is a capital mistake to theorize before one has data. Insensibly, one begins to twist facts to suit theories, instead of theories to suit facts."
—Sherlock Holmes, *A Scandal in Bohemia*

Sometimes, Sherlock arrives at the scene of the crime, only to find that Inspector Lestrade (his somewhat bumbling contact in the police department) has already arrested the victim's wife, claiming that she "must be the murderer, because she was the only other person in the room." Whenever a case comes up, Lestrade looks to nab the criminal right away. He jumps to conclusions, falls for misleading clues, and arrives at overly simple answers. Sherlock, on the other hand, makes a point to ignore that kind of snap judgment and just focuses on clearing up the facts. Sherlock sits in his chair, smoking his pipe and turning the facts over in his mind, trying to figure out what else the data could mean. When he has made sense of it all, he can easily form his own theory, because he has eliminated all other possibilities. Even when the police have declared the crime "unsolvable" based on a lack of evidence—a missing body, or no murder weapon to be found—Sherlock is hesitant to agree. He knows that there are always enough clues to solve any crime.

While you probably won't need to use Sherlock Holmes' skills to solve a murder or major heist anytime soon, you *do* need

Sherlock's skills in school—every time that you open your reading. That's right—Sherlock Holmes needs to teach you how to read.

"What? Uh, I already *know* how to read. After all, I'm reading this sentence right now. Proof!" Yes, yes, we know that you know how to read words and understand what they mean. But have you ever had the experience of reaching the end of a passage you've just read and realizing you were totally zoning out and you have no clue what it was about? Or how about when your English class reads a new novel and some student immediately makes a comment like, "Oh! I love how the author uses this extended metaphor to convey the perils of communism!" (And you're thinking, "Communism? Isn't this a book about talking farm animals?")

We've all been in the position of feeling like we're totally missing the point of a passage. And that's because while we're great at reading the words and sentences, we often have the wrong idea about how reading should work. Most students read in the same way that a cartoon character eats corn on the cob. They chomp rapid-fire down one row, then robotically move down to the next row and chomp their way across again... chomp-chomp-chomp-move, chomp-chomp-chomp-move... once a row is done, there's no going back. They barrel through the passage, reach the end, and then wonder why their brain hasn't digested the material.

Corn-on-the-cob reading works really well for a casual email or a facebook post—in other words, if you have already automated all of the small pieces and ideas. In fact, you can probably corn-on-the-cob read many sections of this book, because it's written in language that you already use all the time. But in school, corn-on-the-cob reading sets you up to have writer's block for your essays and a mountain of memorization to do when it's time to study for the test. Reading something new is not about going directly from start to finish, and certainly the insight is not just going to come to you because you've read the words and sentences. You have to be a detective. Once you've made the facts of a passage Cake-Mix

Clear, bring your best Sherlock to the table. With his approach, you're guaranteed to solve the mystery and get to the heart of what the passage is really saying. If you're reading like Sherlock from the start, then you'll find that everything makes a lot more sense, and a lot of the work of school just disappears.

Cracking the "Impossible" Case

"Good books don't give up their secrets all at once."
—Stephen King

One of the reasons that Sherlock is able to crack any case is that he never lets himself get intimidated. No case is too scary or too overwhelming for him to take on. That's essential, because Sherlock has had cases in which he shows up to a house, and the only "facts" are that they have a missing butler and a missing maid. That tends to not feel like he has "facts" at all. Most of the investigators give up, because they are trying to deal with all of the unfamiliar details at once, and nothing seems like it provides a solid starting point. That's a problem that students face all the time, and it happens the most often when students start to read Shakespeare.

Yup. We said it. *Shakespeare.* The dirty, scary word of English classes everywhere. Teachers love him. You know who else loves him? Your amygdala. Shakespeare has a reputation in high schools everywhere for being scary and impossible. But that's a pretty unfounded conclusion, because most students see that old-school language and develop a judgment about it—that it's hard or boring or intimidating—without ever having tried to dig in and solve the mystery. Luckily, Sherlock can get to the bottom of even the toughest case.

Break Your Fear of Shakespeare: The Case of The Merciless Sonnet

Vikram Gupta had been staring at the computer screen for an hour. The little cursor had been blinking in the same spot the entire time. He was supposed to write a paper on this Shakespeare thingy for his English class, and he had no clue what to say. It was due the next day, and he could already tell it was going to be a looooong night.

Vikram hated English class, because he felt like the kids who did well just made up stuff about the books they read. "*Well, when you juxtapose the multiple allusions to the works of Dante with the subtle imagery of spoons in Chapter Three, it's more than clear that the author was really making a statement against post-*Victorian Society." Vikram never seemed to see those things. How was he supposed to guess what his teacher wanted to hear about this Shakespeare poem? In his mind, math was easy. Science was easy. They made sense, and they were logical. But reading—books, writing, literature—who had time for that kind of fluff?

Katie arrived on the scene, expecting to go through Vikram's first draft with him. But there was no first draft. So far, his essay said this: "Vikram Gupta, English 11B." He sighed and said, "I have no idea what to say about this stupid poem. Ugh! I just want to get this over with." Katie totally knew how he felt. But there was something important that Vikram was missing. If Vikram was drawing a blank when he went to write his essay, then he didn't know what

The Right Way to Use Cliff's Notes

SparkNotes, CliffsNotes, and all of those other literary resources can be helpful, but only if you use them in the right way. They reduce a book down to the most important "clues" so that you can spot those clues while you're reading the full text. But if you only read that basic overview, then how do you think you're going to come up with enough specific quotes and meaty, well-supported ideas to write an essay? "Saving time" in your reading only leads to *wasting* time when you're writing.

the poem was about. He needed to *really read* the poem.

Vikram was not a fan of this analysis. "I've read it already. I looked at it like 100 times. It's not even in English!" Sure, Vikram may have read it corn-on-the-cob style. But if he took about thirty minutes to really dig in and Sherlock the poem, he would save himself about 2-3 hours during the writing process. Better yet, he would know exactly what he wanted to say, and he would never be stuck staring at the screen.

Vikram wasn't convinced that Sherlocking would help. "No way. Look. Writing just takes me forever anyway. So if I spend even more time reading, I'll never get it done! It's like this." (Vikram grabbed some printer paper and drew a very sophisticated bar graph to support his argument.)

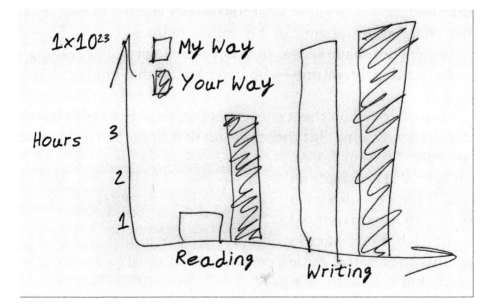

Vikram was right that Sherlocking would make his reading take a bit more time at the outset, but he was in for a *huge* surprise in terms of how much easier the writing process would get. Writing essays may have taken him forever in the past, but it definitely didn't have to. That's true for everyone. Anytime you're stuck and don't know what to say in an essay, then that's actually the perfect clue to tell you that you need a little Sherlock in your life. So let's go back to Vikram and his poem.

Vikram begrudgingly dug around in his backpack, produced a wad of paper, and smoothed it out for Katie to see. It was sonnet time. Katie asked him to start reading. "(Sigh... eye roll...ahem) My mistress' eyes..."

"...Are nothing like the sun? Ahhh, 'Sonnet 130.' A classic. I could've helped you with that, Vikram." Vikram's super-nerdy older brother, Parvesh, had entered the room, and Vikram had steam coming out of his ears.

OMG, Shkspr!

"What the heck, Shakespeare? Why couldn't you just talk in normal English instead of Shakespeare-speak?" Well, in his time and place, Shakespeare *was* speaking in normal English. His plays were written to be understood by the Queen and the peasants alike. So, he made sure that the jokes were common ones and that the language was totally normal for everyone at that time. He didn't make it hard; our language just evolved. Think about it: if you sent Shakespeare a text message, like "OMG! R&J = so L. J/K loved it. g2g," he would be beyond confused. He'd have to work pretty hard to make each piece of that text as obvious as "Eggs."

"Parvesh, I will murder your face!!!!!!" he screamed. Vikram then turned to Katie and calmly said, "Please tell him to leave."

Fortunately, Parvesh disappeared and it was time to continue. Knowing this was a sonnet, and that sonnets are usually about love, Vikram tried really hard to be done. He said, authoritatively, "It's about love. How...amazing love is and a pretty girl and stuff."

Katie didn't buy it. "Where in the poem do you see that, Vikram?" Vikram's conclusion was clear evidence of his belief that you can get through English class by making stuff up. In fact, reading comprehension is just as logical as science—that's why

Sherlock's skills are key when it comes to literary analysis.

"Look, I don't get this. Can't you just tell me what it means and I'll write that?"

A familiar voice boomed from the kitchen: "I can hear you, and if you do that, I'll tell Mom and Dad!" Was Parvesh everywhere? Reluctantly, Vikram read through the poem.

Sonnet 130
My mistress' eyes are nothing like the sun;
Coral is far more red than her lips' red;
If snow be white, why then her breasts are dun;
If hairs be wires, black wires grow on her head.
I have seen roses damask'd, red and white,
But no such roses see I in her cheeks;
And in some perfumes is there more delight
Than in the breath that from my true love reeks.
I love to hear her speak, yet well I know
That music has a far more pleasing sound;
I grant I never saw a goddess go;
My mistress, when she walks, treads on the ground;
And yet, by heaven, I think my love as rare
As any <u>she</u> belied with false compare.

Refers to the girlfriends of other poets.

Before any Sherlocking could happen, Vikram needed to make sure Betty would approve of this poem. Vikram's note on the final line of the poem was a hint that his teacher had given to the class. So, it was already a bit clearer who the "she" was in that line. Next, Vikram went through the poem and made all of the unfamiliar words as obvious as "Eggs," so that he could be sure he had all of the facts lined up before he started to examine them.

SONNET 130: Obvious As "Eggs"

Sonnet 130

My mistress' eyes are nothing like the sun;

Coral is far more red than her lips' red; *of the pink color of*

If snow be white, why then her breasts are dun; *the damask rose* *grayish brown*

If hairs be wires, black wires grow on her head. *(Shakespeare-speak for pink)*

I have seen roses damask'd red and white,

But no such roses see I in her cheeks;

And in some perfumes is there more delight

Than in the breath that from my true love reeks; *to smell strongly and unpleasantly*

I love to hear her speak, yet well I know

That music has a far more pleasing sound; *to admit*

I grant I never saw a goddess go;

My mistress, when she walks, treads on the ground;

And yet, by heaven, I think my love as rare

As any she belied with false compare.

Refers to the girlfriends of other poets.

1. to show to be false;
2. to misrepresent

Then, just like Danielle did with her statistics, once he had finished with the dictionary, Vikram went through the sonnet, translating each line into his own words.

SONNET 130: The Vikram Remix

> My girlfriend's eyes don't look like the sun
> Coral (Like fish? Whatever.) Coral is way redder than
> her lips...so her lips aren't red? Her lips are pasty?
> If snow is white, then her boobs are dull grayish brown (gross)
> And her hair is black and...something about wires.
> I've seen some nice pink, red, and white roses.   5
> But I don't see any of those colors in her cheeks.
> (So...her cheeks aren't rosy?)
> And in perfumes there is a much happier smell.
> Than the funky, rank breath that my girlfriend has.
> I like to hear her talk, but I know
> That music sounds way better.
> I'll admit I never saw a goddess walk around. (I still   10
> don't get why that matters.)
> My girlfriend walks on the floor. (Dunno...)
> But even with all this, I think she's as awesome and rare
> As any other poet's girlfriend who is...misrepresented
> with false comparisons.

By rewriting each individual line in a way that was Cake-Mix Clear, Vikram could concentrate on the *message* of Shakespeare's poem, as opposed to the scary Shakespeariness of how it was worded. It was at this point that Sherlock could take over. The importance of the last line was still mysterious, and Vikram had some questions earlier in the poem too. It was time to start investigating.

Step 1: Assess the clues. What Can You Say for Sure?

Sherlock Holmes doesn't act on any assumptions; he only

builds his case on cold, hard facts. So, Katie asked Vikram, "From what we have in the poem so far, what can we say *for sure*?"

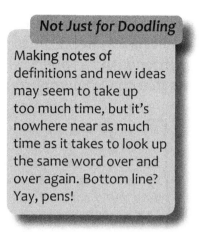

Not Just for Doodling

Making notes of definitions and new ideas may seem to take up too much time, but it's nowhere near as much time as it takes to look up the same word over and over again. Bottom line? Yay, pens!

Vikram snorted, "Her boobs are gray and her breath stinks." Great! "Uh, no, that's gross. I don't get it. Why would he say that? Is the point that his girlfriend is ugly? Man, if I were that girl, I would totally break up with Shakespeare." Exactly. Vikram could now see why it was dangerous to jump to that "it's about a really pretty girl" conclusion earlier. All that he could say for sure was that Shakespeare is willing to talk smack about his girlfriend. Could he use that to get some insight into any of the other lines?

Katie and Vikram decided to start from the beginning. *My mistress' eyes are nothing like the sun.* Vikram's first response was, "Duh! Eyeballs don't look like the sun. The sun is yellow. And on fire." True, true. But if Shakespeare is dissing his girlfriend, then why would he write this? "Well, I guess the sun is pretty and glowy." Right! And that's probably what you'd want someone's eyes to be too. "But they're not." Exactly. What next?

"Ha! Her lips aren't as red as coral, and red lips are hot, and so that means that her lips are also ugly." OK, now he was getting somewhere.

Step 2: Look for Patterns Among the Clues

As Vikram went through the sonnet line by line, he noticed that the speaker establishes a pattern of talking about pretty things and then saying his girlfriend doesn't have them. The speaker eventually changes that, but not until the end. When you're reading anything in school—a poem, a play, or a novel—you can bet that every word is there for a good reason. So, if Vikram's poem had fourteen lines, and twelve of them say that the poet's girlfriend isn't as pretty as a lot of other things, then it was safe to bet that that's an important idea.

My girlfriend's eyes don't look like the sun
Coral (Like fish? Whatever.) Coral is way redder than
her lips...so her lips aren't red? Her lips are pasty?
If snow is white, then her boobs are dull grayish brown (gross)
And her hair is black and...something about wires.
I've seen some nice pink, red, and white roses.   5
But I don't see any of those colors in her cheeks.
(So...her cheeks aren't rosy?)
And in perfumes there is a much happier smell.
Than the funky, rank breath that my girlfriend has
I like to hear her talk, but I know
That music sounds way better.   10
I'll admit I never saw a goddess walk around. (I still
don't get why that matters.)
My girlfriend walks on the floor. (Dunno...)
But even with all this, I think she's as awesome and rare
As any other poet's girlfriend who is...misrepresented
with false comparisons.

WHAT???

She has grey boobs,
rank breath,
wire Hair,
pasty lips,
her cheeks have
no roses...

Shakespeare
spends twelve
lines saying
all the things
his gf isn't
as hot as...

Shakespeare
has an ugly
gf!!!

Whenever you're reading any piece of literature, for English class or otherwise, if a word, phrase, or idea gets repeated, you can be sure that it's because the author REALLY wants you to notice it. Because this sonnet is so short, it is easy to see that repetition of ideas all in a row. But in a novel, you may see repeated words or ideas or images appear once every few chapters or so. It's more spread out, but that's still a red flag that it's important. Noticing the repetition is the key to figuring out the main ideas or themes of any work. Sherlock Holmes operates in the same way. If a particular suspect is present every time a crime is committed, then he or she should definitely be a "person of interest." With enough appearances, it should become really obvious whodunit.

Pay attention to the fact that Vikram's process did not go in corn-on-the-cob order through the poem. After reading the poem one time, Vikram jumped around to make the different words in the passage as obvious as "eggs." Then he picked out the clues that would make the clearest and most helpful starting point, which in this case were the third and eighth lines of the poem. As Vikram went along, he filled in the information around those clues. At this point, he just had to secure whatever the final mysterious pieces were, no matter where they were in the poem. The main idea—the culprit—can be lurking anywhere in your reading. Great detectives never expect to work straight from beginning to end. It's about narrowing in on your suspect.

Step 3: Where are the Holes in my Theory?

Vikram had gotten down to the very core idea of the first twelve lines. But those final two were still confusing, because they definitely didn't seem to fit with the pattern of the poet just saying that his mistress isn't that hot. Here's what Vikram had to work with.

My girlfriend isn't that hot. (Lines 1-12)
But even with all this, I think she's as awesome and rare
As any other poet's girlfriend who is...misrepresented with false comparisons. (???)

One thing that Vikram noticed was that these final lines start with "but" (or "and yet" in the original). That was a sign that the lines contain some sort of message that's going to change things up a bit. What's more, after naming all these terrible things about his mistress, the poet says that he still thinks she's "rare"...which is a good thing, like "wonderful" and "unique." So, based on that, what could a reader tell? "We can tell that even though this girl looks kinda nasty, he still really loves her and appreciates her." How sweet. Vikram had nailed it.

The real kicker was the final line, though. Why was this worth writing a poem about? "As any she belied with false compare." Based on Vikram's translation, Shakespeare is saying that other poets' girlfriends are..."misrepresented" (belied) with false comparisons. So...they get compared to things, but those comparisons aren't really true?

"Aaarrrrgghh! This is so stupid. Why can't poets just say what they mean? If he thinks his girlfriend is busted...just say so!!!! This takes forever!" Vikram was frustrated, and what happened next didn't help:

"Vikram, no need to yell. I'm happy to help you..." (Parvesh was back.)

"GET OUT OR I WILL END YOU!"

Vikram threw his eraser at Parvesh, who melodramatically said, "That really hurt. I will be telling Mom," before leaving. With Parvesh gone, Vikram and Katie got back to work.

Okay, these other poets compare their girlfriends to things, but the comparisons aren't really true. So, on the one hand, this guy is at least telling it straight about his girlfriend's looks. The other poets exaggerate. The basic message would be a poem like this:

My girlfriend isn't that hot,

But I think she's just as awesome
As any other girl whose poet-boyfriend is probably exaggerating about her anyway.

Obviously, Shakespeare's version is a little more appealing and impressive than Vikram's final version. But by making the message this clear, it was starting to make more sense to Vikram why Shakespeare chose the specific comparisons and wording that he did in the first twelve lines. Think about it: all the qualities that his girlfriend doesn't have, like rosy cheeks and bright, twinkling eyes, are exactly the kinds of things that most poets would say their girlfriends *do* have. He's basically saying, "In your face, liars! No one's cheeks are *really* like roses, and no one's voice is *actually* like music. My girlfriend is human, and sometimes she has bad breath, but I still think she's great." It may not be exactly what his girlfriend wants to hear, but he's just telling the truth.

WHAT IS CONFUSION?

The Chinese character for confusion represents a man unraveling a ball of string. Centuries ago, people saw confusion as the perfectly normal process through which everyone goes when he or she is trying to get to an ideal end result.

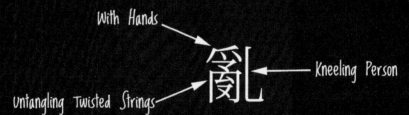

With Hands

Kneeling Person

Untangling Twisted Strings

But thanks to the conspiracy, our idea of confusion has changed. What do you associate with the feeling of confusion? Frustration? Helplessness? Most of us feel as if being confused means that we don't understand what we're working on… and there's very little chance that we ever will. In reality, confusion is an essential part of the process.

Step 4: How Does this Relate to Your Experience as a Human Being?

Sherlock's best technique for making sense of the clues is to really think about them in relation to how people behave. He is fascinated by what people do and why. After all, everybody's life is different, and yet there are some experiences that everyone goes through in some way.

That's important, because the reason that certain literary works become "classics" is that they talk about those universal emotional experiences that we all understand—things like the feeling of having your first crush. Vikram may not have used the word "belied" often, but he *did* live in the world, and he *was* a human being. Therefore, there were things that he knew to be true.

> **The Key is the Couplet**
>
> All sonnets are fourteen-line poems. But Shakespearean sonnets have a very specific structure. The first twelve lines are the "setup." You can think of the final couplet—or pair of lines that rhyme with each other—as the "payoff." They take the setup and either turn it on its head or drive it home in some way. It's usually in the relationship between the setup and the payoff that you can find the real message.

FACT: Most lovey-dovey poems just give a person compliments.

FACT: People do not appreciate hearing that their breath stinks.

FACT: Probably Shakespeare's girlfriend was pretty angry when she read this the first time.

FACT: It's nice to hear over-the-top compliments sometimes, but it's better to be loved for who you are.

FACT: Ultimately, Shakespeare's poem is weirdly romantic, because it's honest. He loves her even with her flaws.

By this point, Vikram was starting to change his tune. "Okay. That's pretty cool. I get this. Shakespeare loved her, but he's funny about it." That's right—this is sort of like the anti-love-poem love poem. And by putting this poem in the context of what Vikram already knew about life—he could finally see what made the poem worthwhile. Vikram looked down at the poem sheepishly. He had to admit, he was actually enjoying Shakespeare.

So, did Vikram just "make up" his conclusions about this sonnet? After all, that's what he said all of the good English students were doing. Of course not! It only looks like people "make things up" when you don't see the steps that are involved. English is a logical subject, just like any other. Vikram's understanding came from doing actual investigation into the poem, so that every conclusion he drew was based on "facts" from the poem itself.

Because he did that investigation, Vikram could talk about what the poem is saying, and why it's interesting that Shakespeare would not only dare to say his girlfriend isn't hot, but would also be willing to call other poets exaggerators. He could talk about how Shakespeare's approach to the "love poem" is way different from most poets' approaches. He could talk about tons of things, because he finally had an *actual understanding* of what was going on in this reading. Not only did this half hour of reading time save him hours when he wrote the essay, but his essay would be much better too.

Does Corn-on-the-Cob Reading Actually Save You Time?

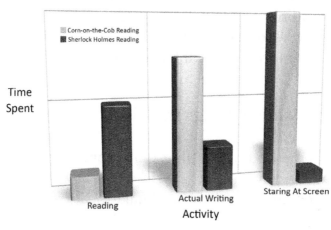

For the purposes of writing his essay, Vikram now had a good enough understanding of the poem to get past his writer's block. Of course, Sherlock Holmes would not stop here; there is much more in this poem to discover. For instance, there are details of word choice that affect the tone and show what literary techniques Shakespeare was using. Perhaps learning more about Shakespeare's own life would bring more meaning to the poem. There are always more questions to ask to better understand a mystery. The deeper you look into what you're reading, and the more you read in general, the more automatic your process will become. With enough practice, things like the meanings of words from Elizabethan English and the ability to recognize literary techniques will become automatic for you.

Vikram also thought that he should be able to understand the poem right away; when that didn't happen, he decided that investigating it at all was a waste of time. "Work" is annoying, but puzzles are fun to solve. By digging in and not worrying about how long the process took, Vikram went from hating Shakespeare to actually kind of enjoying it. Appreciation comes from understanding. The better you understand something, the more exciting it becomes, the more you will appreciate why it matters, and the more fun you'll have doing it.

Knowing The Motive Brings the Clues to Life

Sherlock's method for reading is awesome because it works on any passage in any subject, anytime and anywhere. Some of Sherlock's cases are like Vikram's Shakespeare sonnet; to any other detective, they would seem inaccessible and impossible to solve. Sherlock knows that with enough investigation, he can make sense of even the most intimidating sets of clues.

But there is another kind of case that Sherlock is famous for cracking. It's the sneakiest type of case—the one that from the outside looks like there's not a case to be solved at all. Most detectives see the clues and think that they're perfectly normal and straightforward...and, in fact, boring. They find a reasonable explanation because the case seems to be open-and-shut. Nothing to investigate. But Sherlock is never satisfied until he understands *why* the suspect might have committed the crime. That insistence on understanding every aspect of the case is why he's always the only detective to catch the *real* criminal.

> ### Think They O'er-do It?
>
> One of the conventions of poetry that students find most off-putting is the use of accents and apostrophes to change words that would otherwise be simple. Why do poets write wand'ring and stainéd and even o'er? Most students think poets do this to be "fancy." In reality, the poet is sort of cheating. Many poems have a rhythm that the poet commits to and then has to fulfill. If you can only have ten syllables per line, then changing "over" to "o'er" saves you a syllable of space and that can make a huge difference. This is a poet's way of bending the rules to maximize his poetic punch.

In "The Adventure of the Six Napoleons," Sherlock is called to investigate a series of break-ins in which nothing is stolen. In fact, in each situation, only one thing is out of the ordinary: a statue of Napoleon has been destroyed. When Inspector Lestrade sees this evidence, he reaches a conclusion in record time. Obviously, someone just *really* hates Napoleon. Weird, but no big deal. Case closed, right? Not for Sherlock. Sherlock needs to know the criminal's *motive*; what's more, he needs to find a motive that is actually satisfying. In other words, he needs to believe that it would drive an actual, otherwise normal human being to commit a crime.

For Sherlock, hating a random historical figure from 84 years earlier is not enough reason for the average person to risk jail by breaking into shops and burgling people's homes. That would be like you becoming a burglar because you hate John Quincy Adams's face. There must be something more.

Indeed, as the case progresses, Sherlock discovers that these particular Napoleon statues all came from the same mold and one is rumored to contain a treasure. *Now* there's a more understandable motive. Most people wouldn't risk breaking into a shop just to be mad at Napoleon. But if it meant getting a treasure? That's more believable. By continuing to question the motive, Sherlock finds more clues that help him to solve the case.

The fun of being a detective is the investigation—seeing what other people wouldn't see. So when a case seems obvious, most detectives would get bored. Ugh. Nothing to find here. That's the other key mistake that a lot of students make with their reading. Textbook reading looks, on the surface, like there's not much to discover, and so students go full-Lestrade and treat it like an open-and-shut case. And this is especially true in history textbooks— the undisputed world champions of boring, straightforward factoids.

Sherlock Doesn't Discriminate

Just because Sherlock is a literary character doesn't mean he's only helpful for your English class. Sherlock's approach is the key to solving one of the most universally troublesome parts of math class: word problems. Most students corn-on-the-cob read their word problems and then throw down some Lestrade-like equation. Instead, just as Vikram took apart the sonnet, line by line, you need to take apart a word problem, line by line.
1) Figure out exactly what case you're trying to solve. If the word problem is about a bake sale, b=brownies is not the same as b=cost of brownies or b=number of brownies sold. 2) Separate the facts from the fluff. Search for the relevant clues, and ignore the fact that the bake sale was in support of the Rockingham County High School debate team. 3) Now that you've narrowed it down, figure out how the facts are related. 4) Use them to define and solve an equation. Word problems aren't harder, they just require an initial investigation to weed out the relevant clues.

Be honest. How often do you *really* do all of your history reading each night? Or better yet, how often do you *not* corn-on-the-cob it, whenever you do get around to reading it? "Blah, blah, blah Continental Congress...blah blah blah Winston Churchill... blah blah...wait, did I skip some? Whatever. Blah blah 1957...blah, blah Martin Luther King, Jr....blah blah blah invention of the internet... Done!" It's a classic move to say, "This is just a million facts about dead people. It's annoying, but if I just memorize them, I'll be done." That may get you through a quiz or two, but if you find history "boring" or "useless" then that means that you're approaching your history class in the hardest way possible.

The problem isn't that history is boring. The problem is that it's wa-a-a-ay too interesting. On a practical level, consider this tidbit:

OF ALL THE TRILLIONS OF THINGS THAT HAVE HAPPENED IN THE ENTIRE HISTORY OF MANKIND, THE FACTS IN YOUR HISTORY BOOK HAVE BEEN HAND-PICKED AS THE MOST WORTH LEARNING!!!

Entire civilizations have lived, day by day, for thousands of years. On each of those days, *every single person in every single civilization* did many, many things. And yet only 400 or so pages of events can make it into an average history textbook. So, if something gets an entire paragraph, page, or chapter in your book, you can assume that it's *more important and interesting* than 99.9% of all things that have ever happened to any humans.

What's more, even for the people and events that *do* make it into the textbooks, you're NEVER getting the full story. That's because history is extremely controversial. When it comes to historical events, people have strong opinions about who was right, who was at fault, and whether the actions were justifiable. As you can probably guess, those opinions rarely match up. What's more, as you learned from the genius myths in Chapter

One, people have strong agendas when it comes to how the stories of their own lives and their accomplishments (or failures) are told. Basically, if you're a history textbook writer, you're wading into shark-infested waters. The only way to write a textbook that doesn't anger anyone—or everyone—is to stick to the facts and *only* the facts: the who, what, when, and where.

So what's the result of that? Well, having *just* the facts... is...boring! You're absolutely right to think that a bunch of straightforward facts is not fun to read. But you're *not* right to think that what's in your textbook is the entire extent of what you need in history class.

In history textbooks, the really interesting aspects—the *why* and the *how*—are missing. But it's the *how* and the *why* that make history SO UNBELIEVABLY MIND-BLOWING. History is seriously fascinating. But you have to investigate what's behind the facts in the text in order to find the motives that brought these events about. Those motives are what bring it all to life. Nothing major has ever happened that wasn't fueled by intense emotions, high-stakes drama, big risks, and super-controversial actions. People have done some crazy things, but they do them for real reasons. Take the time to think about *why* the people in history did what they did—investigate the motive—and you'll have no trouble getting through that textbook.

To show you what happens when you apply Sherlock's method to your history reading, let's take a look at an excellently dry sample passage from a textbook. This particular passage is a great example, because the event

The Tutu Guru

Katie was once at the ballet in Los Angeles, sitting behind a father and his six-year-old daughter, who was sporting a very impressive tutu. When the father asked the daughter whether she was going to be okay sitting for the whole length of the ballet, she turned to him and very frankly said, "Dad. Only boring people get bored." Katie was blown away. Best. Advice. Ever. Take a hint from the six-year-old ballerina. If you're bored... whose fault is that?

happened a really long time ago, which can make it feel like it's no longer relevant. Also, it was done by this guy:

That's Martin Luther. How much do you feel like you can identify with him? Already, this is a bit of a turn-off. But if you let yourself go Lestrade like that, it's easy to underestimate what a major deal this man really was.

---

67   CHAPTER 3: THE REFORMATION

In order to fund a rebuilding campaign for St. Peter's Basilica in Rome, Pope Leo X authorized the sale of plenary indulgences. A plenary indulgence was a piece of paper that Catholics could purchase in exchange for absolution from their sins. Martin Luther, a Catholic priest from Germany, was disturbed by this practice and on October 31st, 1517, he nailed 95 theses to the church door at Wittenberg. These theses were a list of his concerns about the current state of the church and Luther's hope was that they would spark a debate. They did much more than that. Martin Luther was excommunicated, and the Reformation began.

Sixteenth Century Europe

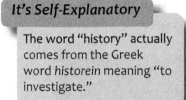

It's Self-Explanatory

The word "history" actually comes from the Greek word *historein* meaning "to investigate."

If you found your attention drifting during this passage, then chances are likely that you were doing some corn-on-the-cob reading. Most students would take away the superficial, just-the-facts conclusion. "Some priest guy got mad, wrote a note to the Pope, and nailed it to a church door." That's true, but it certainly doesn't sound like you've "solved" that case, does it?

What led to this event taking place? What were Martin Luther's motives? Take the straight-up facts from your book and *find* the meaning, the significance, and the connections that show why this event mattered (and still matters) so much.

The passage, like most textbook passages, is pretty close to Cake-Mix Clear already. Let's just make sure that every term passes the Eggs Test.

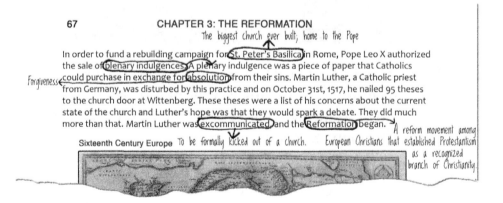

67   CHAPTER 3: THE REFORMATION

The biggest church ever built; home to the Pope

In order to fund a rebuilding campaign for St. Peter's Basilica in Rome, Pope Leo X authorized the sale of plenary indulgences. A plenary indulgence was a piece of paper that Catholics could purchase in exchange for absolution from their sins. Martin Luther, a Catholic priest from Germany, was disturbed by this practice and on October 31st, 1517, he nailed 95 theses to the church door at Wittenberg. These theses were a list of his concerns about the current state of the church and Luther's hope was that they would spark a debate. They did much more than that. Martin Luther was excommunicated and the Reformation began.

Forgiveness

A reform movement among European Christians that established Protestantism as a recognized branch of Christianity.

Sixteenth Century Europe   *To be formally kicked out of a church.*

Step 1: Assess the Clues. What Can You Say For Sure?

In history, this first step is usually very straightforward, because many of the surface facts are presented in a clear way. Now that everything in this passage is as obvious as "eggs," you can take stock of what you know for sure.

1. The pope wants to raise money to build the biggest church ever.
2. To pay for that church, he lets people buy forgiveness for their sins.
3. Martin Luther thinks that's wrong.
4. He makes a list of things the church is doing wrong and nails it to the local church door.
5. He gets kicked out of the Church.
6. He starts a new branch of Christianity.

Step 2: Look for Patterns Among the Clues

Although you can appreciate that these events happened in this order, it's a very different thing to really understand the connections between those events and why each one caused the next.

The events that led to the Reformation started, in part, with Martin Luther getting angry at the Church. So let's examine why the Church made Luther *so upset* that he was willing to risk being excommunicated. Martin Luther thought it was wrong that the Church was selling plenary indulgences. Why? Why was that so bad? Well, think about it. Luther was a priest, and his whole life was dedicated to bringing himself and everyone else closer to God. But suddenly, plenary indulgences made it so that getting into heaven wasn't about faith, it was about money. You could just buy forgiveness coupons! Unsurprisingly, Martin Luther thought the Church was acting in a very shady fashion. So, he questioned the Pope's decision to sell indulgences and brought up a bunch of other things that he thought the Church was doing wrong.

So, now you understand why Martin Luther wrote his 95 theses. You get his motives. But, in order to really give the event a strong context, you also need to know what happened after, and as a result of it. Well, Martin Luther wanted to spark a debate within the Church. But there was no debate, and he got excommunicated. At face value, that would seem like his plan backfired. Luther didn't get to stay in the Catholic Church and make it better. However, his actions still had an enormous effect, because they ultimately led to the Protestant Reformation—not a new version of the Catholic church, but a new church altogether.

Step 3: Where are the Holes in my Theory?

In history textbook reading, most sentences are pretty understandable at face value. But that doesn't mean that you have nothing to "fill in." It is almost impossible to understand or appreciate an historical event in isolation. If you want to know why an occurrence was fascinating, then ask the following questions:

> What led up to this that made it a turning point? What did it take to make this happen?
> What future events did this one make possible?
> What was it like to live then? What were the conditions of the time?

It's important to understand what Europe was like back then. At that point, the Catholic Church had been the biggest, most powerful entity in Europe for hundreds and hundreds of years. *Everyone* in Europe was Catholic, and the Church could do whatever it wanted. Just to give you an idea of how serious this was, when Henry IV—the Holy Roman Emperor—was excommunicated, he crawled on his knees to beg the Pope to undo his excommunication. (When an Emperor gets on his knees to beg you for something, you're pretty powerful.) If the Catholic Church said the Earth was at the center of the solar system, then everybody said it was true. Almost nobody questioned the Church, because people believed that the Pope was "God's chosen representative on Earth." That meant that when the Pope said something, it was the same as if God said it.

And if you were living in Europe, you basically had no options. You were either Catholic or...no "or," actually. You were Catholic. Whether you agreed with the Church's ways or not, you just kept your mouth shut and dealt with it. If you didn't, the authorities strapped you to a pole, surrounded you with twigs and set you on FIRE! Between the lack of options and the refusal of the Catholic Church to change, it's no *wonder* that there were other people out there who were dissatisfied and wanted a new branch of Christianity. That condition was important for making the Reformation possible.

Now, let's talk consequences. In order to understand why you still learn about this little note to the Pope, you have to investigate the fallout. What happened as a *result* of this action? What became of this Protestantism business? Why does the Reformation matter for future events? Well, the Reformation basically split Europe in two. Half of Europe stayed Catholic, and half of Europe became Protestant. This shift in religious practice alone was huge. But once people started to question the church, something major happened: they started questioning other things too. Although it's unlikely that Martin Luther intended this, some historians have argued that the Protestant Reformation created a culture of questioning that played a major role in driving the Scientific Revolution.

What Would That Be Like?

Where do you find the why and the how? There are plenty of ways to look beyond the facts. You can find other books or articles, or even just do a simple Google search. Any extra information helps. You might find conflicting opinions or details, which is even better, because you can really puzzle it out. Then again, you can also get a lot closer to the motives just by actually thinking about what it says in your book. What does it really mean that 12 million people died in the Holocaust? Do you actually stop to picture how massive that is? Alternatively, what would it be like to feel so strongly about an idea that you'd risk your life over it? Or, what would it be like to actually fight in a war? Or to be in charge and have to make decisions about what happens to the soldiers? Sometimes, just by really focusing on a fact, it's much easier to see how important and shocking it is.

Step 4: How Does this Relate to Your Experience as a Human Being?

Of course, Sherlock wouldn't stop at just learning the facts of the church door, the 95 theses, and the excommunication. Sherlock always wants to know what makes people tick, and investigating that aspect of an historical event is what will really help you to understand it—and to remember it. After all, history books are made up of only the *most* impressive feats...people facing the *biggest* challenges and taking the *boldest* actions. So what you want to ask yourself in the final step is, "Why was this a high-stakes move for this particular person?" In other words, what did it take for Martin Luther to do what he did? What was he up against, and why was his action so extraordinary?

So let's put ourselves in Martin Luther's shoes. You've sacrificed your entire life to serving the church as a priest. Little by little, you notice things that the Church is doing that you don't think are quite right. They pile up, but you stay true to your commitment to the Church and try to look the other way. But once the sale of plenary indulgences begins, you just can't take it anymore. You feel like you've got to do something, but what are you going to do? You know what happens to people who challenge the Pope's authority. (They get set on fire.) But you feel so unbelievably strongly about these issues that you go ahead anyway and nail a note to what is essentially *God's door*. Clearly, you know you're not exactly going to get a thank you card for doing this. Martin Luther knew he was taking a huge risk, but he knew it was something he *had* to do.

When you look at Luther's 95 Theses from that perspective, you can get a whole new level of appreciation for what he did and why it was a very, very high-stakes move. He risked a lot, but for him the reward was big too: he eventually got a church in which he could really believe.

And how does that help you today? After Martin Luther's move, for the first time, people in Europe could openly disagree, debate, and question. The intellectual shackles had been taken off. This condition played a major role in the exponential growth in technology, art, and science that happened in the wake of that explosion. Thanks in part to that little note to the Pope, you're not a peasant, you don't worry about the Plague, and you don't empty your toilet onto the sidewalk. Thanks, Martin Luther!

With Sherlock's skills, you can see beyond the surface facts and piece together the full story of things that happened in the past. And when you start doing this, history is no longer just a class where you have to memorize a million separate stupid little details about stuff that has already happened. Instead, by really understanding your reading, you can also see why the things you learn about in history class are hugely important, and why people really are as fascinating as Sherlock thinks they are. The goal of history class is not to learn history but to learn *from* history. Just like studying literature, studying history gives us a way to better understand ourselves. History allows us all to learn and question the choices that people made in the past, so that we can see why our world is in the position that it is today. The more Sherlocking that everyone does, the better chance we all have of making sure that we don't repeat the mistakes of past generations. Only by understanding how we got here can we figure out how to get where we hope to be.

Are You Sherlock Holmes or Inspector Lestrade?

There are two ways to approach your reading. Most students choose the Inspector Lestrade route. Because there's no actual method to his investigation, he ends up running around in circles and jumping to conclusions that get him no closer to an arrest. His "process" is also stressful, because he doesn't really know what he's doing. In the same way, students corn-on-the-cob their reading, try to guess at the real meaning of the text, and then jump to writing an essay. That's just asking for extra hours of being stuck in the writing process with nothing to say. What's more, those students never get to feel like the case is closed, because they never reach some exciting or interesting conclusion about what they read. Lestrade's method of taking the surface explanation *seems* faster, but in the end, it takes more time and is far less satisfying and successful.

And then there's the Sherlock way. We've given you a taste of what Sherlock's method can really do. Sherlock's method may seem, at first, to take longer; after all, it does require more patience and more attention to detail...and even some research. But Sherlocking your reading sets you up to save a ton of time on all of the essays and tests that come after that reading. Writer's block won't be an issue, and everything you read will be more memorable. That means less time studying for your tests and less stress while you're taking them.

Best of all, Sherlocking your reading will make every single class more interesting. Sherlock Holmes is never bored. Already, as a high schooler, you're essentially being handed a Greatest Hits playlist of the best literature and the most meaningful historical events. All you have to do is investigate why what you're studying made the cut. Appreciation comes from understanding.

A Distinct Advantage

The more reading you've Sherlocked in your life, the faster you'll be at finding mind-blowing connections when you read something new. For example, if you've Sherlocked your history up to Martin Luther, then you'd know he wasn't the first person to attempt this kind of reform. But you'd also be able to spot why he was the most successful: he lived in the age of the printing press. Before Luther's time, if you wanted to change the way people thought, you had to rely on hand-copied documents or word of mouth. Thanks to the printing press, just eight years after he first posted his 95 Theses, Luther and his supporters had flooded Europe with three million pamphlets and books.

By approaching your reading like Sherlock would, you can guarantee that the seconds never drag by on the clock; your work will breeze by, and you won't be able to *help* but find it fascinating. So, Sherlock or Lestrade? Well, my dear friend, the choice is elementary.

Getting the Ball Rolling

Depending on your level of familiarity with the text, Sherlocking your reading can take a little while or no time at all. Even if you don't feel ready to dig into a passage as much as we have above, the best place to begin is by catching yourself in the act of corn-on-the-cob reading. Pay attention and stop yourself whenever you get into that left-to-right rhythm. It may be once every couple of sentences, once per paragraph, or once per page, but if you start to pay attention to *how* you read, you'll get more out of *what* you read.

Chapter 8

Produce an Essay That's a Blockbuster

You look at the clock. It's 9:15 pm. Two paragraphs in. So...what do I say next? Umm...something else about...Romeo and how he likes Juliet? Where are all the quotes in this book? *Flipflipflipflip*. Page 43? Nothing there. Sigh...why do essays take forever?

9:33 p.m.
I should make the font bigger. Will she notice if I go to 12.2? 12.3? That helped. I'll also make the margins narrower. But not too much narrower.

9:40 p.m.
I should make my title BIGGER...and **BOLD**. And **UNDERLINED**. Nice. Almost done with page 1. I need a break.

10:12 p.m.
I should just go to sleep and get up early.

10:13 p.m.
I should just keep writing...anything.

10:35 p.m.
This is officially the worst night of my life.

Of all the things that students are asked to do in school, essay writing is the most universally dreaded. Students everywhere know that essays are really involved and really time-consuming. Just one mention of the *word* "essay" conjures up visions of extreme, unending late-night boredom in a way that few other words can achieve. You endure hour after hour of mind-numbing torture at the end of which, hopefully, you have a good essay.

Now, ask yourself the following question: have you ever actually seen a *good essay*? Like, in real life? Few students have. Really good essays are like Bigfoot. And high school is *not* their natural habitat. For this reason, most students are pretty certain that a *good* essay—one you'd actually *want* to read—doesn't exist. Well, we're here to tell you that it *does*. And it probably looks very different from what you were expecting. So what actually makes for a "good essay"—or better yet, an *amazing* essay? You can find the answer playing right now, in theaters everywhere.

Write for Mass Consumption, Not Mass Confusion

A really good essay should be just like a really good movie. And not just any movie. A blockbuster movie. You know, the kind of movie where the hero(ine) fights the aliens/monster/zombies/robots and stops them from taking over the world, one awesome explosion at a time. Everyone in the family can enjoy a blockbuster, because it is an action-packed thrill ride with an epic love story, all packed into one intense two-hour experience. That kind of movie is pure summer-afternoon entertainment. Filmmakers invest years and years of work—and millions and millions of dollars—so that when you, the audience member, sink into your plush theater chair, you know you're about to experience a movie that is exciting, interesting, and most importantly, *easy to watch*.

Think about *Star Wars*, *Jaws*, *Indiana Jones*, *Jurassic Park*, *The Avengers*, *Pirates of the Caribbean*, *Avatar*...these are some of the blockbuster movies that will go down in history for their widespread appeal. It would be amazing if reading all of the essays that you and your classmates write were as fun as watching *Iron Man*. Unfortunately, most high-school writers think that an essay should be like a bizarro black-and-white silent art film. The writer uses the biggest, most obscure vocabulary possible and makes points so deep that you have to be a French neo-post-(sur)-realist art critic to understand them. The final product leaves readers so confused and bewildered that they can only assume something really intelligent must have just happened.

Here's a question. Would you actually *want to read* an essay like that? Of course not! It sounds *terrible*! Those essays are not worth the paper they're printed on, and the writers who write them should have their keyboard privileges revoked. So, the next time that you start down that path of literary pretension, consider this: if *you* don't even want to read your essay, how can you expect your teacher to get fired up about it?

Imagine if Steven Spielberg or George Lucas decided that the point of a movie wasn't to satisfy the audience—it was to forget about the audience and just look really smart. You'd have a new *Jaws* in which the shark only showed up once, and most of the time, Sheriff Brody sat alone in a dark corner, muttering to himself nonsensically and saying, "the shark is a metaphor... the shark is a metaphor"...and then everyone would die...of non-shark causes. And in the middle of *Star Wars*, there would be a ten-minute montage set to weird instrumental music, in which you'd see a shot of rain on a window...and then an onion, peeling itself...and then Yoda would express himself through interpretive dance. Making these movies would be a great opportunity for these filmmakers to try to look smart, but *nobody else* would want to see them.

Just like a major hit movie, a well-written essay is all about the audience. It hooks you at the beginning, keeps your attention from start to finish, has surprising twists and turns, and wraps up in a satisfying way at the end. Sure, you may not be investing hundreds of millions of dollars, but you are investing a lot of your time. Essays are always going to be more time-consuming and involved than other assignments; that's just the nature of what they are. But an essay definitely doesn't need to be boring for you or for the reader.

The key to writing successful essays is to change your entire awareness of what essay writing is all about. You need to start writing essays *for your audience*. If your essay is boring to you, then you can bet that it's boring to whoever has to review it. Fortunately, testing your essay against your own excitement— constantly checking to see whether you find it "gripping!" and "captivating!"—is also the best way to make sure that it's *good*. You need to learn how to write an essay that you'd buy a ticket to read.

A Blockbuster Can Save Your Summer

All of us can relate to the late-night, stare-at-the-blank-screen essay nightmare described at the beginning of the chapter, but that particular wrestling match with *Romeo and Juliet* belonged to our student, Meadow. Meadow Winslow was a tall, willowy, wavy-haired sophomore who would've been a super-hippie flower child...if she wasn't born in the 90's. Normally, Meadow was very easygoing and sweet. She was "one with the universe," and everything was "all good." In fact, in a week, she would be done with the school year and off to be a counselor at an artsy sleepaway camp in Northern California. Best summer ever. There was just one problem.

Meadow needed to do well on her final paper for Sophomore English, or else she'd be trading sleepaway camp for summer school. She'd already spent one torturous all-nighter trying to figure out what the essay should say. To make matters worse, she knew her teacher was going to be tough on her writing; after all, her teacher always made comments like, "You need stronger evidence for your points!" or "You have no analysis here...really dig for *original and specific* ideas!" But come on. How was Meadow supposed to find something *original* to say about a play that people had been reading for 500 years?

Meadow didn't need to accept her summer-school fate just yet. If she was going to make her essay the sort of blockbuster that would save her summer, then she needed to start thinking like a movie producer.

Why a Leaning Essay Is Harder To Write

In reading, students' desire to rush through their work makes them take the corn-on-the-cob approach, which you now know doesn't pay off. That phenomenon carries over into the essay-writing process. Students get a topic, skip the investigation, open a blank document, and just start typing. The result is something we call a "Tower of Pisa Essay."

You may have heard of the Tower of Pisa. It's really, really famous...for leaning. When the tower was first built in the 12th century, the builders made it to about the third floor, and then they realized they had a slight...problem. They hadn't made a deep enough foundation for the soil that was under the tower, and one side was sinking. The tower wasn't heading straight upwards anymore. When construction resumed about a hundred years later, the builders had a choice to make: start from scratch and do it right...or just fudge their way through and force it to work. They chose to keep on building, but the taller the tower became, the more leany it was. Eventually, it got so bad that they tried to compensate by making each new floor uneven. At the end of *that*, the tower was leaning...*and* curved. All of these problems could easily have been avoided if only the architects and builders had thought through every part of their plan *before* they said, "go."

Most students try to write their essays like they are building the Tower of Pisa. They jump straight into writing before they've made sure the foundation of the essay is solid. There are seven basic steps to writing an essay, and students love to skip the early ones so they can get right to piling on the sentences.

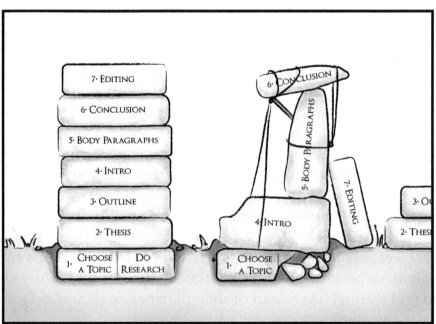

Maybe by the end of a paragraph or two, the students can tell that they're really stretching to make new points. But they keep adding on and pushing toward their conclusion. At each stage, the work gets more difficult, just like it did for the tower builders. By cutting out the planning stages, the students have set themselves up to endure hours of wracking their brains for more ways to say the same things over and over again. And the result? It's always an argument that is really unstable, repetitive, and completely "blaaaahhh." Skipping the foundation makes the essay no fun to write and no good for your grade.

Let's Make a Blockbuster!

The top movie directors are the furthest thing from the builders of the Tower of Pisa. Those directors would never jump right into shooting a film. Years and years of work go into most blockbuster movies before anyone turns on a camera. Do you honestly think James Cameron waits until he arrives on set to decide that the movie should be about some place called Pandora and that the creatures there should be blue? Filmmakers ask *all* of the important questions at the start of the process, building a rock-solid foundation, so that once production begins, they can be sure that they're not just making *any old* movie; they're making the *best possible* movie. Do the right work on your foundation up front, and your essay will earn you a star on the Hollywood Walk of Fame.

STEP 1: Make Sure You Have a Feature-Length Topic

All essays have to start somewhere. Fortunately, in almost every high school class, you will be given an essay topic or topics from which to choose. Meadow's teacher had given the class four possible essay topics, and Meadow looked at #2. This was the prompt:

2. At the end of William Shakespeare's Romeo and Juliet, the Prince says, "A glooming peace this morning with it brings; / The sun, for sorrow, will not show its head." In the aftermath of the lovers' deaths, the characters note that the tragedy is so great that even the sun will not shine. In fact, images of light and dark occur throughout the entirety of Romeo and Juliet. How does Shakespeare use these motifs to inform our understanding of this tragic love?

"Yeah, no *kidding* the sun won't show it's head for *sorrow*. Because it has an *English essay* to write." (Meadow was still far from bubbling with enthusiasm, but she forged ahead.) "Let's just do this one."

Not so fast. Hunter told Meadow that first, before she spent too much time working on this topic, she had to make sure it was feature-length. In other words, she needed to make sure there was enough support from the text—examples and quotes—to drive her argument all the way through the last page of her paper. In order to begin, Meadow needed to get a clear idea of what she was even *looking for* in terms of examples from the play. After she made the prompt Cake-Mix Clear, it looked like this:

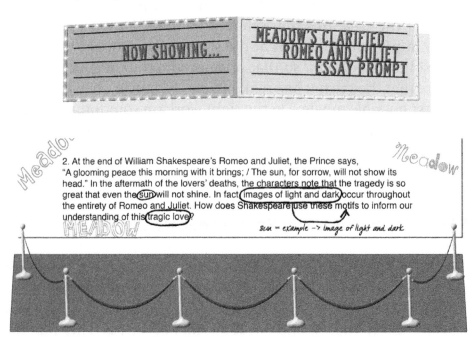

Meadow's teacher had provided her, in the prompt, with one example of how "light" shows up in the play. That meant that other quotes about "light" might also support the prompt—as might quotes with the word "dark." Those would be a great start, but Meadow needed to make sure she found *all* the good quotes related to this *idea*. She needed to generate a list of *keywords* that she could search for. Her keywords were all the words or images that Shakespeare may have used to talk about "light" and "dark." Meadow brainstormed a bit and came up with the following list:

> light / dark
> sun / moon
> daytime / day / morning / dawn
> nighttime / night / evening / sunset
> maybe fire?

Meadow went through the play and gathered all the quotes where Shakespeare not only used some form of her keywords, but specifically used them in a way that dealt with the *tragic love* mentioned in the prompt. After gathering these quotes, Meadow was confident she would have enough to write about, because she had far more quotes than she would need to sustain a 3-5 page paper. Her brilliant essay was lying somewhere in this selection of quotes.

When you turn the page, you'll find the list of quotes that Meadow decided to dig into in her search for the perfect thesis.

NOW SHOWING...

MEADOW'S
BLOCKBUSTER RESEARCH

But all so soon as the all-cheering sun
Should in the farthest east begin to draw
The shady curtains from Aurora's bed,
Away from light steals home my heavy son,
And private in his chamber pens himself,
Shuts up his windows, locks fair daylight out,
And makes himself an artificial night.
(Montague, about Romeo I.i.127-133)

One fairer than my love! the all-seeing sun
Ne'er saw her match since first the world begun.
(Romeo, about Rosaline I.ii.92-93)

What man art thou that, thus bescreened in night,
So stumblest on my counsel?
(Juliet, about Romeo II.i.93-94)

Give me a torch. I am not for this ambling;
Being but heavy, I will bear the light.
(Romeo I.iv.11-12)

O, she doth teach the torches to burn bright!
It seems she hangs upon the cheek of night
As a rich jewel in an Ethiope's ear
(Romeo, about Juliet I.v.41-43)

A thousand times the worse to want thy light.
(Romeo, to Juliet II.i.200)

But soft, what light through yonder window breaks?
It is the east, and Juliet is the sun.
Arise, fair sun, and kill the envious moon,
Who is already sick and pale with grief
That thou, her maid, art far more fair than she.
(Romeo, about Juliet II.i.44-48)

Two of the fairest stars in all the heaven,
Having some business, do entreat her eyes
To twinkle in their spheres till they return
The brightness of her cheek would shame those stars
As daylight doth a lamp;
(Romeo, about Juliet II.i.57-62)

Come, he hath hid himself among these trees
To be consorted with the humorous night.
Blind is his love, and best befits the dark.
(Benvolio, about Romeo II.i.30-32)

O swear not by the moon, th' inconstant moon,
That monthly changes in her circled orb,
Lest that thy love prove likewise variable.
(Juliet, to Romeo II.i.151-153)

O blessed, blessed night! I am afeard,
Being in night, all this is but a dream,
Too flattering-sweet to be substantial
(Romeo II.i.181-183)

Or, if I live, is it not very like
The horrible conceit of death and night,
(Juliet IV.iii.35–36)

O woe! O woeful, woeful, woeful day!
Most lamentable day! Most woeful day
That ever, ever I did yet behold!
O day, O day, O day, O hateful day,
Never was seen a day so black as this!
O woeful day, O woeful day!
(Nurse, about Juliet's death IV.iv.80–85)

For here lies Juliet, and her beauty makes
This vault a feasting presence full of light.
(Romeo, about Juliet V.iii.85–86)

A glooming peace this morning with it brings.
The sun for sorrow will not show his head;
(The Prince, about their deaths V.iii.304–305)

The grey-eyed morn smiles on the frowning night,
Chequ'ring the eastern clouds with streaks of light.
(Friar Lawrence II.ii.1–2)

Gallop apace, you fiery-footed steeds,
Toward Phoebus' lodging. Such a waggoner
As Phaeton would whip you to the west
And bring in cloudy night immediately.
Spread thy close curtain, love-performing night,
    Come, civil night,
Thou sober-suited matron all in black,
And learn me how to lose a winning match
Come night, come Romeo; come, thou day in night,
For thou wilt lie upon the wings of night
Whiter than new snow on a raven's back.
Come, gentle night; come, loving, black-browed night,
Give me my Romeo, and when I shall die
Take him and cut him out in little stars,
And he will make the face of heaven so fine
That all the world will be in love with night
And pay no worship to the garish sun.
(Juliet III.ii.1–25)

For fear of that I will stay with thee,
And never from this pallet of dim night
Depart again.
(Romeo, about staying with
Juliet in the tomb / in death V.iii.106–108)

STEP 2: Find a Jaw-Dropping Thesis

Now that it was time for a thesis, Meadow's Tower-of-Pisa instinct took over...again. "OK, great. 'Imagery of light and dark appears throughout *Romeo and Juliet*.'"

Uhhhhhh. That's true. You know what else is true? Things fall down. And there *are* four seasons. The problem is that *everyone already knows those things*. Remember, your thesis is supposed to be your own unique argument. So, can you go a little deeper?

"Oh. Yeah. OK, 'Images of light and dark are used...to show the tragicness...of love. In William Shakespeare's *Romeo and Juliet*."

Well, that's got some more details. But you still aren't quite there. What about...

"No no! I got this. OK. 'In William Shakespeare's great play, *Romeo and Juliet*, imagery of light and dark is used to *depict* the tragic *nature* of love...for these characters.'" Meadow leaned back from the table, clearly pleased with her insight.

MEADOW.

THIS. IS. NOT. A. THESIS.

Seriously!!! Why not? Because *it's the question!!!* *Anyone on Earth* who got the handout of prompts could write that sentence! It's not new, and it's not controversial. Your teacher *wrote the question*, so clearly she *already knows* that images of light and dark are *present*. This is not poised to amaze her. The quickest way to know whether a thesis works is to put yourself in the audience's shoes. So, Meadow, does this thesis that you have make you super-excited? Can you totally *not wait* to hear more about that? Does this get you fired up because it's so groundbreaking?

Meadow just looked at Hunter like he had lost it.

Guess not. Meadow, if *you're* not excited yet, then your *audience* won't be either. Your thesis should not be a straight-up statement about a general topic; it should *use* the facts from the text to make a case for a new *perspective* on the topic. You should be presenting something that another person reading the play or novel may not have discovered on his or her own. And because the thesis is something that most people might not fully see or appreciate on a first pass, it's *not* likely that the first thing that occurs to you is the best possible thesis choice.

A Good Thesis is Gold

In Hollywood, being the "idea man" is a really lucrative job. Next time you go to a movie, take a closer look at the credits. Often, in addition to the "written by" credit, there will also be a "story by" credit. That "story by" credit means that someone other than the screenwriter got paid a lot of money just to come up with the idea for the movie. That's how valuable a good thesis can be.

Meadow had always tried to make up a thesis out of thin air and *then* go find quotes to support it. That's an impossible mission. So how do you find a thesis that is groundbreaking and exciting? **A jaw-dropping thesis comes from investigation.** Through your research, you *find* your quotes, but through your investigation, you *make sense* of them. Dig into the evidence you have collected in your research, and you will discover all of the interesting specifics that can make for a truly explosive argument that your teacher will never see coming.

Meadow went to her list of quotes and started to investigate the first one that jumped out at her.

"Oh! Right right...where he says that Juliet is the sun! I loved that scene!" Now, Meadow needed to take a cue from Sherlock and use the clues to figure out why the "light" was important here.

So in this quote, Meadow determined that light represents Juliet. Better yet, in some of the other quotes, that also appeared to be true. Juliet was compared to a "torch" later in the play. Maybe Meadow was on to something...

But what about Romeo? After all, it takes two to...have a tragic romance that ends in a double suicide. Meadow found the first quote about him:

Just like light seemed to represent Juliet, in this quote, Romeo was associated with all kinds of things related to darkness: shut windows and locked-out daylight and artificial night. Now, Meadow was really on the way to having something original to say. But she wasn't there quite yet. Maybe Juliet is always light, and Romeo is always dark, but even if that is true, then *so what*? Why do we, as the audience, care?

The SO WHAT? Test

"So what?" is the question that students *always* forget to ask when they're coming up with a thesis. You can use "**SO WHAT?**" as a test, forcing yourself to get more and more specific, until you have a thesis that is truly groundbreaking.

Think about it in movie terms. If someone was trying to convince you that the movie *127 Hours* was worth seeing, it might go something like this:

"Well, this hiker falls down this crack in the rocks and gets stuck."
"**SO WHAT?**"
"Well, he's there for days and can't get out no matter what."
"**SO WHAT?**"
"So to get free...no joke...he cuts off his own arm."
"WHAT???!!! Ewww...that's so...blergh...**I've gotta see this!**"

By using the **SO WHAT?** test, you're able to get more and more specific until it's obvious that this movie is totally unique and exciting enough for you to spend two hours watching it.

So Juliet is light and Romeo is dark...**SO WHAT?** Meadow didn't really have an answer yet. In order to answer, Meadow needed to figure out *why* Shakespeare might have chosen those specific images. Why didn't Romeo say Juliet is a "rose" or a "rainbow" or a "chamberpot?" If Romeo's dad is making the point that his son hides out in his room all day, why not compare Romeo to a turtle going into its shell? Why *light and dark*? In order to get closer to understanding Shakespeare's intentions, Meadow tested her light/dark idea against the following list of questions:

Questions to Help You Pass the SO WHAT? Test:
- What's weird about this?
- How is this the opposite of what you would expect?
- How is this out of character?
- What is true about this idea that may show something about the characters or themes?
- Why would the author have chosen this over every other option?

Hmmm. Nothing seemed weird or unexpected about telling a girl you love that she's beautiful like the sun, so Meadow looked down the list a bit further. Then, she started thinking more about the *idea* from the prompt. What is true about light and dark themselves—even on the most basic level? "Well, light and dark...they're opposites of each other." Nice. And how might that be related to "tragic love"? "Oh. Well, 'tragic love' means the lovers can never be together. Like, they're doomed." Great! So why would light and dark be representing them? "Oh! Because light and dark are opposites...they can't be together either! Like, if it's light out, it can't also be dark out! Wait, so is that my thesis? Shakespeare makes Romeo and Juliet like 'dark' and 'light' because they are opposites, and that's how the reader knows even from the beginning that they can never be together! Whoooaaaahhhhhhh. That's *crazy*! Shakespeare is so sneaky! He's basically telling the audience about the ending of the play—in code—*every time you meet the characters*! That's far out."

Meadow's thesis definitely passed the **SO WHAT?** test. More importantly, this was an idea that actually had Meadow intrigued. For the first time ever, Meadow could see that it was possible to find a thesis that was *exciting to think about*—one that she was interested in pursuing further. And if Meadow was excited, then it was a safe bet that her audience would be too.

Now, this didn't necessarily have to be the *final* version of Meadow's thesis. But she definitely had found something that would be surprising to a general audience. With a thesis this jaw-dropping, she could be sure that her readers would get excited about her essay. But how was she going to make sure she could *keep* their attention all the way to the end?

STEP 3: Set Up an Edge-of-Your-Seat Outline

Everybody knows that summer blockbuster movies are some of the biggest players at the box office. And what makes them so much fun to watch?

Explosions.

Big ones, little ones, fiery ones...train, car, building, spaceship...there is something so satisfying about watching stuff blow up in the middle of a story.

Explosions are just one particularly satisfying way to raise the stakes in a movie. In other words, they make things *more* urgent, *more* severe, or *more* problematic for the hero. The good guys race toward the building where the secret blueprints are held... but right when they get twenty feet from the door and all of their problems are about to be solved...
EXPLOSION!!!!!!!!!!!!!!!!!!!!

The building blows up, and now they'll *never* get those blueprints! That means they need a new way to find the villain's lair! Moviemakers know that audiences love to be kept at the edge of their seats.

If you're unlucky enough to get stuck watching a movie where nothing surprising happens, then what do you do? You lean back, put your feet on the seat in front of you, and focus more on the peanut M&Ms you're eating than on what's happening in the movie. On the opposite end of the spectrum, a movie that consists of *only* explosions loses its excitement pretty quickly as well and sends you back to your M&Ms. Good movies mix it up. They provide an intense action sequence, followed by a sentimental flashback about the hero's wife (who was killed by the villain), and then a sequence leading up to the big attack in which the good guys are about to win...only to have all of their plans ruined by ANOTHER EXPLOSION! That was seriously epic.

Figuring out how to space those explosions out so that each one is as surprising as the last is the key to a successful blockbuster movie. The process of editing one of those movies to keep audiences on the edge of their seats takes months and months. Fortunately for you, you can work with the writer-tested, teacher-approved outline structure that has been saving essays worldwide for generations. You probably have a handout of this somewhere in your old binders. It looks like the following:

Introduction
  - Hook
  - 2-3 sentences bringing the reader into your topic
  - Thesis statement
Body Paragraph 1
  - Transition
  - Supporting Argument #1
    Two to three pieces of evidence plus analysis (4-6 sentences min.)
Body Paragraph 2
  - Transition
  - Supporting Argument #2
    Two to three pieces of evidence plus analysis (4-6 sentences min.)
Body Paragraph 3
  - Transition
  - Supporting Argument #3
    Two to three pieces of evidence plus analysis (4-6 sentences min.)
Conclusion
  - Restate thesis
  - 2-3 sentences to show greater relevance and wrap up

We know that it's hard to see how this seemingly boring outline can turn into an EXPLOSIVE ALIEN MONSTER SHARK ATTACK!!!, but this outline structure will provide your essay with the perfect balance of excitement, reflection, suspense, and big payoffs. Your topic sentences provide the major explosions in the essay. Those leave your audience reeling, but then you swoop in with evidence, spending some time getting into the inner life of the quotes. Then, just when your reader is starting to feel comfortable with that last point you made...EXPLOSION! You make a new point, and the intensity is sky-high again.

When Meadow started to fill in this outline, she realized that the quotes that she had so far were great...but they weren't enough to produce three different explosions. They were really all supporting the same point in slightly different ways. What's more, the other quotes seemed good in relation to the prompt, but didn't *exactly* fit with her thesis.

Not to worry. That just meant that there was something even *bigger* and *more intense* going on here. Meadow needed to find out what other tricks Shakespeare had up his sleeve in this play.

Meadow thought that Shakespeare was using the images of light and dark because they were opposites. On the first level of intensity, light and dark were showing that Romeo and Juliet themselves were opposites. But is that *all* Shakespeare does for the whole play? *What else* might be related to this idea of light and dark being opposites? Meadow needed to figure out what other reveals were in the remaining quotes.

Meadow was pretty sure that the quote, "More light and light, more dark and dark our woes" was useful. After all, it did say "light" and "dark"...twice each. However, it wasn't necessarily paralleling each of the two lovers with "light" and "dark." After some thinking about the context of the quote and doing some Sherlocking, Meadow figured out that the quote meant this:

So Meadow had a better idea of what this quote really meant. Next, by using the **"SO WHAT?"** questions, she started to look for the exciting opposites. What was Romeo really saying? Why is his perspective different than what you would expect?

"Hmmm...I mean, I guess it's weird that they have to be so secretive about being together. Like, they sneak around during the day, when it's light outside. They're only safe at night." Good! And is there any opposite in that? "Yeah, it's the opposite of what it should be. Nighttime is more dangerous usually. So night and day are the opposite of what they normally are. Whoa—that's kinda cool, because their whole relationship is all messed up."

Excellent! Think about it: this is still about *them*...it's just that here, Shakespeare is using light and dark to represent them *together*. Now, their whole *relationship* is the opposite of what a normal relationship should be, because it's dangerous in the light and safe in the dark. This fits with your original idea, but in a different way—which means that it's the topic of your second body paragraph. Two explosions down, one to go.

At this point, Meadow realized that her teacher had given her a big clue. There was a quote about the sun *in the prompt*, which probably meant that her teacher wanted her to consider it in the essay. She Sherlocked that quote too, and she realized that the Prince was relating the sun (or lack of sun...meaning darkness) to the deaths of the two main characters. So by the end of the play, "light and dark" were even *more* intense, because they were representing "life and death." That worked well, because life and death were certainly opposites, and just like Romeo and Juliet could be together only at nighttime, they eventually could be together only in death.

This process requires a lot of back-and-forth testing and brainstorming to figure out how to keep your audience's jaw dropping. You'll have moments of total certainty...and then figure out something new that makes it seem like you were *way* off. But don't give up until you've *really* thought it through! Usually, you will discover that what you're actually doing is making your thesis even *more* exciting. Creating an edge-of-your-seat outline allows you to figure out and solve all of the problems up front, so that by the time you're writing, it feels easy. All of the ideas—the thesis, the quotes, the structure—are taken care of; you just have to connect the dots.

With this final outline, Meadow felt, for the first time, that writing her essay would be no problem at all. She hadn't even technically started *writing* it yet, and she was already sure it would be one of the best essays she'd ever turned in. There was *no way* her teacher could say that her ideas were unoriginal or that she didn't have enough support for her argument. Meadow was sure that her summer was already saved. "Art Camp, here I come!!!"

Note: Unless your teacher requires that you turn in your outline, you don't need to worry about this being fancy...or even having complete thoughts. Just note the major points and mention the quotes in a way that you will remember them. All that matters is that what you write is a cake-mix-clear recipe for action.

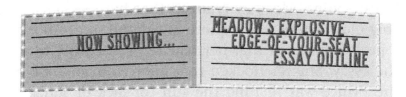

I. Introduction

    A. Hook: What would you do if the one person you loved was the one person that you couldn't be with?

    B. Thesis: Throughout Romeo and Juliet, the imagery of darkness and light foreshadows the fact that
        Romeo and Juliet come from opposite worlds and are doomed to never be together while they are alive.

II. Romeo and Juliet = Dark and Light, which are opposites

    A. Romeo shies away from the light, so is "dark" (quote about artificial night)

    B. Juliet is light (quote about teaching the torches)

    C. They're both saying these things about each other

        1. Light and dark are opposites

        2. Foreshadowing/clue

III. Dark and light intensifies to night and day, which can never be together

    A. Juliet is the sun (quote)

        1. Romeo points out that the moon and sun are at odds

        2. They can't share the sky -- Romeo and Juliet can't share their life

    B. Juliet says Romeo would become stars at night (quote)

        1. Romeo is linked to nighttime/moon/stars

        2. They both set this up

IV. Relationship vs. Everyone Else

    A. Nighttime and Daytime are Opposites

        1. Quote: "Gallop apace..."

        2. They can only be together in darkness, so she's wishing for that

    B. Nightingale and Lark (Quote)

        1. They're not on the same side ever in this argument

        2. Quote: "More light and light..."

        3. Things should get easier in the day, but because it's all opposite, it's harder

V. Life vs. Death

    A. Torch in the tomb

        1. Juliet is still "light" because she's still alive (quote)

    B. Quote from Prince: glooming peace

        1. They are together in the darkness of death

        2. Death means darkness because after their deaths, the sun won't shine

VI. Conclusion

STEP 4: Sell Your Essay With An Attention-Getting Preview

As an essay writer, you're a bit spoiled. All students are. No matter how much or how little work you put in, you are always guaranteed an audience of at least one: your teacher. Your essay could be the most boring, clichéd, non-believable, confusing paper out there, and your poor teacher has no choice but to sit through it until the bitter end.

Moviemakers don't have that luxury. Not only do they have to make the movie, but they also have to *convince people to come and see it*. And they do that with a fantastic trailer. Fortunately, thanks to years of moviegoing experience, you already know *exactly* what makes the best trailers so awesome. They get you excited! You see *just a snippet* of something *so totally amazing* that you know you *have* to see more! Trailers may be only a few short minutes long, but they're super-important, because they are the first impression an audience has of a new movie.

Just like a moviemaker does, you need to start treating your essay as though it needs to attract a mass audience. And what's the best way to reel in an audience? A killer introduction. The introduction of your essay is your chance to make a fantastic first impression. It's also your chance to get creative and have some fun. Get your readers excited with your intro, and your audience won't be able to help but love all of your amazingly explosive points.

Blockbuster movie trailers know *exactly* how to get an audience excited, and there's a formula to making the audience eager to buy their tickets. They **hook** you with something that makes you sit up and suddenly pay attention. Often, that's a dramatic sound paired with an arresting image so that you want to know more. You don't understand what the movie will be yet, but you're definitely intrigued. Then, the trailer **sets you up** with just the information you need—who the main characters

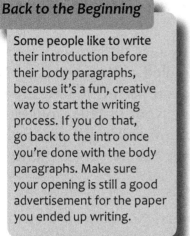

Back to the Beginning

Some people like to write their introduction before their body paragraphs, because it's a fun, creative way to start the writing process. If you do that, go back to the intro once you're done with the body paragraphs. Make sure your opening is still a good advertisement for the paper you ended up writing.

are and where they are—in order to fully appreciate why this movie offers **something you haven't seen** before.

A great introduction has the same three elements as a great trailer: **the hook, the setup, and the thesis**. It starts with a hook to grab the reader's attention. The following list is a great jumping-off point for finding a way to create that excitement and intrigue. Most importantly, don't be afraid to **use your creativity** with this! What would grab *your* attention if *you* were the audience?

1. Ask a question that makes your audience think.
2. Tell them a weird, interesting, or shocking fact.
3. Use a quote that will make them want to know more.
4. Tell a story or set the scene using vivid specifics.

While there are infinite ways in which a writer can grab a reader's attention, this list of suggestions that Hunter gave to Meadow was a helpful start, and Meadow tried a few of them out. Much as she wanted to divulge the drama of her last relationship, a personal story didn't seem like the best choice *for the audience*. Instead, Meadow decided to hook the reader with the question, "What would you do if the one person you loved was the one person you couldn't be with?" That way, the reader would be thinking about his or her own experiences with love as Meadow started to explain Romeo and Juliet's doomed relationship. Choosing this hook would make the reader feel personally involved in the essay from the getgo.

Now Meadow was ready for the setup. In an essay, this is where you tell the reader which book or play you are discussing and explain the general problem that you plan to address. **Assume the reader is already familiar with the work you are discussing**. You just need to set up any specific story details, themes, or relationships the audience needs to know in order to fully appreciate your thesis. Keep this section moving; movie trailers rely heavily on quick-fire pacing, and so should your introduction. If it starts to drag, the audience will get bored. Each sentence should get more and more specific and exciting as you get closer and closer to your thesis.

All of this leads up to the moment in which you show your audience why your essay is **something they haven't seen before**. The final sentence of your introduction should be your thesis. Use all of the great analysis that you've done to create your outline to rework your thesis so that it really expresses the essence of your three explosive topic sentences.

Meadow revisited that first claim about light and dark representing Romeo and Juliet and worked on expanding it to include all of her new points. After trying some options, she ended up with the following:

Throughout <u>Romeo and Juliet</u>, *Shakespeare uses imagery of darkness and light to hint at how the lovers can never be together and foreshadow the relationship's tragic end.*

This thesis was a million times more exciting than Meadow's first attempt had been. It still had "light and dark." It still had "tragedy." But it also went *way beyond* what was already in the prompt. No one would say "**SO WHAT?**" about this. Instead, after an intro this strong, all of Meadow's readers nationwide would definitely buy a ticket to read her essay.

STEP 5: Make It So the Reader Can Just Press PLAY

Finally, Meadow had done all of the groundwork that she needed in order to figure out *what* to say. Building that foundation had taken a while, but it also had guaranteed that Meadow wouldn't have a Tower-of-Pisa essay. From this point on, the process would move very quickly, because **when your points and evidence are rock-solid, writer's block doesn't happen**. You know exactly which points you need to make; all that's left is to figure out *how* to argue those points in the best possible way.

Moviemakers try to create lots of experiences for the audience—excitement, intrigue, suspense, nail-biting fear, humor, devastation, and even love. But one experience that they work hard *not* to create is confusion. Confusion takes the audience out of the flow of the movie, and it takes your reader out of the flow of your essay.

Your reader should be able to "just press PLAY" on your essay. This is probably the opposite of what you've been led to believe, because students tend to think that dense, complicated essays with snooty vocab are more "impressive." In reality, your reader should never have to spend even a moment figuring out what you mean. Remember how we talked about those majorly popular movies and how they are so *easy to watch*? **Your job is to make your essay so easy to follow that anyone who picked it up could grasp what you were saying perfectly...on the first try.**

Making the Move From Outline to Paragraph

Even with a solid outline, it still sometimes happens that you freeze up when it's time to translate your ideas into a full paragraph. You know that the items from the outline *go into* the paragraph, but where do they go? What else should you say?

YES! AND...

Imagine that you are on a stage with no script, no plan, and an audience of two hundred people staring at you and waiting for you to make them laugh. This is the world of improv comedy, and it is the essence of creativity under fire.

When really good improvisers perform, it seems magical. But underneath the crazy characters, impressively intricate scenes, and the relentless avalanche of jokes, improv is entirely based on rules and structure. Even when the performers seem to be coming up with ideas out of thin air, they are really relying on tried-and-true rules to help them create a scene. And at the core is the most important rule in all of improv: SAY YES. Be ready to take whatever your partner says to you, accept it fully, and make it work. You are forcing yourself to stay open-minded about what you're creating. And actually, it's not just any "yes." In improv, students learn to say, "Yes, and..." Not only do you agree with what your partner gives you, but you add more to it. Improvisers train themselves to keep running with an idea, honing it, and building on it. Just ask Tina Fey, creator of *30 Rock*, former head writer of *Saturday Night Live*, and lifelong student and performer of improv. In her book *Bossypants*, she describes it this way:

If I start a scene with "I can't believe it's so hot in here," and you just say, "Yeah..." we're kind of at a standstill. But if I say, "I can't believe it's so hot in here," and you say... "Yes, this can't be good for the wax figures" or if I say, "I can't believe it's so hot in here," and you say, "I told you we shouldn't have crawled into this dog's mouth," now we're getting somewhere. To me YES, AND means don't be afraid to contribute.

The conspiracy has taken away most people's willingness to have an idea and run with it—to say "Yes! AND..." No matter how uncreative you feel, don't be so quick to abandon your work; make bold moves and keep crafting it. You might be surprised at how creative you really are.

Writing your body paragraphs can be as methodical as any other process. Just follow this pattern, using 1-2 sentences each:

1. Topic sentence: _____
2. Set up first example: _____
3. Quote/Proof: _____
4. Explain quote: _____
5. Set up second example: _____
6. Second quote: _____
7. Explain quote: _____
8: Wrap up: _____

Note: Steps 4 and 7 are the most important parts of your paragraphs, and the parts that students often skip. Once you've included the quote, really make it obvious to the reader why that quote proves your point. You don't want to leave anyone behind.

That's it. Just follow that plan of action and fill in the blanks, one by one. Of course, this may seem more formulaic than the popular free-flowing, muse-inspired view of writing. It is. There's a reason why teachers talk about the "mechanics" of writing. Using this structure guarantees that your points will come across strongly. That's the way to make sure that your paragraphs pack as much EXPLOSIVE content as your outline did.

Now, it's time for the fun part: how you say it. You can play with the structure as you become more comfortable with it. As you work your way through presenting your points, make sure to keep the audience members on their toes. Use specific images and details; choose words because they make your point, not because they're impressive; use transitions to lead your reader by the hand through your argument; vary your sentence structure so that you have

Choose Wisely...

"The difference between the almost right word and the right word is really a large matter—it's the difference between the lightning bug and the lightning."

— Mark Twain

some long, complex thoughts and some short bursts of ideas. The more fun and exciting you make that journey, the more you'll have your audience right where you want them when it's time for the big finale.

STEP 6: Leave The Audience Wanting More

The final section of your essay is the conclusion paragraph—an oft-neglected and desperately underappreciated piece of writing. Above all other essay components, the conclusion tends to get treated like "filler" that just needs to take up space after your final major point.

In conclusion, here's the stuff I've said. Now, I'm saying it again, 'cause that's what I'm supposed to do here. I am so, so close to being able to go to bed. Here we go...four to six sentences of reminding you of the things I've said. Here they are again, in a few different ways. Please feel conclusive about that.

What does a great movie conclusion do? First, it gives you a satisfying resolution. The bad guy dies, or the dog and cat find their home, or the sparkly vampire takes the brunette to the prom. In an essay, most people think of this moment as "restating your thesis." But it's more than that. In the introduction, you told your thesis to an audience that couldn't fully appreciate it yet; it was just an intriguing claim. But in the conclusion, you can present your thesis to the reader more impactfully, because the reader, having seen the facts for him or herself, will really believe it.

The second role of the conclusion is to leave the audience wanting more. It provides some sort of cliffhanger ("Did she get on the plane?"), or a shot of the thought-to-be-dead villain's hand breaking up through the rubble. That has sequel potential written all over it! It leaves the audience with fun questions to consider as they file out of the theater. It leaves them wanting more!

Your conclusion should start with the central argument of your essay and then build out from there, showing how your essay illustrates something bigger about life or literature or anything else that you want the reader to think about. In fact, the conclusion should have the inverted structure of the introduction. Your intro began with a large idea and became more specific until you arrived at the thesis; your conclusion should begin with the thesis and get more general until your audience is contemplating life from a whole new perspective.

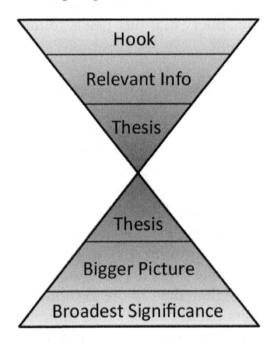

Meadow decided that she liked how her hook had encouraged readers to think about their own experiences with love. Now that they better understood the tragedy of Romeo and Juliet's experience, she brought that idea back in her conclusion. She chose to ask her readers what sacrifices and risks are really worth it in the name of true love, and to consider how things could have been different for Romeo and Juliet if they hadn't been so blinded by their love for each other.

STEP 7: Get the Crew Member Out of the Shot!

Camera rolls. The Golden Knight races through the corridors of the Castle Elsinore. Suddenly, he hears a sound and ducks, narrowly avoiding the slash of the Dark Knight's cursed sword. He raises the sword of Valindere high above his...wait...wait...who's that guy in the background in the ill-fitting Hawaiian shirt? Is he eating...is that beef jerky? WHAT?!!

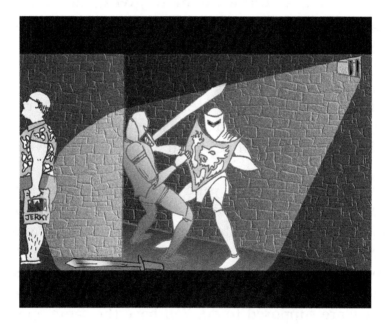

"Was that a crew member in the shot? Wasn't that car dented in the last scene? Wasn't her dress yellow a second ago?" As a seasoned audience member, you know that even a miniscule error is incredibly distracting. It can actually ruin a movie for you. Essay readers have the same experience. A beef-jerky-munching production assistant may not show up in your essay, but you may have typos or other errors that distract from the points you are trying to make. After all, the audience knows what the people in the castle are supposed to be wearing, which is why it's easy to catch that hula-shirt guy, and your teacher knows how to spell "separately"which is why "seperately" would instantly be distracting. Points are points, and no matter how dazzling your ideas are, your grade won't reflect them if you don't edit for things like spelling, punctuation, agreement, and even formatting.

Write an Essay That You'd Buy a Ticket To Read

Great essays—like great movies—take analysis, planning, and most of all, **a commitment to giving the audience an unforgettable experience**. Clearly, with this way of approaching essay-writing, your teacher wins, big-time. But there is a real benefit to you, the writer, as well. Rather than spending hours staring at the computer screen, waiting for inspiration to show up, you can have an actual *process* for your writing. Writing with the reader in mind gives you a way to guarantee that every essay you write will be a box-office smash with audiences everywhere.

Keep in mind, once your foundation—your thesis and outline—is in place and you're on to the actual writing, you can do as many takes as you need to get it right. If the lighting is wrong, or the actor flubbed a line, or it's just not believably scary, a movie director will make everyone do another take. That director will keep going until all of the parts of the production are doing just what they are supposed to do. You have the same opportunity. Is this hook *really* grabbing my attention? Do these sentences *really* keep me excited? Is my quote *really* clear in supporting my argument? Essays, like movie sets, require lots of pieces that all do different jobs; keep trying different options until you're sure that your essay will satisfy your audience.

But let's be honest. Why do you care about your audience? Your teacher has to read your paper no matter what. Is it worth going to the trouble of making it easy to read?

Uh, yes. It definitely is. Here's why. By becoming a champ at essay-writing, you're really learning how to communicate in a way that convinces people to get on your side and agree with you. While you may not care what people think about your ideas of Romeo and Juliet's love, you will definitely care what people think about your ideas in the future. In your career, in your family, and in everything you do, you'll be better off if you can get people to care about what you have to say, and then lead them through your argument until they agree. Want your boss to give you a raise? Want your neighborhood to start recycling? Want people to produce your album? Convince them. No matter what you do, if you want to do it well, then being a good communicator is going to be essential.

And it all starts with essays. From the first dramatic sound to the final credits, you have the opportunity to give your reader the ride of a lifetime. Just don't be surprised when your blockbuster essay comes back and you not only get an *A*...but also the first-ever Oscar for Best Double-Spaced Performance in a Three-to-Five-Page Role.

Getting the Ball Rolling

Changing your perspective to really think about the audience begins with something easy—and fun. You just need to start thinking about what happens when you watch movies. What are the things that make you stop enjoying a movie or take you out of it? Do you hate when movies start to drag, or when they get confusing? Does it annoy you when you feel like you've seen the story before? Take note of those problems, and then look for them in your essays. Each time you're done with an outline or a draft, take off your writer's hat and switch to being a popcorn-munching moviegoer. Put yourself in the audience's shoes, and a box-office smash will be yours.

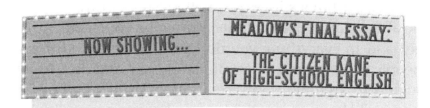

Meadow Winslow
English 10B

You Are My Sunshine:

Images of Light and Dark in Romeo and Juliet

What would you do if the one person you loved was the one person that you couldn't be with? People all over the world know what it is like to fall in love and to feel the fireworks so strongly that it's easy to forget about any of the problems that love brings. But few relationships have ever been as passionate or as doomed as Romeo and Juliet's. In Romeo and Juliet, William Shakespeare provides the reader with imagery to show how in love the two teenagers are—and how much trouble they face. In particular, throughout the play, Shakespeare uses imagery of light and dark, such as the sun and the moon or daytime and night. As the play progresses, darkness and light become the perfect symbols for this love; dark and light are equally strong, powerful images, but more importantly, they are opposites and can never exist at the same time. Throughout Romeo and Juliet, the imagery of darkness and light foreshadows the fact that Romeo and Juliet come from opposite worlds and are doomed to never be together while they are alive.

From the first moments that Romeo and Juliet are introduced in the play, Shakespeare uses the images of dark and light to set them up as opposites. When Romeo first appears, and he is depressed about Rosaline, Lord Montague describes how Romeo prefers to be in darkness. "Away from the light steals home my heavy son, / And private in his chamber pens himself, / Shuts up his windows, locks fair daylight out, / And makes himself an artificial night" (I.i.143-146). Romeo goes "away from the light" and tries to make it night all the time, and so he is immediately associated with darkness. In contrast, when Juliet first

1

 = HOOK  = JAW-DROPPING THESIS = EXPLOSIVE TOPIC SENTENCE

Meadow Winslow
English 10B

appears at the Capulet ball, Romeo says, "O she doth teach the torches to burn bright" (I.v.46). Romeo is simply commenting on Juliet's beauty, because he thinks that Juliet is so full of light that she is brighter than the blaze of a torch. However, through this association with light, Juliet becomes an opposite to Romeo's darkness.

 This link between the characters and the images of light and dark is intensified by the addition of symbols of daytime and nighttime. These symbols show that the lovers are not just opposites, but are destined to be apart. When Romeo comes to Juliet's window after the ball, he says, "But soft, what light through yonder window breaks? / It is the East, and Juliet is the sun" (II.ii.2-3). Romeo is again praising her beauty, but he immediately goes on to describe how the sun and moon work against each other. "Arise fair sun and kill the envious moon, / Who is already sick and pale with grief" (II.ii.4-5). Romeo is pointing to the fact that the sun and moon cannot share the sky; just like dark and light, they are at odds. In the same way, Romeo and Juliet can never be together. Later, Juliet associates Romeo with nighttime, saying, "Come night, come Romeo...Take him and cut him out in little stars, / And he will make the face of heaven so fine / That all the world will be in love with night" (III.ii.17-24). Without knowing that Romeo associated her with light, Juliet praises Romeo by associating him with night and darkness. By this point in the play, not only does this imagery show that the lovers are opposites, but also that it will always be impossible for them to be together.

Meadow Winslow
English 10B

As the play continues, the images of light and dark grow to represent the opposition between the lovers' relationship and the "real" world of their families. For young lovers, love should be light and carefree, but instead, Romeo and Juliet's love can only exist during the night, in darkness. By act III, night and day are at war, because night is when the lovers are together, and day is when they must face the harsh reality of their situation. While Juliet waits for Romeo, she says, "...bring in cloudy night immediately" (III.ii.4). Juliet wants day to be over, because Romeo can only come see her at night. Being together in the light is not an option. In scene five, after Romeo and Juliet finally get to spend the night together, they once again argue about whether it is night or day, and whether they heard the nightingale (the bird of night) or the lark (the bird of morning). Even in this argument, Romeo and Juliet are opposites; when Romeo changes his side and says that it was not the lark and that he should stay, Juliet immediately switches so that they are opposed again (III.v.1-30). Because it is daytime, their love cannot exist, and Romeo must leave. Upon exiting, Romeo says, "More light and light, more dark and dark our woes" (III.v.36). Romeo is pointing out one last time the contrast between light and dark, and how the two are working against each other. Things should get easier during the daytime, but because everything is the opposite of what it should be, in daytime, their love is doomed.

By the end of the play, light and dark have gone beyond representing just the lovers to now representing the contrast between life and death. Just like the meaning of night and day were switched, life and death start to take on their opposite meanings, because death is when

3

 = EXPLOSIVE TOPIC SENTENCE

  = POSSIBILITY OF A SEQUEL???

Meadow Winslow
English 10B

the lovers can be together. When Romeo reaches Juliet in the tomb, he says that her beauty makes the vault a "feasting presence full of light" (V.iii.86). Juliet is still "light" because she is actually still alive at that point. But Romeo believes she is dead and wants to be with her in death, and so the lovers each commit suicide, ultimately coming together only in the "darkness" of death. In the final lines of the play, the Prince notes that, "A glooming peace this morning with it brings; / The sun, for sorrow, will not show its head" (V.iii.305-306) The sun will not come out on the morning of the deaths, and darkness has finally overtaken even the literal light in the play, just like death has overtaken Romeo and Juliet's lives.

Although light and dark symbolize different things throughout the play, Shakespeare's use of light and dark imagery in Romeo and Juliet sets up a constant contrast between the lovers so that it is clear to the reader that they will never be together. Ultimately, the contrast is between the characters' dream for their life, which exists in the dark, and the harsh reality that they are living by the light of day. In the end, they can only be together in death, and after the struggle between light and dark that has lasted the entire play, darkness wins. Love at first sight can be overwhelming, and true love can be powerful. But what could have happened if Romeo and Juliet had tried to see past their feelings? Ultimately, they got their wish to be together forever, but only in death. If Romeo and Juliet had known that their love would cost them their lives, would they still have ignored all the signs and followed their passion?

4

Chapter 9

Navigate Your Test Prep Like a London Cabbie

Esther Xiang had discovered a new level of boredom. Beyond ordinary boredom, beyond extreme boredom, there was a level that could only be reached by flipping the same eighty flashcards eleventy jillion bazillion times. A small rivulet of drool meandered out of the corner of her mouth and dripped slowly onto the rug. Drip. Drip. Drip. Flashcard after flashcard swept by her deadened eyes. Flip. Flip. Flip. Half a stack. Half a stack. Still eighteen terms that she didn't know. Onward into the Valley of Boredom rode poor Esther.

OK. So, maybe it wasn't *that bad*, but during Esther's many nights of endless studying, she definitely reached points when she felt like banging her head against the wall. At least banging her head against the wall produced a cool beat. Esther was a sophomore in the jazz ensemble at school, and she loved it. She was all about jumping into new tunes and improvising to see how they turned out. Who needed sheet music? Just go. Monotonously flipping through flashcards didn't sit well with Esther, but what other choice did she have? Isn't that how studying works? You get the material from the unit, you drill it until it's practically your sixtieth birthday, and then you hope you remember it the next day when the test is in front of you.

This is how studying feels for a lot of students, and they're not wrong. Endless repetition *is* a way to memorize facts. And endless repetition *is* boring. What students aren't right about is thinking that endless repetition is the only way to learn material before a test. So why have we all spent so many years going straight for the flashcards and flipping them until we drop? And while we're at it, why do so many people think they are bad at memorizing things? Bad at memorizing! Are you kidding us? You have memorized millions and millions of facts in your life, and if you think we can't prove it, simply consider how many stories you know. Everything counts, from the "story" of *Snow White and the Seven Dwarves* to the "story" of that time that you escaped from your mom at the store and hid under the rack and she yelled at you to the "story" of your best friend's love note getting discovered and read by the teacher during third period. You can recount the many facts that make up those stories in incredible detail with no hesitation. So, it turns out, your memory is pretty great. You just need to give it what it wants.

Stories, songs, nursery rhymes—these are all great examples of the things that your memory really prefers to hold onto, which are pieces of information connected in a truly meaningful way. And it's always been that way. Before we had books, our ancient spear-chucking ancestors huddled around a fire in their cave and told stories. Before mass literacy was en vogue, medieval bards traveled the countryside reciting epic poems and singing ballads to the uneducated peasants. Since our earliest days, human beings have used storytelling to share vital information, preserve culture, and pass lessons on to future generations.

The sheer power of the human memory to retain meaningfully connected information is undeniable. For example, if you've had to read any of *The Odyssey* in your English class, then you know that Homer's epic tale of vengeful gods, lost love, and high-seas adventure is close to 500 pages long. What you may not yet appreciate is that it was composed before the Greeks had writing. In order to keep the 12,100-line poem from being lost forever, people had to memorize the whole poem and pass it on. If you think that's impressive, the same is true of the Indian Mahabharata, which at over 200,000 lines long, may in fact be the world's longest poem. It was passed down orally for centuries before being committed to writing around 500 BC. We owe a large portion of our cultural and historical heritage to the power of human memory and the meaning and connections that stories provide.

Our brains love to find meaning and connections in what we learn. Yet when it comes to school, we've all been trained to think that the way to make something memorable is just to repeat it... out loud...over and over again. So what's the better, more effective way to memorize, and how can you use it to make your test prep quicker, cleaner (drool-wise), and more fun than it's ever been before? Well, for the answer to that, you have to go to London.

Be Sure to Tip the Genius

"Awright, Guv'nor! Getcher bags in the boot and we'll be off. Where you headed?" Every day, people jump into the roughly 21,000 black taxi cabs in London, tell their drivers where they need to go, and sit back as the taxis speed off toward their destinations. And as that's happening, it's likely that *none* of those passengers are appreciating the out-of-this-world level of memorization that it takes for the driver to instantly calculate the shortest route... and then have that route so well automated that his attention is free to *chat about the rugby match* while he zips through the city streets. London's taxi drivers navigate so effortlessly that for hundreds of years, almost no one has realized what geniuses they are.

That's right. The taxi drivers in London are *geniuses.* They have to be. That's because compared to navigating most cities around the world, such as New York City or Paris or Kyoto, navigating your way around London is a *nightmare.* Despite significant advances in transportation, nothing about the city of London's layout has changed since the roads were initially constructed for peasants pushing vegetable carts...and the occasional passing knight. The result is that there are close to 25,000 streets within London's main city limits. What's more, all of those streets are twisty and turny, they end for no reason, and they have typically Harry Potterish names like "Throgmorton Avenue" and "Shoulder-of-Mutton Alley." It takes a really smart chap to be able to navigate London without a map. In fact, in order to even get an all-London taxi license, a cab driver needs to know *every single* one of those streets by *heart.* Basically, he has to be a human GPS. To really appreciate that, take this quiz:

Guess The Name of the Highlighted Street

If you figured out that the highlighted street on the New York map was West 38th Street, then good job counting. You deduced that 38th comes between 37th and 39th. That street name was easy to guess based on its surroundings. And what's the name of the street on the London map? Finnsbury Circus. Finnsbury what?!? There's no way you could guess where that street is, let alone how to get there. You'd have to know it by heart.

So, all of the cab drivers in London are really some secret society of freakish map-people? Nope. Not at all, mate. The drivers don't all come from fancy educational backgrounds or have tons of experience to start. They're a bunch of regular blokes and birds. They like rugby. They like going to the pub. They enjoy a hearty plate of bangers 'n' mash in the morning. But they *are* hiding one huge superpower. London's cab drivers hold the world's greatest secret to acing every test they take.

By the time they're done preparing for the taxi license, London's cabbies need to know *tens of thousands* of facts about London and access them in an instant. Those "facts" make up an extremely comprehensive and detailed understanding of every street within a six-mile radius of Charing Cross, a central point in London. That understanding is known as "The Knowledge." Cab drivers are tested on The Knowledge in order to obtain their licenses. But also, their understanding is tested over and over again every day, each time a new passenger hops into the backseat. The number of potential destination requests is seemingly endless. And yet to learn The Knowledge, the cabbies don't need to make a single flashcard.

Now, imagine if you got into a cab with a driver who studied like Esther. It would probably go something like this:

Passenger: "Hi! Thanks for stopping. I need to get to Shaftesbury Avenue, and I need to be there as quickly as possible. I have a career-making meeting in twenty minutes!"

Driver: "Riiiiight...shooooot...yeah, no, ok! Wait! I know this! Don't tell me. It's...I mean, I looked at the map like a bunch of times late last night, so... Um...OK. We're facing south, so let's just start driving forward and then..."

Clearly, that's not ideal. How do cabbies make sure that they remember how to get to the correct destination every single time? **They create as many meaningful connections within the information as possible.** For London's cabbies, the main pieces of information are the 25,000 streets, and the connections are fairly easy to identify, because the cabbies are working from a standard map of the city. But anyone can look at a map. What makes the cab drivers so good at what they do is that rather than studying the minimum number of facts they will need or treating the streets like separate items to memorize, they connect and relate the streets and destinations to each other until the entire map of London is one big, super-connected, super-meaningful picture.

Don't Learn Streets. Learn Routes.

So, where do those connections begin? Since 1865, the standard practice for attacking The Knowledge has been to memorize the main *routes* first. The 320 popular routes that go through the center of the city give cabbies a foundation of essential **central logic** on which they can build. By knowing how one street connects to another...which connects to another... ending up at a major destination, the cabbies can lock in *several* pieces of information in a chain of logic, making it difficult for any one piece to escape. Logic comes from relationships in space, in time (order/sequence), or in function. For instance, consider how easy it is to figure out and remember where 38th Street might be in relation to 37th Street when you're first learning the map of New York City.

Fortunately, you already know how to find logic in what you're studying. You've been doing it throughout this whole book. The first way to do that is to make things Cake-Mix Clear. For example, remember Charlie Wexell? Because he took the time to *really understand* the logic behind his math, he had a recipe for action that he could then practice (through repetition) for the rest of the unit. By test time, Charlie barely had to study at all. Making things Cake-Mix Clear can eliminate almost *all* of your study time, especially for math and science classes. When you find the routes in your material, whether it's the *sequence of steps* in a math procedure or the *spatial relationship* of the parts of the atom or the *function* of different parts of a cell in making a protein, you're finding the *logic* that connects all of those facts, making them memorable from the getgo.

The other way to identify logic is through Sherlocking. Whenever you Sherlock your reading in history or English class, you're solidifying the logic, in terms of the sequence of events that occur. Remember, when we took the time to examine the events of Martin Luther's 95 theses in terms of their logic—Martin Luther nailed his 95 theses to the church door *because* the church was selling plenary indulgences *because* it was corrupt—it made Martin Luther's actions more memorable. Connecting the facts through time or understanding them as a process makes them far stickier than it would be to try to learn "plenary indulgences" or "Wittenberg" alone. What's more, in the Sherlocking process, you also took advantage of *emotion*. You made a point to put yourself in Martin Luther's shoes. *How angry* must he have been to take a stand against the Pope? *How passionately* must he have believed in what he was doing? Relating to his emotions made the events truly unforgettable; emotions are the precise kind of "extra" information that you can add to your material to make it really sticky.

Contrary to what most people believe, when it comes to remembering information...**the more you learn about a topic,**

the easier it all is to remember. When you're making things Cake-Mix Clear and Sherlocking passages, what you're really doing is looking past the immediate facts in order to see how they're connected or why they matter. If you take time to connect the facts in any unit and understand *all* of them as one bigger picture, you're saving yourself *tons* of study time later.

And the reality is that working this way is not that difficult to do. In any class, a *unit* or *chapter* of material *already has* an underlying logic to it. The best way to improve your studying is to *find* and *understand* that logic. After all, the various facts of any section of material are grouped together *for a reason*. It is *always* going to be better to treat those facts and ideas as a group and work to understand the relationship among them. That way, you're giving yourself the strongest and most memorable *route* through the material.

By the time the cabbies have learned all 320 main routes through the center of London, it is practically impossible for any one street along any one route to be forgettable. Even if they can't recall how a particular street fits into one route, they can use the other 319 routes to figure out its location; they can always find a way to get back to any street they've learned. In the same way, if your facts and rules and concepts are all connected like routes— and full of the logic and emotion connecting them—then you can always find *some* way back to the answer. Learn the routes, and at test time, it will be almost impossible for any one fact to escape.

Why You'll Never Forget Carting Lane

Learning main routes is helpful, but cabbies still need to know all of the quirky, twisty back alleys and side streets by heart. If there is no logic on the surface of the map, then the cabbies need to look beyond the map to *find* logic that will make those streets memorable.

Unsurprisingly, memorizing the 25,000 streets in London is just the beginning of what they're required to know. Check out the following selection from the official instructions for mastering "The Knowledge" and preparing for the cab drivers' test:

In order to complete the Knowledge you will need to know any place where a taxi passenger might ask to be taken and how to get there. To do this you will need to know all the streets, roads, squares etc. as well as specific places, such as parks and open spaces, housing estates, government offices and departments, financial and commercial centres, diplomatic premises, town halls, registry offices, hospitals, places of worship, sports stadiums and leisure centres, stations, hotels, clubs, theatres, cinemas, museums, art galleries, schools, colleges and universities, societies, associations and institutions, police stations, civil, criminal and coroner's courts, prisons, and places of interest to tourists.

Most people, upon receiving this insanely long list of "extra" things to know, would probably be *really* intimidated, or even annoyed. The cab drivers, however, are thrilled. Art galleries and town halls and courts may not seem like things you need to learn if you just want to memorize a map of streets. But these are exactly the kinds of "extra information" that cabbies use to transform random street names into meaningfully connected information.

Looking for "extra information" was exactly what Esther needed to do to prepare for her big vocab exam. During the semester, Esther had used repetition to cram for quizzes and managed to more or less remember each set of ten words the next morning. But now that she needed to remember all of the words from the whole semester, she felt as if *none* of them were still in her brain. She had been staring at the list for an hour, but she didn't feel like the words were actually sinking in.

Esther was through with the endless repetition approach for good. That being said, she couldn't see how any of these words were logical enough to make them unforgettable. Not to worry. She just needed to start looking beyond the list of words and definitions to see what logic *wasn't* on the page. Here are the first six words that Esther set out to make more memorable:

culpable — (adj.) deserving blame
deleterious — (adj.) causing harm or damage
gregarious — (adj.) fond of company; sociable
malcontent — (adj.) dissatisfied or rebellious
nefarious — (adj.) extremely wicked or villainous
tenacious — (adj.) characterized by keeping a firm hold

STEP 1: Look for Logic Hidden Within

If Esther was going to make the most of her study time, she needed to first look for words that already contained some clues within them. That's what cabbies do. London has a road called Great *Tower* Street, which leads to the *Tower* of London. Knowing more about that street—adding the information that there is a very famous tower near it—makes it easier to remember. Separately, the location of Great Tower Street and the Tower of London are forgettable. Together, they are memorable.

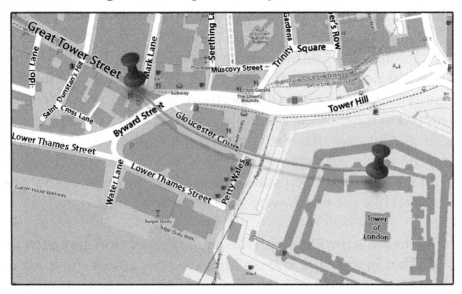

"Great Tower Street" may initially seem like a random name, but by examining the parts within that name and looking for more information about them (Why "Tower?"), it becomes clear that unforgettable logic is close by. Often, you might look at the definition and not immediately see how it connects to the word, term, or idea itself. However, by breaking the word down into pieces, you might discover that all the parts provide clues that you can use to remember the whole.

malcontent: For this word, the meaning was hiding right in front of Esther's nose. Esther noticed that the definition of this word was "dissatisfied." By starting from Step 1, she broke the word down and recognized the word "content" right inside of it. She knew that "content" meant something like "satisfied" or "happy." What's more, "mal-" was at the beginning, and Esther recognized that as a prefix meaning "bad" or "not," like in "malfunction." So if the word was really "bad/not + satisfied/happy," then it suddenly made perfect sense why the definition would be "dissatisfied."

In this process, because Esther already recognized the prefix "mal" as meaning something negative, that helped her jump to the definition. Whenever you see a new word, rather than treating it like its own isolated fact, think of *any other words* that you might know that have similar prefixes, suffixes, or roots. You can even go to related languages. If you take Spanish or French, you also know that *mal* is the word for bad. Suddenly, your new word turns out not to be so "new" to you. It is actually connected to a whole *chunk* of words that are already stuck in your brain.

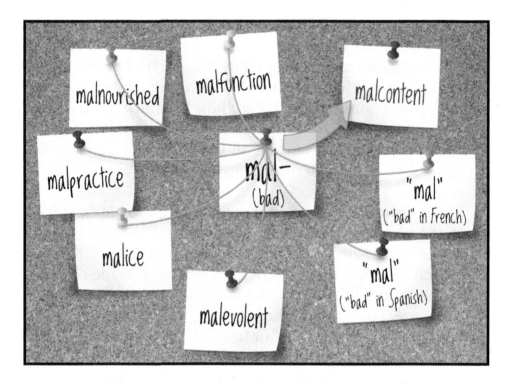

STEP 2: Dig a Little Deeper to Make Your Facts Stickier

The cabbies don't have to go too far beyond Great Tower Street itself to find the helpful logic of a *very famous tower* nearby. And just by breaking down "malcontent," Esther realized that word's definition was far more intuitive than she had expected. But sometimes, you need to dig a little deeper to make something memorable.

Many of the streets in London have names that offer no memorable logic at all, and a perfect example of this is Carting Lane. After all, it doesn't contain Greater Carting Hospital or pass any large, stone monuments commemorating the invention of carts...it's not even shaped like a cart. So surface logic is out. When that happens, you need to turn to the other top memory super-tool: *emotion*. Some experiences are so sad, some jokes are so funny, and some images are so terrifying that the memory of them lasts a lifetime.

So how would taxi drivers make a street as seemingly forgettable as Carting Lane emotional? Just like they dig for additional information that provides logic, they dig for additional information that can provide emotion. If there's nothing *obvious* to use, that doesn't mean that there's *nothing* to use. The process of finding memory glue may take some time, but you just have to continue digging and keep an open mind. Often, something really unusual will become the key to your success.

It turns out that Carting Lane does have one thing that sets it apart from all other streets in London: it is home to the city's last remaining sewer-powered gas lamp. Underneath the lamp is a dome that collects certain...vapors...from the bathrooms of the nearby super-famous Savoy hotel. So, if you were walking home late at night along Carting Lane, you could thank the hotel's very rich guests for the very rich vapors which light your way. Now, is there *any word* that, say, might *rhyme* with Carting...that is *related* to those *vapors* that light the *gas* lamp??? Parting Lane? Starting Lane? Darting Lane? Noooo...that's not it...keep going through the alphabet. We don't like to *toot our own horn* or anything, but clearly, we're *FAR Too* classy to spell it out for you here. We're sure you'll get the picture. The important thing about this story is that whether you find it hilarious or disgusting, you've got all the emotion you need attached to this street to make sure that Carting Lane and its proximity to the Savoy hotel will stick in your memory. It doesn't matter what glue you use to secure a fact, as long as that glue is meaningful to you.

Would you have ever thought ahead of time that the key to remembering Carting Lane would be a "gas"-powered lamp? Probably not. But that's why gathering more information makes memorization more successful. You'll never, ever forget Carting Lane as long as you live. (Sorry about that.)

Just like Carting Lane has its own rich history, words and facts rarely come out of nowhere, and very often, by finding where they come from, what inspired them, or why they're important, you will stumble across some simple, permanent glue that makes the word and its definition really meaningful.

Etymology is the study of the origins of words, and every word's dictionary definition includes the word's etymology. Most people skip reading that part, but when it comes to learning words, it's often the *most helpful* and *most interesting* section! Words are usually related to either the time in which they were invented or to another language from which they are borrowed. While breaking down a word might not always give you parts as straightforward as "mal" and "content," understanding the pieces can still provide you with the meaning you need.

tenacious: By looking at the word's etymology, Esther found out that "ten-" has to do with holding. Because Esther was taking Spanish, she realized that was just like the Spanish verb *tener* which means "to hold." (The French verb for "to hold" is *tenir*.) Esther made this even stickier when she realized that ten is also the number of fingers on your hands. She may not have remembered the Spanish and French verbs on the test, but she would definitely remember that she had ten fingers. Putting these two different kinds of glue together ensured Esther's "firm hold" on the meaning of "tenacious"—"characterized by keeping a firm hold."

culpable: The only word Esther could think of that sounded like "culpable" was "culprit." Sure enough, when Esther looked it up, she found out that *culpa* means "blame." Oh! So "culpable" means "able to be blamed." The culprit was culpable. Totally.

STEP 3: Who Cares Where the Glue Comes From As Long As it Works?

Step 1 is easy. Step 2 is interesting. But Step 3 is the most fun. If you have gone through Steps 1 and 2 and have yet to find glue that will *really* make your fact memorable, then you need to start thinking outside the box. *Way* outside. Go crazy and use your imagination. Cabbies don't stop until they have some sort of guaranteed glue for every street on the map—something that will really make the fact "stick" in your brain—no matter *how* strange or unexpected that glue might be.

Inventing some sort of logic or emotion is still better than finding no logic or emotion at all. To find glue for the "stragglers" that didn't pass Steps 1 and 2, go through every possible association you can make with this word or fact—regardless of whether it's related to the actual test material. The goal is just to find something you can't forget. So, ask yourself questions like the following: What does this remind me of? What does it sound like? Does it look like anything familiar? Who can I think of that has the qualities of this word? What does it rhyme with? Can I make a sentence out of the first letters of these words? (That's how people sometimes learn the planets in order. My Very Excellent Mother Just Served Us Nachos. = Mercury, Venus, Earth, Mars, Jupiter, Saturn, Uranus, Neptune. Sorry, Pluto.) Can you act out the word without speaking? Is there a funny voice that this word or fact matches? Does this word or fact match up with something about one of your pets? The list of ways to relate the word to something you know can literally go on forever. Your job is to go through the *entire universe* of facts, until you find a way that is funny, weird, disgusting, shocking, or exciting enough to make you never forget! Anything goes, as long as it's glue.

Getting Glue from Pirates

When you find some good glue, you *never* forget the glue or the fact that it's holding in place. When Katie had to learn the word "harangue" during sophomore year of high school, she couldn't find *any* good glue. There wasn't a good way to break the word down, and it meant, "a lengthy and aggressive speech; a lecture." But Katie found a way to remember this word that she still uses today. "Harangue" is pronounced "huh-rang," and it was some sort of angry lecture. "Harangue" and "angry" sort of sound similar, so... Katie used a funny voice, kind of like a Scottish pirate. "Harangue... her-anger... Her anger made her yell at everyone!"

deleterious: OK…"causing harm or damage." Esther looked for something she would remember about the word. She chose to use the fact that the beginning of the word contained "delete." How can "delete" relate to "causing harm or damage?" That was easy. If Esther accidentally deleted an essay she'd been working on for hours, then that would certainly cause harm and damage… to her grade and her happiness. Piece of cake.

gregarious: "Gregarious" means "fond of company" or "sociable" and apparently comes from the Latin word "grex" meaning flock…as in sheep. Some students would stop there and just picture a big flock of sheep chatting amongst themselves in a very sociable fashion. That's memorable, but it wasn't sticky enough for a city slicker like Esther. For this one, Esther really had to look outside the box. Okay. It looks like there's a "Greg" in there…like the name. Esther didn't know anyone named Greg, but she imagined that there was a Greg out there who was "fond of company; sociable." He always wanted to go to a movie or chat or just hang out. If there was a party, you could bet the first person to arrive and the last person to leave would be Greg. Oh, Greg!

nefarious: For the last word on her list, Esther had to really use her imagination to find some glue. The etymology showed her that the Latin word *nefas* meant "unlawful deed." Not so much. Esther started breaking the word down to look for something that caught her attention. "Ne…far…" "Far" is a word, but there's nothing about distance in here. So that route is a dead end.

The "ne" part isn't helpful. And it sounds a bit like "furious," but that isn't exactly right. Oh! But you pronounce it "nuh-FAIR-ee-us." That sounds like it has the word "fairy" in the middle! Great...except that the word means "wicked or criminal," and fairies are mostly sparkly and smiley and helpful. So, Esther ended up remembering "nefarious" because it meant "the opposite of what fairies are." That works too.

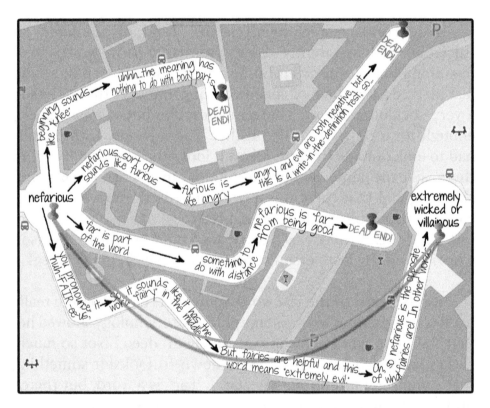

Esther had a blast coming up with each form of memory glue, because it required her to be flexible and *creative*—something she associated with jazz but had never associated with studying vocab in the past. What's more, by the time she got to the end of her list, she already remembered each of the words really well. At *this* point in the memorization process, once the glue is in place, repetition finally comes in handy for students. With just a few rounds of repetition and reviewing her glue, Esther had ensured that the definitions would be there for her at test time.

Finding The Glue When You Study

When you study, don't reach for the flashcards right away. Cabbies know that they could repeat "Carting Lane, Carting Lane, Carting Lane" over and over again and stare at the map for hours and get nowhere. But as soon as they go beyond the map and find something like the gas lamp, that street sticks instantly. Don't waste your time mindlessly drilling individual words or facts; *use* your time to look beyond the study guide and find each fact's "gas lamp."

When considered in isolation, none of these words had the kind of logical or emotional meaning that would make them unforgettable to Esther. But by asking the right questions, it became easy for her to start finding glue just as memorable as Far-...ahem...CARTING Lane. Whether the logic is within the word or whether you need to come up with something way out there in order to glue a fact in place, the important thing is that you feel sure the word will stick.

In all of these cases, Esther was the most surprised to realize that in terms of memorization, **more information really did make things more memorable**. By knowing more about the parts of a word or its etymology or by adding on more information from her imagination, Esther was making it *faster* and *easier* for herself to memorize each word.

Keep in mind, the process of coming up with all these different types of glue *is in itself* the process of studying. In fact, it's the very best way to study. By having to really think about the logic connecting these terms and attach emotion to

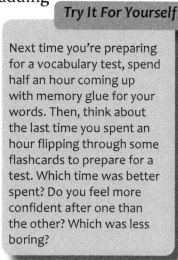

Try It For Yourself

Next time you're preparing for a vocabulary test, spend half an hour coming up with memory glue for your words. Then, think about the last time you spent an hour flipping through some flashcards to prepare for a test. Which time was better spent? Do you feel more confident after one than the other? Which was less boring?

them, you are doing most of the work to make it memorable. Your attention is super-engaged, and that means that you're automating the concepts. With a few final repetitions, the information will be stuck for good.

Take your Glue for a Road Test

Having the necessary knowledge is great, but you also need to make sure it will be ready for action. A large part of what makes cabbies such great test takers is that they make sure that they're prepared for exactly what will be required of them. When they are officially tested on The Knowledge, part of the process is verbal, and part is written, and so the cabbies make sure to prepare for those types of exams. But a third part of the test happens on the road, using The Knowledge the way it would be used in real life. It's not enough to be able to write down the answer; the cabbies need to be able to *drive* the answer, at a moment's notice. Cab drivers must know the map so well that their attention is free to focus on other things: keeping an eye on traffic lights, watching for absent-minded tourists, and chatting with passengers! That means that some of their practice has to happen *in* the driver's seat.

> ### Don't Wing Your Essay
> If you have to write an essay on exam day, then you can take that for a road test too. Practice writing an essay using what you've studied. Even if the essay doesn't come out exactly the same on the real day, at least you'll be prepared for recalling the specifics and forming an argument from them.

Students, however, often forget that the best way to tell whether information is really glued in place is to take a practice test *in the exact format* that the real test will be given. If a vocabulary test is going to be fill-in-the-blank, then practice that way—you'll need to know not only what the answer is, but also how to spell it. If your teacher wants you to write sentences using the words, then you should know the words' spellings and

IMAGINING YOUR WAY TO A GOLD MEDAL

Simon Reinhard of Germany can memorize the order of an entire deck of cards in 21.19 seconds. His countryman, Johannes Mallow, holds the world record for memorizing historical dates: 132 out of 140 memorized in 5 minutes. In the same 5-minute window, Wang Feng of China can memorize the order of 500 random numbers. Each year, Grand Masters of Memory from around the world gather at the World Memory Championships. And if you were to attend, you would likely conclude that all of the competitors had crazy photographic memories. How else could someone memorize that much information that quickly? There is a hidden secret to what they do, but it's not a natural gift. The memory champs will all tell you that photographic memory is, as one put it, "a detestable myth."

In his book, *Moonwalking with Einstein*, journalist Josh Foer chronicles how he went from writing an article about the memory champions to becoming one himself. In his training, Foer discovered that to remember the order of a pack of cards in under a minute, memory champs use every trick in the book, including emotion, logic, repetition, and story. By associating each playing card with a particularly memorable image, Foer could see the six of diamonds not just as any old playing card, but as Pope Benedict XVI—something much more memorable when, say, it is launching a spit glob (nine of clubs) into Albert Einstein's thick white hair (three of diamonds). A meaningless sequence of three cards becomes an instantly unforgettable short story.

Foer ultimately won the U.S. Memory Championships and even set a new record for speed cards. But the real focus of his book is on how possible it is for the average person to memorize large amounts of information in a way that is enjoyable and doesn't take forever. As Foer's mentor, Grand Master of Memory Ed Cooke, told him, "Even average memories are remarkably powerful if used properly." Foer still routinely forgets where he puts his car keys. But when he needs to, he knows how to use his creativity to make things unforgettable.

Thought You Were Ready?

One student we know practiced her multiplication tables until she was lightning fast at answering any problem out loud, but when it came time to write the answers down on a 100-problem speed test, she completely froze up. Practice in the exact way that you'll need to perform.

understand what the words mean *and* what part of speech they are. Clearly, if the test questions are based on matching, then knowing the spelling is not required at all. The moral? Prepare for what's needed, and you'll be able to guarantee that you're ready. You're done when you can do exactly what's expected on the test—with 100% acuracy.

After Esther had finished finding glue for all of her vocabulary words, she took out a blank sheet of paper. She knew that her teacher always read the words and then made the class write down the word, the part of speech, and the definition, so she got her sister to read them and pretended it was test time.

By making it feel exactly like the real test, Esther could figure out precisely which words and definitions still needed more glue. Best of all, having to write the information down from scratch meant that Esther was doing some extra automating. After her practice test, she set aside the words that she'd gotten correct and focused on the two or three that needed a little more work. There's nothing worse than having studied a lot, only to find out that you don't remember everything as well as you expected to when you're taking the actual test. By taking her information out for a "test drive" the night before, Esther was able to make sure that all of the vocabulary words were stuck for good, and that she felt unstoppable on the day of the test. When you can pass your Road Test with no problems, you have successfully reached the *end* of the study process.

Get Serious About Making Your Study Time Fun

If there's one thing that we hope to accomplish with this chapter, it is to bring about the end of "serious" studying forever. We don't mean "serious" as in "focused and intensive"...obviously, that's fine. But we *do* mean "serious" as in "boring and humorless." Take a page from the cabbies—there's a reason that Carting Lane is so memorable. From now on, your study process should be full of color and loudness and jokes and disgusting images and *anything* that will actually make the information memorable and fun. (This will likely be a whole different way of studying from what you've done in the past. But based on the fact that most people's past studying involves repeating phrases like, "Smoot-Hawley Tariff Act...1930...raised tariffs...Smoot-Hawley Tariff Act..." over and over in a drone-like voice, hoping it sinks in by osmosis, we're pretty confident that this new approach will be an improvement.) Engaging your brain in the process of learning by **finding meaningful connections** is *always* more effective and more fun than cramming by repetition alone, hours before the exam.

In the wake of all this "anti-cramming" talk, we do want to recognize one thing. We totally get why some students *like* to cram for tests. For one thing, it's a really satisfying idea to try to "beat the system" and pass the test, having done almost no work. Who needs to study for hours and hours? I have the secret! (Of course, this benefit can only be enjoyed if it *works*, and you do pull it off.) But the other reason students think cramming is a good idea is that they are under the impression that you only need to know the material for long enough to scrape through the test. The next day, it's on to a new unit, and you can forget that other stuff until the mid-term. No sense storing it all that time!

Sure, cramming may make you *feel* like a beat-the-odds rock star, but it's actually a recipe for making every subsequent test you take more difficult. Trust us—we've seen students "pull off"

B's and even *A*'s in everything from quizzes to oral presentations to actual tests. And they are proud of it: "I totally made it up on the spot and *still* did well!" That may seem impressive in the moment, but cram-lovers everywhere are totally missing the point.

If you've left three chapters of reading to do all on the night before the test, because you didn't do them when they were first assigned, then you won't have *time* to make it logical or interesting—and therefore memorable. With only a few hours of time to prepare for the test, you're forced to focus on getting *through* the reading, rather than getting anything *out of* it. Maybe you'll show up to the test and remember a few major points, but you're not going to be able to confidently ace every answer.

The even bigger issue is that the way that we learn new things is by connecting them to what we've learned in the past. If you forget all of the information you've learned as soon as the test is handed in (or if you never learned it in the first place), then the next time that you have to learn something new—either in the next unit or in a different class entirely—you have to start from scratch with finding things to connect it to. That means that every time you study, you have to spend a lot of time trying to either drill things endlessly until they stick, or searching desperately for something to stick it to. The next test will be twice as hard to trick your way through...and the test after that will be even worse. By cramming, you leave yourself nothing to work with in the future.

But what if you didn't cram? Let's say that for each test you took, you found a way to make the information *really sticky*, so that it stayed with you not just through the test, but for good. If that was the case, then it would mean that the more you learn, the more your brain becomes like flypaper. When new information comes along, like a new vocabulary word, there is *so much* to relate it to that it just sticks. That glue is already in place, waiting for new facts to come along. Pretty soon, you will have cut out the "glue-seeking" process entirely, and the connections will happen right away. *That* is why some people barely need to study or seem like they "know" things as soon as they first hear them.

One way that you can set yourself up to have a flypaper memory is by changing your perspective on each subject that you study. Rather than seeing each unit as a totally new topic that abruptly stops being important once you're tested on it, start to see *everything* as part of a bigger picture—just like the cabbies' map. Units that you cover in class such as the Industrial Revolution and World War I may seem like totally different stories with totally different sets of characters. But if you have a good understanding of the Industrial Revolution it will make your study of World War I *far* stickier and *far* more interesting, because you'll see how industrialization fueled the competition and conflict between countries and how it changed the face of how wars were fought. The whole key to studying history is to draw parallels between different important events and people. Even though it can feel like you're studying individual snapshots, history really is one long, unified narrative. And if you dig past the surface, it's a really sticky one at that.

While finding the glue between units in an individual subject is super-helpful, you're going to be the most blown away by what happens when you start to make the information sticky in *all* of the subjects that you learn. Knowing all of your subjects well makes it possible for you to find glue *anywhere* in the spectrum of knowledge that's in your brain. This is the cabbies' real secret. They know that the more glue they have for each street, the more quickly they'll be able to recall its location. A cab driver may know Bridge Street by the fact that it leads to Westminster Bridge. But when he or she also connects it to the fact that it runs past the Houses of Parliament and Big Ben, or even the fact that it is at the southern end of Canon Row, then it becomes even stickier. With that many different types of glue, Bridge Street is not getting lost, and it won't take long to learn either.

Likewise, all of the information you learn can serve as glue *for all other subjects as well.* Learning your vocabulary well the first time means that whenever you see those words in any of your reading for English class, history, or even science, you won't have to look them up again. On the flip side, you can use your Spanish, French, science knowledge, or even stories where you've seen the words before to learn a new vocabulary word. Why limit yourself to only one source of stickiness? The best part of all is that the more you know, the more the right glue will be obvious right away.

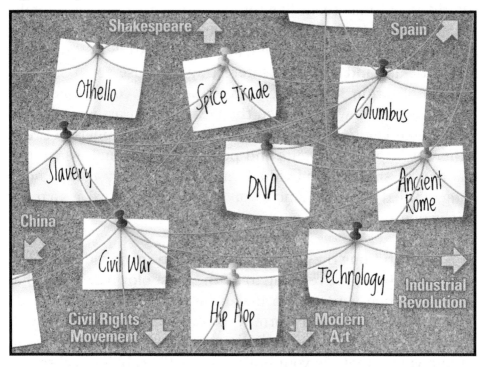

In school, your subjects are not separate topics that you learn. You are given the post-its—the major topics—but if you look *beyond* them to discover how all of those topics are related, then *everything* you learn will be memorable. What's more, you'll see why everything you learn really matters beyond the test you're taking. You'll end up with so much more than just an *A*; you'll end up with an education. As you can see from the diagram above, those connections are infinite, and your teachers don't have time in one class period a day to cover all of them. But they *are* out there, ready for you to find, and they *are* really interesting. For instance, did you know that some historians think that the African slave trade existed because Africans were the only people who were genetically resistant to malaria? Or, did you know that Brutus, the man who killed Julius Caesar, may have actually been Caesar's *son*? And if you follow the history of the Civil War all the way through the migration of freed slaves to Northern cities, then you could get all the way to the reason why Jay-Z is from Brooklyn. Facts like that are certainly harder to forget.

The bottom line is this: cabbies know that more is more. **More knowledge equals more ability to remember that knowledge at a moment's notice.** Since 1865, London cab drivers have known that the fastest way to learn every detail of London's 25,000 streets with lightning speed is to demand more out of their memories. They pile on 30,000 "extra" points of interest. Throughout the course of their careers, things are constantly added to the story of London, from new restaurants to new plays to newsworthy events throughout the city. The more they learn about London, the easier their job gets.

So what can you really learn from London's secret geniuses? Get greedy for knowledge. Your goal should be to possess the broadest and richest base of knowledge possible. The more you know, and the more "alive" that knowledge base is, the *less* you'll ever need to study for a test in the future. Often, new glue will form almost instantly. What's more, everything you have to learn will be more interesting. The cabbies master tens of thousands of facts in just a couple of years. That means that you can certainly learn the material from one unit of one class. Take a cue from the chaps in the front seat, and remember: the fastest route to *A*'s runs through Carting Lane.

Getting the Ball Rolling

How can you get started on your new road to being a test-taking genius? Try the Glue Guide out on a short list of terms. Start a few days before the test (or even when you first see the new term or word) and find some memory glue options. Wait a bit, and then test your glue. Did it stick? Which things are you still remembering after a few days go by? This should give you a good sense of which types of glue work best for you. Now, try it out when you study for your next test, and prove to yourself that your time is better spent coming up with great glue than just repeating terms until you're blue in the face.

Chapter 10

Go Cyborg on Your Mistakes

Until this point in your process, you've been the sweet but meticulous baker. You've been the detective who patiently uncovers all of the clues, and you've experienced the thrills and spills of producing a blockbuster essay. Working in all of those ways requires a certain level of flexibility, open-mindedness, and above all, patience. And throughout, you are the creator of your homework...the writer of your essay...a feeling, thinking person struggling to control your academic destiny in a world that's turning way too quickly... Oh, the humanity!

But at a certain point, you "finish" the problem that you're solving, or the draft of the essay that you're writing. And when that happens, you should feel a change coming over you. Your posture becomes rigid as you grow a cold, metal endoskeleton. Your vision goes red, and you have laser focus. And as you remove your sunglasses and stare into the mirror, you experience an overwhelming desire to ride a motorbike and engage in some history-altering time travel. You've transformed into an emotionless, systematic, and efficient killing machine. And your homework is now the enemy, poised for takedown. Hasta la vista, Betty. You're the Terminator.

In the *Terminator* movies, an incredibly smart computer named Skynet decides that it's high time humans were extinct. Launching a nuclear war gets rid of most of those pesky humanoids, but a few stragglers survive and fight back. Skynet needs to get rid of the human resistance leader, John Connor, but it's proving impossible. So, in order to kill this one person, the super-smart computer system invents time travel. If you go to the past and kill John Connor's *mother*, then your John Connor problem is solved—*because it never existed.* As soon as the time-travel thing is worked out, Skynet gives the Terminator his mission: travel back in time and *kill John Connor's mother, Sarah Connor.*

When the Terminator has a job to do, *nothing* will stop him from doing that job. Perfectly. When he is given his mission, the first thing he does is go to the phone book. There, he finds three possible listings for Sarah Connor. Which one is his target? Faced with this setback, the Terminator does not go back to Skynet and say, "Sorry, evil computer boss! My bad! There are three Sarah Connors! I didn't know who to kill, so I just stopped." No! Robots don't play that way. What's the Terminator's solution to making sure he gets the job done? Easy. Wipe out ALL the Sarah Connors, no matter where they are. That's the only way he can guarantee that he did his job well, so that's the *only* thing he'll do.

Yes, the Terminator is a scary death machine. But, he is also a stellar example of how to make your schoolwork airtight and mistake-free. In school, teachers always say, "Check your work!" And on some level, students know it might be a good idea. After all, putting hours of work into an essay or a homework assignment and then getting a bad grade only because of spelling, punctuation, and neatness errors is the most frustrating feeling in the world. So why do so many students decide to skip the checking and just hand their work in? They think checking doesn't make a big difference. Who cares about the little details if your ideas are good, right? Wrong. Every part of the finished product counts. If you wouldn't be happy with restaurant food that was half-cooked, or a movie where the sound and picture don't match, or a car that has its tires falling off, then there's no reason that homework with spelling and punctuation errors should be acceptable either.

The key to the Terminator's success—and to yours on any assignment—is to turn against your homework and make it the enemy. You can't go through the checking process and hope that your work is right; you should be bloodthirsty. You should be desperate to find weaknesses and get rid of them before anyone else can. Actively hunt down any possible source of failure...and then terminate it.

Sarah Connor Doesn't Want to be Terminated

When students actually do check their work, many just scan the page quickly and fix any mistakes that are obvious at a glance. That's like if the Terminator sat on his front porch, drinking a tall, refreshing glass of motor oil and waiting for each Sarah Connor to wander onto his lawn and ask to be terminated. What most students *don't* do is hunt their mistakes down until every mistake is dead. Checking your work is an "extra step?" HA! Tell that to the Terminator. The Terminator has a job to do and doing it 100% perfectly is a necessity. In the Terminator's line of work, the *fate of the world* is at stake. Robots can't annihilate humans and take over the Earth by doing a sloppy job.

Checking is essential. The need to cehck your wrok has nonithg to do wtih how good you are at the sujbcet. It is never a wtsae of your tmie. The peolpe who awlays do wlel do wvhateer tehy can to garuantee the qualtiy of their wrok, no maettr how much tmie it taeks or how tehy feel aobut the mstiakes tehy mdae. Everyone makes mistakes. But only a Terminator is guaranteed to catch them.

Did you notice anything about the last paragraph? Hopefully you *did* notice that there were some...uh...ERRORS in it. But what you *really* should have noticed is that they didn't really affect your ability to read and understand the text. Part of the reason that it's difficult to catch mistakes sometimes is that you have a *human* brain. Robot brains are extremely literal and they can't handle variation. If the Terminator saw the word "awlays," an alarm would instantly go off: "Not a word. Nonsensical letter combination. Does not compute."

On the other hand, the human brain is *really good* at seeing beyond the exact information it has in front of it, in order to fill in meaning where there is none. Your brain has been automating words and reading for so long that you can actually make sense of that error-laden paragraph just fine. In fact, as long as the first and last letters of any word are in the correct place, your brain will automatically rearrange any combination in the middle. That's amazing! But it's also dangerous. It makes it easy for us to miss simple mistakes, unless we're *really* looking for them. If your friend signed a note, "love <u>awlays</u>," you would still know what she *meant to say*. But for graded assignments, there's a big difference between *meant to say* and *did say*—and you'll see it in your score.

What's the Big Deal?

There's a huge difference between 10mg (milligrams) and 10μg (micrograms) of medicine. In fact, 10mg is a thousand times bigger. In the United States alone, roughly 7,000 patients die each year simply due to medication errors. Some of those are caused by patients not reading their prescriptions properly, while others happen because sloppy doctor handwriting leads to incorrect dosages.

And that goes for everyone. In junior year US history, Katie wrote a beautiful paper. It was all about the Constitution and the birth of a new nation and the bravery of the founding fathers. It was epic. It was inspiring. It was a love letter to the patriotism of a few men, stepping out on their own...challenging the Man... fighting for freedom. Katie finished the paper and printed it out. "Ahhhh, finally done! That took all night! But what a masterp... Wait. What the..." Katie happened to glance at the paper while she stapled the pristine final copy and realized that *all* through the paper—like, almost every time—she had written "**The Untied States**." (As you can imagine, those words appeared pretty often in a paper *about* the United States.) If Katie had turned this paper in to her teacher, it wouldn't have mattered at all what fabulous arguments she had made. It said "Untied States!" She felt like a bit of a moron as she went back and changed every single appearance of "Untied." It was just sheer *luck* that she caught it when she did! Anyone can make a mistake, and Katie certainly wasn't in Terminator mode when she decided to print out that paper. She was totally focused on content and on being done...so much so that she forgot to check the littlest details (for instance, *spelling*).

Guaranteeing that you can bring out your inner Terminator whenever you need it requires a simple RESET. Rather than choosing a better emotional mode...switch to anti-emotional mode. In other words, become a robot. When it comes to error-finding, mistakes are not a reflection of your personal worth or intelligence. The process of checking is not about judgment. It's about Judgment Day. The Terminator doesn't let *feelings* get in the way of his mission. (Please. *Feelings* are for *humans*.) Separate yourself from the work and just get the job done perfectly. No pain. No fear. Just terminate.

Create Your Checklist

As a futuristic robot, the Terminator has a very detailed, concrete procedure for checking his work. In the *Terminator* movies, any time the Terminator has to make a decision about *anything*, a digital menu appears in his vision with all possible sources of error and all options for how to proceed. He is extremely methodical, and he thoroughly analyzes each of these options before making the next robotic move.

That pull-down checklist is exactly what you need to ensure that the work you've done is really complete. That's what Shawn, a high-school junior, discovered when he had to raise his French grade. Shawn was the super-jock of his school. He was tall with broad shoulders, and he was built like a brick wall. He had a buzz cut and a deep voice—he was like the high school version of Mr. Clean. And although he had never worried about his French grade before, it was suddenly extremely important that he get it up to at least a *B*; otherwise, according to his coach's rule, he would be kicked off the football team.

Shawn was really worried about letting down his teammates, and thinking about his team was just the RESET he needed to get him to buckle down. The funny thing was, when Hunter tested him, it was clear that Shawn had been doing a pretty good job of staying on top of all the rules, vocab, and conjugations he needed to do really well in French. So then why did he have a *D*?

Hunter asked him about his work over the last couple of weeks. "Ugh...I'm trying my best, but my teacher just doesn't let anything go! On every quiz and test and whatever, she takes off points even for tiny stuff like accents." Shawn, points are points, and you're not doing everything that you possibly can to make sure that you stay on that football team. Just because you answer all of the questions does not mean that you're done. And that's why you keep getting marked down for things you actually know pretty well.

Shawn couldn't afford to keep noticing his mistakes *after* the teacher did. He had some homework that he was planning to turn in the next day, so Hunter asked to see it.

Shawn Williams   <u>Après Avoir/Être Homework</u>

1. After having done all of her homework, Michelle left the library.

Après avoir fait tout son devoir, Michelle a sorti bibliotheque.

2. After having left the library, Michelle met me at the movies.

Après être sortie la bibliotheque, Michelle a rencontré moi au cinema.

3. After having met at the movies, we went to eat.

Après avoir rencontré au cinema, nous sommes allé manger.

Let's see how Shawn was checking his assignment. Because Shawn had already mentioned that he sometimes lost points for "accents," Hunter decided to start there. Shawn, you wrote "bibliotheque" in the first question. Are you sure that word doesn't have any accents?

"Uhh...I don't know. I guess?"

I guess?!?!?!? How positively *human* of you. The Terminator would *never* tolerate even the slightest possibility of error, so that's something that needs to be checked. What about "après?" Are you sure that accent is correct?

"Yeah. Definitely. No question. ...Right?"

You don't even need to speak French to see that the problem here was that Shawn wasn't *100% certain* about his answers. To be a Terminator, during the checking process, there cannot be room for "maybe," "sort of," "I guess," or anything ending with "-ish." And if someone asks you how your test went, and your answer sounds like a question ("Great?"), then you're toast. You need to make sure that you have checked everything that could possibly be wrong. For Shawn to guarantee he didn't lose any points on his assignment, he needed to create a quick pull-down checklist for himself, just like the Terminator uses when making any decision. With that checklist in place, Shawn would be able to run that scan in his mind every time he finished an assignment or test.

Shawn was ready to do some terminating. He went through the homework answers and stopped at any word he didn't know was correct with 100% certainty. That meant identifying each and every place that could possibly contain an error. First item on the checklist? Accents. No hard feelings, no mercy.

ACCENTS: PROCESSING...

Shawn Williams   Après Avoir/Être Homework

TARGETING AREAS OF UNCERTAINTY...

1. After having done all of her assignments, Michelle left the library.

Après avoir fait tout son devoir, Michelle a sorti bibliotheque.

2. After having left the library, Michelle met me at the movies.

Après être sortie la bibliotheque, Michelle a rencontré moi au cinema.

3. After having met at the movies, we went to eat.

Après avoir rencontré au cinema, nous sommes allé manger.

CONSULT TEXTBOOK? (Y/N)

Shawn (rather begrudgingly at first) looked up each of those words in his textbook. One by one, he fixed the accents until he was completely positive there were none missing or misplaced in any of the sentences.

```
                              ACCENTS:  TERMINATED

  Shawn Williams    Après Avoir/Être Homework

ACCENT ERRORS
TERMINATED...   done all of her assignments, Michelle left the library.

    Après avoir fait tout son devoir, Michelle a sorti bibliothèque.  [·]

  2. After having left the library, Michelle met me at the movies.

    Après être sortie la bibliothèque, Michelle a rencontré moi au cinéma.  [·]

  3. After having met at the movies, we went to eat.

    Après avoir rencontré au cinéma, nous sommes allé manger.  [·]


CONTINUE CHECKING? (Y/N)
```

Once the accents were all correct, Shawn could add more items to his checklist and check the homework for other potential weaknesses. He could already see the difference that going into Terminator mode was going to make on his homework grade.

Shawn built his checklist by thinking about where he usually lost points, but there's a much easier way that you can build your checklist. When you start a class, each time you learn a new topic—verb conjugations, adjective agreement—you need to add that topic to your checklist. At first, especially in a foreign language, you'll need your checklist to include every topic, because you still need to be careful about making sure that you're following all of the new rules that you've learned. But as you go through a class, you will automate some of its

Save Yourself Some Time

Many students avoid "showing work" as they do math problems, because they believe that it takes longer or is unnecessary. Showing no work makes it impossible to quickly terminate your mistakes. How can you locate where the error happened? Your only option for guaranteed success would be to redo every step of the problem to check the answer. Do yourself a favor and write it out the first time.

Make it Easy!

It helps to start out by writing down your checklist. Put it inside the front cover of your textbook or notebook so that you can refer to it during class or while you do homework.

topics so well that you won't need to have as much attention on them anymore. You'll also learn new topics that need to be added to the list. Your pop-up checklist in any class is a constantly-evolving list of targets.

Once he fixed the accent errors, Shawn could continue down his checklist, one item at a time, terminating any "bonehead mistakes" that appeared in his homework. (Hunter suggested saying, "I'll be back," in a deep, Austrian-robot kind of voice at the end of each pass.) When Shawn was through with the list, he had guaranteed that he would get full credit for all of the work that he had done. No losing points for things he already knew how to do.

ACCENTS:	TERMINATED
AGREEMENTS:	TERMINATED
ARTICLES:	TERMINATED
AVOIR/ETRE:	TERMINATED
PRONOUNS:	TERMINATED

Shawn Williams   Après Avoir/Être Homework

1. After having done all of her assignments, Michelle left the library.

       tous ses devoirs   est sortie
Après avoir fait ~~tout son devoir~~, Michelle ~~a sorti~~ bibliothèque.
                                                        de la

2. After having left the library, Michelle met me at the movies.

                                                m'a
Après être sortie la bibliothèque, Michelle ~~a~~ rencontré ~~moi~~ au cinéma.

DIRECT OBJECT PRONOUNS:
CORRECT FORM: MOI -> ME...
SHOULD PRECEDE VERB...
ME BEFORE A -> M'A

3. After having met at the movies, we went to eat.

Après avoir rencontré au cinema, nous sommes allés manger.

PRONOUN ERRORS TERMINATED...
CHECKLIST COMPLETED

By going through this process, Shawn could finally see how avoidable it was to lose all of those points and let his grade suffer. He knew these rules—he just wasn't taking the time to make sure his homework was 100% error-free. Before he had beefed up his pop-up checklist, his "checking" process had looked something like this:

IS IT FRENCH?   LET ME SEE

Shawn Williams   Après Avoir/Être Homework

1. After having done all of her homework, Michelle left the library.

Après avoir fait tout son devoir, Michelle a sorti bibliotheque.

2. After having left the library, Michelle met me at the movies.

Après être sortie la bibliotheque, Michelle a rencontré moi au cinema.

3. After having met at the movies, we went to eat.

Après avoir rencontré au cinema, nous sommes allé manger.

UH....IT LOOKS PRETTY GOOD....

Essentially, Shawn had been the *Indeterminator*. His approach to homework was carefree and shiny and full of gumdrops and sugarplums...but it didn't do much to catch any errors. Fortunately, now, he had a pop-up checklist as thorough as the Terminator's. What he needed to do next was to train himself to slip in and out of cyborg mode at any moment. On his future assignments and tests, when he completed a first pass of an exercise or an essay, he would know to reach the end and say, "I'll be back." Then, he would boot up his checklist, go cyborg, and start

Spell Check Is No Cyborg

Students have come to rely on the little squiggly lines from spell check and grammar check. Those squiggles will detect incorrect spellings, but they won't detect incorrect usages. If you write, "The students were eager to see *there* friend," then spell check will breeze right over that sentence... and if you're not in Terminator mode, then so will you.

Cyborgs Can RESET

Remember RESET's? Shawn's RESET wasn't a phrase; it was a physical object. Shawn taped a printed copy of this season's football schedule to the inside cover of his French notebook. Anytime he started to feel bummed or frustrated, he could look at that schedule and remember why the hard work was worth it.

targeting his mistakes until he had terminated all of them. No matter how correct or how "French" his homework looked, Shawn wouldn't be fooled. He would assume there was a problem; he just hadn't found it yet. As he got into this habit, his grade improved, and he stopped experiencing the frustration of losing points for things he already knew.

Shawn never would have given 100% in a football game only to stop trying with a few minutes left because it *looked* like his team would win; he always played with Terminator-like ruthlessness *until the final whistle,* because he wanted to keep scoring points to *guarantee* a win. His French work needed that same ruthlessness. In the past, he had treated losing a half-point here and a half-point there for things like spelling and accents as "no big deal." But dozens of half-point errors add up to *many* lost points over time. Ultimately, his "bonehead mistakes" weren't costing him half a point—they were costing him his place on the football team.

With his checklist in place, Shawn had a mission to search and destroy...every error. The Terminator has no choice; he can't do a mission halfway. And Shawn realized that checking wasn't a choice either; it was something that had to happen every time. Mistakes might slip through his grasp on the first couple of passes, but ultimately, no mistake escapes the cold, emotionless precision of a Terminator.

Simple Questions Save the Day

Using the rules that you're learning in class is a great way to build your pull-down checklist. However, even if you're brand new to a class, there are plenty of rules that you already know. You just may not realize that they can help your checklist too.

The rules that we're talking about are the rules of real life—common sense about how the world works. For example, one student, Carly, was working on a word problem about a discount on an iPhone. The price started around $300, and then there was a 20% discount and then a 10% discount applied. But when Carly got her final answer, her paper said that the store would be selling the iPhone for $1.43. No math is even required to recognize that this answer is too good to be true. (Although if you ever find the store that sells that $1.43 iPhone, let us know, because we'll be first in line.) Simple questions like these can save you from making absurd errors.

Because you're so familiar with real life and how it works, using real life examples or comparisons can be the best tool for spotting when something isn't quite right. Here are some similar questions that you could add to your checklist in order to catch answers that are way off:

- **Should the answer be positive or negative?**
- **Did I copy down the question correctly?**
- **Should the answer be big or small? This big? This small?**
- **Does my answer say that gravity works upwards?**
- **Does this math make sense in terms of something concrete, like money?**
- **Is it likely that Henry the Seventh of England ruled before Henry the Fifth of England?**
- **Does my answer say that it took negative two hours for the train to reach Manchester? Am I sure I want to**

say that this train is capable of traveling backwards in time?

Your checklist should not be limited to the rules you've learned so far within the subject that you are studying. Common sense is one of the best tools you have at your disposal when you're on the hunt for mistakes to terminate.

Red-Letter Day: A Great Time to Terminate

Creating a checklist before you hand in your work is great, but there's another essential part to preventing future mistakes. Your final—and most helpful—opportunity to do some terminating happens *after* you've already gotten a test, paper, or assignment back.

When students get tests back, they tend to just see the grade—that big red *B* or *C* is all that they remember. But a letter grade doesn't say anything specific about what caused it or what needs to be fixed. That's why it's so important to *terminate the errors on the work you've already done.* Analyze why each mistake happened. Sure, you can't change your grade this time, but you can strengthen your checklist for the future. Better yet, you might see that the grade doesn't reflect some major issue with understanding, but just the simple need for a Terminator.

A Cosmically Big Error

The Mars Climate Orbiter Project cost $327 million to build, so it's pretty unfortunate that the satellite exploded. Why did it explode? Because despite the perfect execution of the engine, the computer chips, the solar panels and every other part, the engineers made one tiny mistake. One team was calculating in pounds and the other team was using metric units. Fortunately, mistakes on your homework don't cause it to explode. But this is proof that Terminator-grade checking is essential in real life too.

For example, when Hunter started taking physics in his junior year of high school, his first quiz grade was a disaster, and he felt majorly ashamed. He was supposed to be one of the smart kids, and now he was totally bombing physics. From that point on, whenever Hunter got back any assignment or test, he would shove it into his folder quickly so no one else could see his humiliating grade. Eventually, his physics grade was ruining his GPA so much that he realized he had to do something. So, he went home, pulled out all those papers and had the shock of his life. His bad grades had nothing to do with his understanding of physics. Hunter couldn't read his own handwriting. His 4's looked like 9's and his 1's looked like 7's. That had caused weeks and weeks of calculation errors. And that was all he needed to fix to get back on track.

Hunter's discovery was that he had simply underestimated the importance of clear handwriting. For years, he had believed it was a waste of time to improve his handwriting. Knowing that *handwriting* was the culprit was all it took to get back on track. If he had been more of a Terminator when he first took those

Diva... Or Terminator?

David Lee Roth, the lead singer of the band Van Halen, got a reputation for being a demanding diva, particularly because in his contract, he demanded that every concert venue have a bowl of M&Ms waiting for him in his dressing room. The catch was that every brown M&M had to be removed from the mix. If even one was in the bowl, Van Halen would not perform... but the band still had to be paid in full.

The thing is, people only saw this as diva behavior because they didn't know the full story. Van Halen had a *huge* touring show, and often they would play venues in smaller cities that were only used to accommodating performances a third of their size. Van Halen's staging was complicated, intricate, massive... and potentially very dangerous. It also came with pages and pages of instructions for how it needed to be set up so that the concert went smoothly and safely. So, within that list of instructions, David Lee Roth added a little detail about brown M&M's—"Article 126." If Roth showed up to perform and the brown M&Ms hadn't been removed, then he instantly knew that the instructions hadn't been thoroughly read... and therefore it was likely that the staging wasn't 100% perfect and 100% safe for the band. More than once, the M&M test led Van Halen to discover safety hazards. In other words, the M&M test was there to save their lives. David Lee Roth wasn't being a diva; he was being a Terminator.

quizzes, he could have prevented lost points. But being *willing* to do a checklist-scan of past work is what really allowed him to pull out of his rut and raise his grade. A Terminator ignores *no* piece of data. Scan the errors that already occurred, and you'll give yourself the most specific plan of action for next time.

You're Not Done Until Every Mistake Has Been Terminated

In the world of the Terminator, there is only right and wrong. "Right" means 100%-guaranteed right. If "sort of right" or "I hope it's right" are the most you can say for your work, then assume that it's wrong. Settling for "sort of" is exactly how students needlessly throw away easy points. If you're not sure it's right, then you'd better check. Look it up in your textbook or ask your teacher, but *make sure* it's right.

The Terminator sets out to beat mistakes to the punch. He deals in hypotheticals. How could this fail? How might this mess me up? Could I bet my life on this?

That's exactly what you need to do every time the "I'm done" reflex goes off after homework or a test. Rather than finishing the problems and then spending the remaining twenty minutes on an elaborate and impressive doodle, or skipping checking altogether because you want to look "fast," go cyborg and seek out potential problems. Could this spelling be wrong? Could I have said this more concisely? Am I absolutely sure that's the answer? The time that you spend checking your work is not "wasted time." It's the time that it takes to ensure a victory.

The added bonus is that Terminator-style checking contributes to your fix-it-focused practice. The more thoughtfully you look for mistakes in your work, the more strongly you are automating the "right way" of doing that work. When you have looked up the correct spelling of a word twenty times, you will have no doubt about whether it's spelled the right way. That means that the checking process itself will get easier and easier, until eventually, you can do a robot-style microscan and catch everything in nanoseconds.

NO ONE IS ABOVE A CHECKLIST

One million people die every year from preventable errors that occur during surgery. These are things like surgeons leaving sponges inside bodies after they're closed up or forgetting to administer the right medication or wash their hands. The irony in these cases is that the surgery itself—the massively complicated procedure that takes years to perfect—goes well. It's the details that cause the deaths.

American physician and journalist Atul Gawande has attempted to solve this problem by implementing checklists in operating rooms nationwide. The surgery checklist that his team developed, which ensures that the simplest, smallest steps aren't overlooked, has been proven to reduce the rate of death by preventable surgical error by 47%. Despite the checklist's great results, when surveyed, 20% of the surgeons in the study still claimed that they "didn't need" it, or that it would "take too much time" to use.

This is the conspiracy at work. Over many centuries, the Straight-A Conspiracy has made us all so focused on how impressive it is to do complicated things, that we start to think the simple tasks don't matter. A doctor forgetting to wash his hands is no reflection of his talent as a surgeon, right? And your misuse of some tiny commas shouldn't matter, because all of your ideas in the essay were brilliant, huh? Sure, the complicated tasks might be more impressive. But at the end of the day, the survival rate—and your success rate—depends just as much on remembering the little, seemingly insignificant, "easy" parts of any process as it does on the "advanced" actions.

Getting the Ball Rolling

The easiest way to start building your checklist in any subject is to look at what you say when you're annoyed. "Ugh. I *always* lose points for _____." It may be "accents" or "spelling" or "not showing work" or just general "neatness." Whatever you routinely say is your most common "bonehead mistake" is actually the first item to add to your checklist. For one week, *just* start to terminate that *one issue*. See what a difference it makes, and you'll likely be inspired to make that checklist bigger—and your mistakes nonexistent.

Chapter 11

Decide To Go Pro

Where to even begin? He's a six-time NBA Champion, a five-time NBA MVP, two-time gold medal-winning Olympian, NBA Rookie of the Year, fourteen-time NBA All-Star, two-time NBA All-Star game MVP, two-time NBA Slam Dunk Contest winner, a member of the NBA's fiftieth-anniversary "All-Time Team," NBA Hall of Famer, ESPN's Top Athlete of the Twentieth Century...and he's been on the cover of *Sports Illustrated* a mere fifty-six times. Oh, yeah...and he also was responsible for revolutionizing the sneaker and creating a line of shoes that still generates over one billion dollars in revenue per year. People often describe other successful people as being the Michael Jordans of their respective fields. Michael Jordan isn't just the Michael Jordan of basketball. Michael Jordan is the Michael Jordan of being the best.

Many people have heard the legendary story of how Michael Jordan was cut from his high school basketball team as a sophomore. Those same people likely know exactly what Michael Jordan looks like when he's flying through the air in a red Chicago

Bulls uniform and his famous Air Jordan sneakers, dunking a ball from higher in the air than seems humanly possible. But what most people *don't* know is what happened in between. How did Michael Jordan go from being the high-school team reject to being consistently ranked as the greatest athlete of our time?

After working his way onto the high school team and becoming one of its best players, Michael Jordan earned a scholarship to play basketball at the University of North Carolina. He had a superstar freshman year, and everyone knew him as a phenom who came in, got onto the starting five, was named ACC Freshman of the Year, and made the game-winning jumpshot to earn the Tar Heels the NCAA Championship. Michael Jordan was already *really good* at basketball. But it's what he did next that deserves the most notice. As one biographer puts it:

"The summer after his freshman triumph, he took on all comers in five-man pickup games in the Tar Heels' gym. As he racked up win after win, he dismantled and reassembled each piece of his game. His outside shot was still shaky, and so was his defense. There had been too many mistakes that first season, too many gambles he lost with the ball. He knew he was a clutch player. Now he wanted to be a perfect player."

While most people would have taken that victory and left for the summer to give themselves a hard-earned break, Michael Jordan was just getting started. His goal was to become a professional athlete, and, as well as he was already playing, he knew he could be better. Until the day that he retired from professional basketball, Michael Jordan never stopped analyzing his own game and putting in extra practice. He never stopped looking for ways to improve.

In fact, Michael's **refusal to ever settle** is the secret to how *all* pros rise to the top of their fields. Pros don't settle for staying as good as they are right now; they work to become even better. Pros don't settle for what other people *tell them* they can accomplish; they just focus on accomplishing all of their goals, so that they can prove those people wrong. Whether it's professional sports, business, writing, politics, music, acting, science, or anything else, the actions and the attitude that it takes to be the best are all the same.

> ### They Said it Can't Be Done
>
> For many years, people in the world of distance running believed it was physically impossible for a human to run a mile in under four minutes. Then, in 1954, Roger Bannister ran a mile in 3 minutes and 59.4 seconds. Everyone was stunned. Just three years later, sixteen athletes had broken the four-minute-mile mark. The real barrier that Bannister broke wasn't a physical one; it was a mental one.

Most importantly, pros know that they can't just "bring it" when it's time for the big game, presentation, or performance. In the last chapter, we taught you how to get ready for what is essentially your "game day" as a student: the test. There are ways to prepare yourself starting early in the unit, a few days before, or (if you have to) the night before, that will still help you to get through...and likely do well. But why be good when you can be *great*? Michael Jordan would *never* show up to play on game day, having only prepared as much as was absolutely necessary to get by.

Doing just enough to "get by" is fine in situations where you never need to get past the amateur level. For instance, plenty of people all around the world play sports in recreational leagues. After a tough week in the office, they show up on Saturday morning, feeling kind of tired but still interested in getting some sort of exercise and seeing their friends. They probably stayed up late and ate some junk food the night before. They know it's fun to win, but it doesn't really matter if they don't. This is how a lot of students treat school, because they think they're only good enough to be amateurs. Most students currently have a **getting-by mindset**.

Pros are in a different league for a reason. As fans, we all see professional athletes on TV or at the stadium, when they're doing what we consider to be the most important part of their job: playing the game. But if you asked those athletes, they would say that there are lots of other parts to their jobs that are just as important. Professional athletes know that they can't go to practice for a couple of days, skip some days, eat fifteen slices of pizza, and still be in top form when it's time to play for real. Every decision that they make in terms of how they approach each day is made based on what will best help them when game day arrives. From the minute the season begins (and usually even in the off-season), what they eat, how they practice, and how they schedule their time is all decided with the upcoming games in mind. Being a pro is a 24/7 job, because every minute is an opportunity to be better, faster, stronger, or more skilled. In fact, pros *never* settle for just getting by; instead, they insist on **always getting better**.

The Neverending Book Report

Having a pro attitude isn't about things being easy; it's about always pushing yourself to the finish. In sixth grade, Katie's class was assigned a book report. Katie decided that she would do her report on Emily Brontë's *Wuthering Heights*. (Note: What on Earth would possess eleven-year-old Katie to choose that book? Who knows? But it was way more than she could handle.) When she told her teacher, Mrs. Palmer, her plan, Mrs. P. smiled knowingly and said, "O...kayyy..." And off Katie went. By the time the report was due, she had only crawled her way through about one-third of the novel. Katie was ready to surrender but, Mrs. P. wouldn't let her back off. It took almost the entire sixth-grade year, but Katie read that whole book. She turned in the report a record 187 days late—but taking on a challenge she wasn't actually ready for was one of the best lessons in perseverance that she ever experienced.

As a student, you don't necessarily need to start pounding bottle after bottle of Gatorade, but you *can* change your habits so that even when it's not game day, you're still setting yourself up to win. You may not need your body to be at a pro level, but if you want to continue through school and have a successful life, you *definitely* need your *brain* to reach the pro level. All you have to do is decide that you're ready to bump your game up a notch, beyond just improving your scores on a few homework assignments and tests.

What a pain! Ugh! It's hard enough to motivate myself to do the work it takes to get by. How am I supposed to motivate myself to go that far above and beyond? Question: Do you think it's hard for Michael Jordan to motivate himself to get out of bed for that crack of dawn practice? Nope. Know why? Because he knows that in return for his hard work, he gets to be MICHAEL JORDAN! Getting by isn't going to get anyone fired up. But knowing that you're making yourself the Michael Jordan of...*anything*, really...is enough to convince you to always get better.

By going pro, you can have all-around success, so that everything in your life is not only better, but also easier, and less stressful. You can take control of everything that you do, and you can do everything you can to ensure that you come out on top. Best of all, what it takes to raise your game to the pro level is really just lots of small but consistent actions. Even Michael Jordan didn't become the best overnight. Take it from him:

"I've always believed that if you put in the work, the results will come. I don't do things halfheartedly. Because I know if I do, then I can expect halfhearted results. That's why I approach practices the same way I approach games. You can't turn it on and off like a faucet. I couldn't dog it during practice and then, when I needed that extra push late in the game, expect it to be there."

Being a pro isn't about being better than other people; it's about constantly taking any and every opportunity to be better than you were the day before. Being a pro isn't a job. It's a lifestyle.

Michael Jordan Never Forgets the Fundamentals

Creating an entire lifestyle can be a tall order. So where can you begin, once you've decided that you want to go pro? Being a pro in *any* field always begins with the basics. Michael Jordan had a great coach—UNC's Dean Smith—to thank for this mindset. There have been lots of great three-point shooters, ball handlers, and defensive players in the history of basketball. What made Michael Jordan such an amazing player was that he made *every part* of his game exceptional. That wasn't an accident. Dean Smith didn't care that Michael was an amazing shooter; he wouldn't rest until his players were amazing at *all* aspects of the game.

This approach stayed with Michael for his entire career. Even once Michael reached the NBA, when most people would assume that he had "already learned" how to play basketball, he never let himself off the hook. He never decided that he was "done" learning how to do any of even the most basic skills. And Michael was the first to admit that.

"Fundamentals were the most crucial part of my game in the NBA. Everything I did, everything I achieved, can be traced back to the way I approached the fundamentals and how I applied them to my abilities."

For Michael, the principle of keeping the fundamentals strong meant that he revisited his ball-handling, practiced shooting from the free-throw line, and did drill after drill of easy layups at every practice, and even on his days off. He might have focused on just the placement of his wrist when he shot three-pointers, or how quickly he could plant and pivot to get around a scary power forward. He took it down to the tiniest details, working each move out *slowly* until he was sure that it was perfect. This slow, methodical, fix-it-focused practice is how the pros do it. There's no rushing, and there's no assuming that the skill will be good enough. You do whatever it takes to improve.

For you, as a student, that means that you get into the habit of doing all of the things we've taught you in part three of this book, *all the time*. Every time you have to read something new, it's a chance to Sherlock it. Every time you learn a new rule, you can make it Cake-Mix Clear. Every mistake can be terminated every day, and so on. Never forget the fundamentals.

It's very easy to think that you already know how to read, or that you already know how to check your work or write an essay. Probably you *do* know how to do those things, in the sense that you know *one* way to do them. But that's like your super-awkward friend who knows *one* way to shoot a three-pointer. He holds it in two hands, swings it down between his legs, and then chucks it in the direction of the hoop. That granny shot is not going to work for Michael. Michael Jordan is never interested in knowing *one* way to do something; he wants to find the very best way to do it. A pro would never settle for mediocre results. Pros pay attention to the basics, because that's how you become an all-around all-star.

"The minute you get away from fundamentals, the bottom can fall out."

So true, Michael Jordan. (How awesome is he?!) If you're really ready to take your game to the next level, then you have to be on constant lookout for ways to get closer to doing basic actions *perfectly*. That doesn't mean that you ever have to reach that level—or even know what it is. It just means that you have to always be improving, little by little. Basically, what we're saying is that you have to start doing fix-it-focused practice, not just on your work, but on *how* you work. After all, Michael Jordan is the king of fix-it-focused practice:

"There is a right way and a wrong way to do things. You can practice shooting eight hours a day, but if your technique is wrong, then all you become is very good at shooting the wrong way."

We know that it may seem obvious at this point in the book to suggest that you do...well, all the things that we've told you in this book. But the real issue is whether you only do it when you absolutely have to—to **just get by**—or whether you do that every day, so you're **always getting better**. The students who work this way every day are the students who don't really have to study much when the test comes. They don't get stressed, and they don't ever feel bad, because they always know that they've done everything they can, and so they're ready for whatever comes up. Every day, Michael Jordan left everything on the court.

"Players who practice hard when no one is paying attention generally play well when everyone is watching."

Doing this kind of work on your fundamentals is eighty percent of the job, in terms of improving your results. So, if you're even the slightest bit curious about what it takes to go from being "successful" to being, say, the Michael Jordan of high school academics, then you might as well keep reading, because there's only a very secret (but very doable) twenty percent further to go.

You know what? It's been *a whole paragraph* since we quoted Michael Jordan. Let's have another!

"Get the fundamentals down and the level of everything you do will rise."

He did it again! What else do you have to teach us, Your Airness?

Put Your Schedule on Offense

Imagine that you're a pro athlete. When you wake up in the morning, you know that today, you should fit in the following things: attend team practice, do some additional work (an hour maybe) on your jump shot, eat three to five healthy meals, and go to the gym. You go to team practice, because that's always first thing in the morning. But then, just as you're deciding whether to stay after for that jump shot practice, go to eat, or hit the gym, your teammate comes up to you and says, "Hey! Wanna go test-drive some Ferraris with me?" (You are million-dollar-contract professional athletes, after all.) With those options in front of you, what do you think you're going to pick?

Ferraris. After all, can't you still fit in that other stuff later in the day? Sure, you *might* be able to. But we've all had unscheduled days, and we all know where they go. After Ferraris, you and your teammate grab some bacon-wrapped chili cheese dogs, and when you get back, you don't exactly feel like heading to the gym. Maybe later on that night, you fit in a few jump shots at home... but your grand plan definitely didn't happen. That's because your schedule wasn't "on offense."

Pros in every field, from business to sports to science to writing, have to set schedules for themselves, because *that's the only way that they can make sure things happen.* Don't get us wrong; we know that there are some things that you don't have to schedule, and they still manage to always get accomplished. It's just that those things tend to be video games and Facebook posting and watching funny cat videos on YouTube. Michael Jordan might also love to just watch cat videos on YouTube all day (we don't know Michael Jordan personally, so it's possible). But he knows that if that's the choice he makes, he can't also expect to have a championship ring at the end of the season. Your schedule needs to be on offense against the opposition. For those of us who aren't facing a team of frighteningly agile giants in shiny sneakers, the opposition is

> **Forget About It**
>
> Isn't it annoying trying to remember all the things you need to get done? One of the great things about offensive scheduling is that you don't have to worry about forgetting to do something. You just have to do what's scheduled right now.

all of the little things that waste our time, bit by bit, throughout the day.

To understand what offensive scheduling really means, you first need to understand *defensive scheduling*. Defensive scheduling is what the athlete above did. It's when you wait for things to come to you. (I should practice sometime today. Buuuuuuut, my test isn't until Friday sooooooo...) Then, when those things roll around, you haven't left enough time to actually do them, and you have to try to frantically shove them in at the last minute. Obviously, they very rarely all get done...and it's even rarer that they *get done well*.

On the other hand, offensive scheduling makes sure that nothing gets forgotten, and you *still* have time to fit in that *hi-la-rious* cat video (if you're so inclined). With offensive scheduling, you're always in control of the game, taking charge of your time and planning it out *well before* it can get away from you. As soon as you know something needs to happen, you find a time to *make* it happen, and you lock it down. That way, you're never scrambling to make up a bunch of baskets as the buzzer is sounding.

You need to use offensive scheduling: check it off or block it off. Very often, the best time to make something happen is *right now*. If you were in the habit of doing everything as soon as it came up, then you would never have to remember to do anything later on, and you would always be up-to-date (or ahead) on all of your work. There are lots of times that you can do that (and maybe you already do, without realizing it). Tasks that should be done right away are simple things like putting away your quizzes and homework assignments in the right place in your binder, checking to make sure you have the right supplies for class, and writing down the homework assignment for that night. These take less than a minute, but checking them off right away makes your life far easier, because they're already out of your brain and off of your schedule.

Of course, we know that it's not realistic—or possible—to do *everything* as soon as it shows up on your radar. If you can't check it off, then you need to block it off. Go to your calendar and block off time for that task, so that you can be sure that it is going to get done.

Team Practice: The first thing that you want to lock down is whatever happens at a certain time, no matter what. These are things like your regular classes, weekly practices for sports teams, performing groups, or student council...even family dinner at 7 p.m. each night. You can't change those, but you do have to be there, so make sure you know when they will happen. If you use a calendar on your computer, then set these events early in the semester and make sure they will show up each week. If you're using a handwritten assignment notebook, try to fill in your schedule either at the beginning of every week (maybe Sunday night, when you have some downtime), or before every two weeks. That way, you don't have to think about it again until you've gotten through all of those requirements.

	Sunday	Monday	Tuesday	Wednesday	Thursday	Friday	Saturday
7am							
				Student Council			
8am							
		8am-3pm School	8am-3pm School	8am-3pm School	8am-3pm School	8am-3pm School	
9am							
10am							
11am							
12pm							
1pm							
2pm							
3pm							
4pm		3:30pm-5pm Play Rehearsal		3:30pm-5pm Play Rehearsal		3:30pm-5pm Play Rehearsal	
5pm							
6pm							
7pm		7pm: Dinner	7pm: Dinner	7pm: Dinner	7pm: Dinner	7pm: Dinner	
8pm							
9pm							
10pm							
Key: Team Practice							

Get Some Teammates!

If you think you're going to have a hard time motivating yourself to do something, then the best trick is to plan to do it with someone else. Athletes often set times to hit the gym together. Set up your study session with a friend, or tell your parents you'll do homework while they do their taxes. (Trust us, you'll be having more fun.) Just make sure you and your teammate are watching out for each other, and it's more likely that you'll both get it done!

The Daily Drill: Next, fill in anything that has to happen, but can happen at any time during the day. For a basketball player, this might be going to the gym for weight training. For you, this might just be setting aside an hour or two when you are going to do your homework. You get to decide when it will go the best, and then choose to plan it for that time of day. (Usually the best time to do it is as early as possible. Michael Jordan went to the gym *before* practice every day.) You can do your homework as soon as you get home or better yet, plan to really utilize your study hall time and practice cutting down on how much homework you need to do outside of school!

	Sunday	Monday	Tuesday	Wednesday	Thursday	Friday	Saturday
7am				Student Council			
8am		8am-3pm School	8am-3pm School	8am-3pm School	8am-3pm School	8am-3pm School	
9am							
10am							
11am							
12pm							
1pm							
2pm							
3pm							
4pm	3:30pm-5pm Play Rehearsal	3:30pm-5pm Homework	3:30pm-5pm Play Rehearsal	3:30pm-5pm Homework	3:30pm-5pm Play Rehearsal		
5pm							
6pm	5:30pm-7pm Homework		5:30pm-7pm Homework		5:30pm-7pm Homework		
7pm	7pm: Dinner	7pm: Dinner	7pm: Dinner	7pm: Dinner	7pm: Dinner		
8pm							
9pm							
10pm							

Key: Team Practice
Daily Drill

Hang Time: Hang time is the part of scheduling that really separates the pros from the recreational league players. After you've locked down the other two categories, it's really up to you to decide how to use the time that's left over. You can use it as hang-out time—after all, you will have gotten all of your regular work done. But you can also use it to *improve your game*—if you're a basketball player, to increase your hang time. Find ways that your game could be better, and take advantage of those time slots.

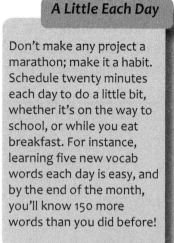

A Little Each Day

Don't make any project a marathon; make it a habit. Schedule twenty minutes each day to do a little bit, whether it's on the way to school, or while you eat breakfast. For instance, learning five new vocab words each day is easy, and by the end of the month, you'll know 150 more words than you did before!

When you're going pro, you want to be on the hunt for *any new thing* that comes up that you will need to do. If Michael Jordan is going to give an inspirational speech to young basketball players, he needs to find a way to get in the time to prepare it. Students commonly encounter this type of event when an essay is assigned or a test is announced. It doesn't matter when you fit in time to work on these things, but it does matter *that they get done*. Rather than waiting until the night before, make your life less stressful and block off time in advance. If you want to make it part of your homework, add thirty minutes per day to that time when you get home. If you'd rather work after dinner, that's fine. You can even do more on some days, and take other days off. What you do need to do, though, is make your hang time *specific*. Instead of giving yourself an hour to "study for history," say that you're going to "study key terms from Chapter 7." That ensures that the hour you spend studying is focused, and you don't just spend it randomly flipping through the book. Get more bang for your buck, and you'll have to use less hang time for history later in the week.

Once you've added in all of the extra practice that you need, then by *all means*, plan on the rest of your hang time being reserved for hang-out time. You've earned it. Best of all, you'll actually enjoy that time more, because your mind will rest easy knowing that you've taken care of everything else.

Key	Sunday	Monday	Tuesday	Wednesday	Thursday	Friday	Saturday
7am							
8am				Student Council			
9am		8am-3pm School	8am-3pm School	8am-3pm School	8am-3pm School	8am-3pm School	
10am							
11am							10am-2pm Lit Essay
12pm	11am-2pm Video Games & Computer						
1pm							
2pm							
3pm							
4pm	4pm: Go for jog	3:30pm-5pm Play Rehearsal	3:30pm-5pm Homework	3:30pm-5pm Play Rehearsal	3:30pm-5pm Homework	3:30pm-5pm Play Rehearsal	3:30pm-7:30pm Hang out with Max & Janie
5pm							
6pm	5:30pm-7:30pm Extra French Practice	5:30pm-7pm Homework	5:30pm-7pm Lit Essay	5:30pm-7pm Homework		5:30pm-7pm Homework	
7pm		7pm: Dinner	7pm: Dinner	7pm: Dinner	7pm: Dinner	7pm: Dinner	
8pm							7:30pm-9:30pm Movie?
9pm							
10pm							

Key:
Team Practice
Daily Drill
Hang Time

Of course, in order to make sure that this glorious calendar of events really does happen, there needs to be one unbreakable rule in place. **Once it's in your calendar, there's no negotiating— it's there to stay.** You can move it, you can split it into two parts, but you **can't delete it**. You have to be honest with yourself to make sure you don't let things slide. Ferrari test-drives can be very distracting. But you know what's even shinier than a Ferrari? A championship ring.

Does making a schedule take time to do? Sure. But it also saves you time later, because it frees you from worry. You don't ever have to be concerned about what still needs to get done or whether you forgot something, or whether you'll run out of time. Just check the schedule. As you start to practice putting your schedule on offense, you'll notice something else too. Checking off the things you've done is oddly satisfying. It feels great to know that you've gotten something done. And at the end of the week, your calendar will provide you with an at-a-glance assessment of all that you've accomplished. Pretty sweet deal.

Count Those Sheep

To anyone who has ever pulled an all-nighter, it should be no surprise that a full night's sleep boosts almost every aspect of thinking, from response time to memorization to creativity. But the latest research suggests that the time you spend sleeping is the time that your brain uses to solidify what you learned that day. Interrupt that process, and you're likely to sabotage a lot of the hard work you did during daylight hours. What's more, studies show that students who get C's, D's, and F's get an average of twenty-five minutes less sleep per night than students who get A's and B's do.

Even Pros Need Their Coaches

Beyond school and extra-curricular commitments, there is one other activity that takes up a major chunk of the week for most students: being nagged. Parents do it, teachers do it, and no matter who does it, it stinks. Fortunately, there's a foolproof solution to making your life a nag-free zone. Just tell people what's going on.

Because we've all been so brainwashed by genius myths, most of us have a tendency to not want to let people in on the process of our work. We'd rather go it alone. The thing is, just like basketball, being a student is a team sport. And your teachers and parents got drafted to be a part of this too. Any athlete who's on a team, any boss who has employees, any doctor running an operating room knows that the best way to show that he or she has the situation under control is not to be silent—it's to be vocal. Teammates huddle before each play. Bosses distribute weekly reports. Surgeons call out each incision before they make it.

Communication is key and if your parents and teachers don't get any from you, they have no way to know whether you have the situation under control. His Airness agrees.

"Those around you have to know what to expect. They have to be confident that you'll be there, that your performance will be pretty much the same from game to game, particularly when things get tight."

If you bring home a *C*, that could mean a lot of things. Maybe that's an improvement from how you did at the beginning of the unit. Maybe that happened because you decided to experiment with *non*-studying. Maybe this means that you need extra help outside of class. If your parents freak out about the *C*, it's because they had no way to prepare for it or to put it in context. Parents have expectations too. One of those crazy expectations is that if they start a conversation with one of their offspring, to whom they have given the gift of life itself, that their darling little one will actually answer them. In fact, they're so determined to have a meaningful conversation that if you do none of the talking, they'll do *all* of it. They'll talk and talk and talk...and they'll keep talking (in varying degrees of agitation) until they lose their voice (unlikely) or you just run out of the room, covering your ears and screaming (common).

Instead of waiting for that nag-bomb to drop, launch a preemptive strike. Make a decision that each day, whenever your parents or teachers ask how things are going, you'll *tell them*. (We know. It's a crazy idea. So crazy, it just might work.) Look, it doesn't need to

> ### World's Worst Businessman
>
> One person who really would have benefited from listening to his coaches and teammates was Thomas Edison. Customers, co-workers and friends all suggested that his phonograph should be used to record and distribute popular music, but Edison rejected the idea for decades. Because he didn't value other people's advice, he missed out on *huge* moneymaking opportunities for several of his inventions. In fact, his friend Henry Ford even nicknamed him, "The World's Greatest Inventor...and the World's Worst Businessman."

be a lengthy analysis of your life, moment-by-moment. But if you provide a little status update, it can go a long way to reducing the need for nagging. At first, you may not think there's even much that's important to say; maybe it just felt like any old day. If that happens, go through your schedule and update them on anything. It doesn't even matter. The more information you give them, the more relaxed they'll be.

Once you've "shared your feelings" in a mini-Kumbaya kind of way, you have two options. The first is to immediately follow your open, honest moment of confiding with the phrase, "...but don't worry. I've got it under control." In this scenario, your goal is just to stop the nagging. Nothing more. You've done your job, and now you can escape.

That works just fine. But why not go *full pro* and actually make it a *conversation*?! It works like this. After you finish saying your piece, you then continue with the following phrase:

"What do you think, (name of adult)?"

CAUTION. After so many years of living *without* heartfelt conversations about school, your request for advice will trigger a very strong, almost animalistic reaction in your chosen adult figure. Hyperventilating, excited shaking, and tears of joy are common side effects. But the main response is a flood of advice. "Oh! Oh! *The Great Gatsby*?! I remember when *I* read that book. I was fifteen and dating Chris Turner at the time. He played soccer. I loved it...I could reread it...we could read it together..." Students respond with an equally uncontrollable urge to roll their eyes and wish they hadn't brought it up.

That's all natural. But if you're Michael Jordan, you know that suppressing that urge and actually *listening* to the advice is the surest way to take the next step toward the top.

Even Michael Jordan needs a coach. Bosses need employee feedback. Pros understand that they *don't know everything*. In fact, Michael Jordan needs a coach more than any other player in the NBA does, because he doesn't just want to play well; he wants to be the best player *ever*. That's going to take a team effort—he'll need all the help he can get. And in working toward his goal, Michael Jordan realizes that although his coach gets on his case sometimes, and pushes him to do things he may not want to do, and makes him eat broccoli, that coach still has been around the game of basketball even longer than Michael has. That means that he just may have a thing or two that's valuable for Michael to know. The coach has spent a lifetime building his basketball knowledge; Michael doesn't need to spend *his* life building that knowledge too, if he just asks the coach for it instead.

In that same way, you want to train yourself to start *actually listening* to the feedback, guidance, and advice that you get from parents and teachers. **Let yourself be coached.** Now, let's be clear. We're not saying that you have to *take* the advice. But if you're going pro, then you do have to *consider* it. Some advice is good, some advice is bad, and some advice is good...but just not for you. When anyone gives you advice, pretend that it didn't come from them, and it's not meant for you. Weigh the advice on its own merits, and ask yourself, "If someone else was in this situation, would I think that he should listen to this?" Chances are, once you can get your own desire to be right and independent out of the way, you'll find that a lot of what you're told is actually going to make your life easier and better.

Of course, Michael Jordan is not exactly a passive guy. He doesn't wait for advice to come to him; he goes and gets it. Michael wants to be the best, and so he always needs to be doing something to get closer to being the best *right now*. Now, it's not always easy to ask for advice, either because we don't want to impose on other people or because we don't want to seem like we need any help. But if you ever feel hesitant to ask for advice, just put yourself in the other person's shoes. How do you feel when people ask you for advice? It makes you feel awesome, because this person trusts you and thinks that you'll have some wise words to share. And that's how the people that you ask will feel too. They don't care that you're unsure of something. They care that you keep them in the loop, and they're flattered that you respect them enough to go to them. Everyone on your team just wants you to win.

"You have to gain the respect of those around you by your actions. You have to be consistent in your approach whether it's basketball practice, a sales meeting, or dealing with your family."

Another slam dunk, Michael! Working hard and being attentive to your schoolwork is just one part of your job as a pro. You also have to put in the work to foster good relationships with your parents, teachers, other mentors, and even classmates. There are a lot of people who feel some investment in how your education is going. By controlling the communication among all of the teammates, you have better control over how quickly you improve—and how stress-free your life is while you do it.

Building a Better Brand

Once Michael Jordan had reached the very top level as a basketball player, it was time to expand even further. It was time to become an icon.

The reason that we all know Michael Jordan so well is only in part because of those insane game highlights and his outstanding stats. He also became the spokesperson for several brands, including Gatorade, McDonald's, Wheaties, Coke, and Hanes. But his real baby—his passion project—was working with Nike to create the Air Jordan brand.

> **Hope It Works!**
>
> Try to catch yourself the next time you say that you "hope" you'll do well on a test. Students say this a lot, but "hoping" that you do well means that you're okay with having no control over your brand. After all, if a car company said, "We hope the brakes work!... Fingers crossed!" how would you feel about making that purchase? What kind of reputation would the company get?

When Michael began working with Nike, there were already plenty of athletes who endorsed various sneakers and other athletic apparel. It was a quick money maker, and most of them simply agreed to slap their name onto the product; they weren't overly concerned with the product's quality. But Michael wanted to take charge. He had spent years building his reputation, in high school, at UNC, and in the NBA. The name "Michael Jordan" was not just synonymous with "basketball." The name "Michael Jordan" was synonymous with "excellence." Michael was known as the *most* dedicated, the *most* hard-working, and the *most* professional player in the NBA. There was no way Michael Jordan would just slap his name on any old shoe.

And so, Michael Jordan set out to create the greatest basketball shoe ever. The first Air Jordan sneaker had the most stylish design, was the most durable, and was made of only top-of-the-line materials. With each subsequent year, the sneaker only got better and better. While other players just lent their names to sneaker companies and thought no more of it, he spent hours and hours in meetings with designers and marketers, making sure he was involved in every aspect of perfecting his product. His brand became a major success worldwide because he proved to people that *anything* bearing the "Michael Jordan" name would be the best of its kind—just like Michael himself.

"I believe in leading. There was never anything contrived about the way I played the game, and there is nothing contrived about what we have created at Brand Jordan."

We just talked about how many people are invested in your education. Make the most of your teachers, parents, extended family and friends. But even with all of those teammates and coaches helping you out, you need to keep in mind that it's *your* name on the homework. It's *your* name on the transcript. It'll be *your* name on the diploma. And once you're done with school, and starting to work, you're on your own. When people decide if they want to work with you in the future, they won't care what anybody else did or didn't do. They'll be basing their decisions on your brand. So, what do you stand for, and what do you guarantee that you will bring to the table?

Just like Brand Jordan, you have a brand too. You've been building it since your first day of school (whether you realized it or not). Your brand is determined by the level of work you do and the attitude you bring to the table. So, would you want to invest in the brand that you're currently selling? Maybe. Maybe not. But you can reinvent your brand at any time. It starts with a change in perspective. You have to take complete responsibility for everything that happens in your education.

Ask yourself the following questions, and try to be really, really honest in answering them:

Who is responsible for making sure that you understand the material from class—your teacher, or you?

Who is responsible for making sure that you know what assignment you have for homework?

Who is responsible for the fact that you got grounded for having bad grades? Your super-mean parents? Or...perhaps...you?

Really, what these questions boil down to is this: Who is the leader of your education right now? Is it your teachers? Is it your parents? They are there to help, but in any brand, there can really

GENIUS IS NOT IN THE ACCESSORIES

When you see these people, what do you assume about them?

While wearing Air Jordans might make you feel like Michael Jordan, it doesn't actually make you Michael Jordan. Unfortunately, the Straight-A Conspiracy has taught us to confuse the image of genius with the actual product. If you're wearing a beret outside of France and you seem tortured and sullen, then we assume you are a brilliant artist. Similarly, if you have crazy hair and glasses, then you must be on the verge of discovering a new nuclear particle. Sorry. Crazy hair doesn't make you Einstein. It's all about the work. And this translates to the classroom. You can be the first to finish the reading, or do all your math problems without "needing" to show any work, but if the results aren't as impressive as the show, then the image is just an illusion.

be only one effective leader. You. You have to take charge. **Think about the brand you're building.** Michael Jordan may have help from coaches and teammates and Nike designers, but at the end of the day, his image is on the highlight reel, his name is on the books of the statisticians, and he is the one wearing the sneakers. He knows that if he misses a shot or allows a turnover, or if the Air Jordans fall apart, *he* is the one that will be held responsible in the public's eyes. So he's not taking any chances; he makes sure that he is 100% responsible for how his career is going.

"If the person out front takes a day off or doesn't play hard, why should anyone else?"

Guess what? Even we are not responsible for your education; we're just here to help you. We chose the concepts in this book because we found that they work for a lot of our students. But that may not mean that they work for *all* students. You may find nothing about Sherlock Holmes interesting, or you may hate sports and therefore think Michael Jordan is boring. (Gasp! We won't tell him.) If that's the case, then you need to take responsibility for making these concepts something that *you* care about.

And that is true for all of your schoolwork, even on the smallest level. For example, one seventh-grade student really got bored whenever she had math word problems that started with, "At the Imperial Tire Company," or "The percentage of commission on a real estate transaction..." She immediately tuned out. So she

> **Sneak by with SparkNotes?**
>
> Think you're a "slow reader?" How many books have you read start-to-finish? Using SparkNotes is no substitute for actually reading the book. By all means, use SparkNotes ahead of time to know what to look for, or as you go, to make sure that you're picking up on the right themes and ideas. SparkNotes are a tool to help your reading, not to replace it. The students who really understand their reading and write amazing essays built up those skills by reading actual books. Does your brand stand for "getting by" or "getting better"?

took charge and translated it into terms she could care about: "At the Glitter Bedazzle Factory..." "The percentage of commission on a pair of Prada heels..." Suddenly, all of the math was something she just might be interested in using. You might be getting advice from great sources, but you are ultimately responsible for making sure that you will remember it and will be engaged in your work.

And you need to take that responsibility on a larger level too, as you build your brand. In fact, customization is all the rage nowadays. Circle the words below that you would want to apply to your own custom brand:

Getting Your Head In The Game

During a basketball game, Michael Jordan can rely on his coaches and teammates for a certain amount of feedback. If he runs the play slightly incorrectly, or if he starts to hook his shot, or even lets up a bit in terms of how aggressive his defense is, his coach can call out to him to give him advice. His teammates can come over to help him get his head back in the game. Most of Michael's game is visible, and so to some extent, he can depend on other people to keep him playing at 100%.

But as we all now know, most of the time and effort that it takes to be a professional basketball player is not visible to the fans in the arena. When Michael wakes up at the crack of dawn to train before practice, no one is monitoring what he does. He could easily just do five pushups and then tell everyone that he did 100. After the gym, he could eat a stuffed-crust meat lover's supreme pizza and then tell everyone later that he had a protein shake. Michael Jordan has to be responsible for giving *himself* constant feedback. Doing five pushups and eating pizza are fine, but they won't help Michael get the job done, so he doesn't let himself do them.

"They don't understand the foundation I had to create to support everything that came afterward. They don't know about lifting weights at 7AM, practicing hard every day, finding ways to motivate myself for every game, sitting up half the night with an ankle in a bucket of ice, or hooked up to an electronic stimulation machine. They don't know anything about those things. What they do know is that I have my own shoe line, and that I did McDonald's commercials."

Actually, Michael even has to be giving himself that feedback when the coaches, teammates, and fans *are* watching. That's because only Michael knows what his attention is doing at any given moment—and that's what will ultimately determine how well he plays. After he takes a shot and misses by an inch, Michael can put his attention on a lot of different things.

1) I can't believe I missed that shot.
2) Basketball is stupid anyway.
3) Do I look fat in these shorts?
4) Get on defense! Go!

He could think any of those things, and no one else in the arena would ever know it...but only *one* of them will help Michael get the job done. He constantly makes sure that his attention is on what he's doing *right now* and how he can do it better.

The same is true in school. While bad test grades and missing homework assignments are visible signs that will make parents and teachers jump in and help, there is also a lot you do in between those moments that people can't see. *Thinking and learning are invisible processes.* And thinking and learning are what you're doing (or at least pretending to do) for most of your school day. When you're listening to your teacher explain the new lesson, or while you're working your way through a test, *you* are the only person who knows where your attention is. And it could be anywhere.

1) I can't believe I didn't know that.
2) Biology is stupid anyway.
3) Do I look fat in these shorts?
4) Figure this out! Go!

That Move Is a Classic

Here is a list of things that students do to avoid the work and put their attention on anything other than what needs to get done. Have you ever used any of these tactics? (Did you think you were the only one who did?)

1) The "Ohh, yeaaaah...I get it" move, best used when you don't get it at all. Effective in getting your teacher to move on and stop testing you.

2) The classic "bad handwriting" to cover up an unsure answer. What does that word really say? Is that an accent mark, or just a pencil smudge?

3) The unnecessary bathroom break.

Pros don't try to sneak their way out of getting it right, because they know it's easier, faster, and less painful to get it wrong now and fix it for the future.

It's really easy to *look* like you're thinking about something. You furrow your brow, stare off into space, turn some pages of any book, and go, "hmmmm" very studiously. Great! Everyone is fooled...except you.

Now, ask yourself these questions:

Who is responsible for your attention?
Who is responsible for your emotions?

Whenever you are working on anything in school, the most professional thing that you can do is to take total charge of your attention at all times. So how can you be sure to use it like a pro? Choose to always put it on something that can move you forward. This includes all of the parts of being a pro. Choose to put your attention on communicating. Choose to put your attention on revisiting your fundamentals. Choose to put your attention on making sure you have time to get the job done. And then, when it matters most, choose to take your attention *off of* feeling ashamed, hating the subject, or wishing you could be doing something else, and put it *on* winning. **The only thing that matters is what you're doing right now.** It doesn't matter whether Michael Jordan won or lost the championship last year, or what his chances are for winning it this year. Every choice that Michael Jordan makes throughout the day is a choice to put his attention on something that will help him to improve. *That* is how being a pro becomes a lifestyle.

> ### How to Predict the Future
>
> In Game 3 of the 1932 World Series, Babe Ruth famously pointed over the outfield wall, allegedly to "call" his home run—*before* he hit it. If you want to really make sure that you keep your attention on getting the job done, then start to broadcast what you plan to do. Walk into the kitchen and tell your parents, "Hey! I'm getting A's this semester. Good night!" Tell your friends that your presentation is going to be *amazing*. Making your goals public puts the pressure on you to stay on track to achieving them.

Choose the Interpretation that Serves Your Success

In your old way of thinking, you may have thought it would be cool to be a doctor one day, but you might not have felt certain you were smart enough to do that. If you failed the first biology test of the year, you might have said, "Oh! Maybe I was wrong. I guess I'll never be a doctor." You could do a temporary RESET, but your interpretation would always have enough doubt in it to keep you from really going for it.

Well, what if you just changed the interpretation entirely? What would happen if you decided that no matter what, you will do whatever it takes to become a doctor...and you will cure cancer. If you decided this were true, think about how you would respond to failing your biology test. Instead of giving up on your entire dream, you'd say, "Ha! Ha! When I win the Nobel Prize for curing cancer, this will make for a great story. In the meantime, I'd better talk to my teacher and see if I can do some extra credit."

To you, this point of view may seem a little out there—or at least overly confident. Really, all that matters is that you choose an interpretation that leads you to take successful actions. Maybe you end up pursuing a completely different career. The important part is that you will have developed enough good habits to make sure that all options are open to you, no matter where you go.

Just like you can choose how you deal with your emotions, you can choose your perspective on everything you do. You can choose to see school as an obligation and drag yourself there every morning, or you can choose to see it as your ticket to an awesome future. Neither one of them is a fact. They're both interpretations. But only one of them helps you to succeed.

As you automate some of the parts of the pro lifestyle, such as scheduling and locking down your fundamentals, you will free up your attention to take your work to the next level. A pro is continually raising the bar on what it means to "get the job done." Win the game. Next week, be the MVP. After that, win the championship. Already won the championship? Get a sneaker line. Make that sneaker line #1. On to the Hall of Fame. There is no limit on what your pro lifestyle can help you to accomplish.

Having Your Own Agenda

"Everyone had a different agenda for me. But I had my own."

People always talk about Michael Jordan getting cut from his high school basketball team, but the best part of the story is what happened *after* that event. Rather than giving up on basketball forever, Michael Jordan looked for an opportunity to keep making his goal happen. He *had* to get onto that team. So, he became the team statistician, sitting on the bench and writing down all the great plays the people on the court were making. At away games, the other schools would only let the *real team members* into the gym, so *Michael Jordan* would carry the other players' uniforms into the building, just so he could be involved with the team in any way possible.

What would have possessed the greatest basketball player of all time to do grunt work for the people who beat him out for a spot on the team? Easy. Michael Jordan has always followed his own agenda. No matter what other people tell him, no matter what stands in his way, and no matter what people say is "impossible," he finds opportunities to improve and keeps moving toward his goals. He never takes "no" for an answer.

A pro doesn't accept anything that people tell him at face value and decide that's the end of it. He or she will investigate it, find out as much as possible, and always come to his or her own conclusion. If the shoe that Nike made for Michael Jordan looked cool but wasn't comfortable, he wouldn't

Caring Doesn't Just Happen

You might go through phases in which you have a really hard time getting yourself excited about school; you just don't care. The solution is *not* to wait until something happens that fires you up again. It is your *responsibility* to investigate, scrutinize, and figure out how to get excited. You are completely capable of *making yourself* care about your classes again. Desire *will* show up and surprise you...but you'll find it hiding in the work itself. Just get busy.

say "good enough." He would figure out how to make it the best. And if he noticed that his game felt a little "off," he'd be in the gym first thing the next morning, trying to figure out how to fix it.

Similarly, if Michael Jordan heard the genius myths of the Straight-A Conspiracy, he wouldn't believe them right off the bat. He'd get the real story, and then use that to fire him up even more. If Michael Jordan's teacher told him he just "wasn't a math person," he would see that teacher's statement as a *challenge*, work even *harder* at math, and ultimately prove that teacher wrong by acing every test. And if Michael Jordan's friends told him he should hate school because school is boring and lame, he wouldn't swallow that. He'd figure out what school could do for him and his goals, and then decide for himself. Come on! You're a *teenager*. Aren't you supposed to hate being told what to think? Aren't you supposed to hate being told what you can and can't do? Why should other people be allowed to determine what you make of your future?

"Part of this commitment is taking responsibility. That's not to say there aren't obstacles or distractions. If you're trying to achieve, there will be roadblocks. I've had them; everybody has had them. But obstacles don't have to stop you. If you run into a wall, don't turn around and give up. Figure out how to climb it, go through it, or work around it."

Pros take *nothing* at face value. They scrutinize, they question, and they pick things apart, looking for opportunities to help them toward their goals. First, pros do this to anything that other people tell them, so that no one else's opinions get in the way of their goals. But then, pros do this scrutinizing, questioning, and picking apart *to their own work*. Michael Jordan would never take it at face value that his layup is as good as it can be. There is always the opportunity to make every part of your performance better. That fighting spirit is the real pro perspective.

Which looks like a better use of YOUR time?

PROCRASTINATION	ACTION

PROCRASTINATION

Ugh. That biology assignment is due tomorrow. What's it on? Mitosis? (Hesitates looking up assignment: **2 min**)

Really? We have to draw and label a diagram? That's not fair. I suck at drawing. What a stupid assignment. (Debates worthiness of assignment: **8 min**)

I wonder how much I have to include. Can I skip one of the steps? (Explores options to do less work than assigned: **10 min**)

<Phone beeps> Oh hey – Lucy commented on my post. I wonder what she said... (Checks post, looks at every photo of Lucy, and all of her photo albums: **40 min**)

Alright back to this lame diagram. Why do I even care about mitosis? I bet my dad doesn't know about mitosis, and he's a lawyer. Hey Dad, do you know what mitosis is? (Challenges worth of assignment, again. Embarrasses father, who doesn't remember mitosis: **15 min**)

Hmm, I'm kinda hungry. (Microwaves leftovers, eats on couch watching TV: **35 min**)

Alright, I should really start this biology diagram. I'll just check my email really quick then start. (Checks email: **2 min**. Gets IM from Bobby. Complains to Bobby about biology assignment: **18 min.**)

Okay, I guess I'll start now. (Starts diagram: **30 min**)

I don't really get this part. Do I need to? I wonder how many points it's worth. Maybe it's just like 5 points. I can do without 5 points. (Guesses at unclear part: **15 min**)

That's probably enough, right? I mean, she can't expect some amazingly clear diagram. (Decides whether or not assignment is complete: **4 min**)

Whatever, I'm tired. I'm going to sleep. I'll just turn this in tomorrow. (Done-ish: **1 min**)

zzZZZzz...

ACTION

Okay! Time to do the biology mitosis diagram. (Gets it done. Well: **1 hr**)

Done! Nice... not quite bed time – I'll check out that DVD I've been meaning to watch! (Movie and popcorn: **2 hrs**)

One of the biggest ideas that we're *all* guilty of taking at face value is the idea that getting A's would be more stressful than getting B's or C's. The truth is that getting A's is the *least stressful* thing you could do in school...with the exception of doing absolutely nothing and getting all zeros. It may feel like it makes sense to want B's or C's—to aim for a lower goal. But in that process, you are also adding a *ton* of questioning, additional work, and ambiguity about what needs doing, what's worth doing, and how far you really need to go. In contrast, getting an A is incredibly straightforward. You just do the work as well as it possibly can be done, all the time, and you're guaranteed a good result. There are no questions, no wondering, and no time spent feeling...any way at all about how it's going. **Being excellent is less stressful than being average.**

That's it. There's a very clear reason why everything Michael Jordan says about basketball is always so unemotional and matter-of-fact. Michael's goal was always to be the best player *ever*. Once he made that decision, the things that he needed to do became obvious. And Michael still operates that way in everything he does today. When any task comes up, he does it. As well as he possibly can. You never know which actions will be the key to your success; you might as well consistently bring your A-game.

Once you've taken this pro approach to your work for a while, you'll see how easy it is to just stay "in the zone." A-students don't stress, because they *actually don't* need to study all that much. It *is* easier for them. But the reason it's easier is not because they're naturally smarter; it's because they've been working like a pro for a while. By laying the groundwork, having solid fundamentals, making time for everything to get done without cramming, and keeping your team strong around you, you lay the foundation for your own success. Then, whenever it's time to test how far you've come, you're already ready to go. Rather than having to *get ready*, A-students constantly *are ready*. And there's barely a moment of doubt or questioning or any unhelpful emotions, because they're using all of their energy to take actions that move toward their goals. Once you're in the zone, you won't even need to remind yourself to make your calendar or check in with people or look for mistakes. It will be so much a part of how you work that it won't feel like work at all. You'll just be living the pro lifestyle. Confidence...success...happiness...and maybe one day your own sneaker deal with Nike.

THE SIX RULES OF BEING
THE MICHAEL JORDAN OF...ANYTHING!

1. **Never forget the fundamentals.**
2. **Use offensive scheduling: check it off or block it off.**
3. **Let yourself be coached.**
4. **Think about the brand you're building.**

5. **The only thing that matters is what you're doing right now.**
6. **Being excellent is less stressful than being average.**

Getting the Ball Rolling

Of course, changing your *entire lifestyle* doesn't feel like a small task. You've been treating school like recreational basketball for so long! So where can you begin? Just take *any* of these "pro" actions. Start a calendar—just for this week. Talk to your parents once. Go back through your work and look for ways to strengthen your fundamentals...even on one assignment. Just trust that doing any one step will pay off, and then see how it goes.

But here's the real key. *After* you have taken that step, you need to congratulate yourself right away. The action you took may not lead to a huge, obvious payoff right this minute, but it still helped you to move forward. And you need to get in the habit of reminding yourself of that. Think about it: while Michael Jordan was in high school, carrying other people's sweaty uniforms and writing down how many points they scored, it probably wasn't easy to stay excited about what he was doing. After all, "high school team statistician" and "winner of six NBA championships" sound pretty far apart. But Michael knew he needed to do whatever he could in order to take *any* step closer to his goals. So if he got into the arena one day, it was a win. If the coach talked to him, it was another win. Those wins added up, because Michael kept at it, and by the following year, Michael was actually on the high school team. It still wasn't the NBA, but it was a lot closer. If you don't celebrate the little steps that you're taking *as you take them*, then it can feel like they're not worth doing. But just because the payoff may not be here today, it doesn't mean that it's never coming. All you need to know is that being a pro *will get you wherever you want to go*. The trick to becoming an all-star...is to start.

PART four

"Each second we live is a new and unique moment of the universe, a moment that will never be again. And what do we teach our children? We teach them that two and two make four, and that Paris is the capital of France. When will we also teach them what they are? We should say to each of them: Do you know what you are? You are a marvel. You are unique. In all the years that have passed, there has never been another child like you. Your legs, your arms, your clever fingers, the way you move. You may become a Shakespeare, a Michelangelo, a Beethoven. You have the capacity for anything. Yes, you are a marvel. And when you grow up, can you then harm another who is, like you, a marvel? You must work, we must all work, to make the world worthy of its children."

— Pablo Picasso

Chapter 12

Generation Genius

You are alive for a major turning point in history. In the opening chapter of this book, we told you that this was the best time in the history of the world to be a student. And now you can understand why. You are a member of the first generation *ever* in which everyone can know exactly how to become a genius in whatever field they choose. That means that you're unstoppable.

Sure, there have been other major turning points in history. There was the Enlightenment, and the Industrial Revolution, and the discovery of penicillin. Your parents or grandparents can say, "I remember when we got our first color television." The authors of this book can say, "When I was a kid, no one I knew had the internet yet." All of those changes affected the way that everyone interacted with the world. But the change that's happening in your lifetime affects the way that *people view themselves*. Think about it: one day, you'll be able to look back and say, "Can you believe this? When I was a kid, people really thought that you had to be *born* a genius! Like it was luck or something. Crazy!"

Your parents, your grandparents, and the people of every other past generation ended up deciding what they were capable of achieving at an early age. Then, they spent the rest of their lives assuming that there was a limit to how smart they could ever be. They made their decisions and based their lives around those notions, stopping themselves short of trying for things that seemed "out of reach." But you have the opposite problem. You're the first generation of students who really can *be anything*. So now, you have to ask yourself a question.

What kind of life do you want to live?

When most people get asked this, they come up with a very modest answer. "Oh...I just want to be happy." "I just want to be able to...get by." Um, sure, yeah. That's nice. But deep down, what do you *really* wish you could have? Like, if a genie asked you this question, and you were feeling greedy, what would your response be? You probably wouldn't stop at "getting by." Wouldn't you say you wanted to feel super-confident and successful? That you wanted to be in control of your life, and have the respect of everyone around you? Wouldn't you want to feel like things were easy for you, and that nothing was out of reach? Of course you would! That's what everyone wants. It's just that now, you can actually guarantee that you have all of those things...and more.

For Generation Genius, it's no longer unreasonable to think that you could ask for all of that and *get*

If He Can Do It...

William Kamkwamba grew up in a rural village in Southern Africa. When a famine hit his country, and his family couldn't afford the $250 per year to send him to school, he went to the local library to educate himself. Inspired by one particular book, he decided to build an electricity-generating windmill, transformer, and wiring system for his house. He built his own power grid with an old bicycle wheel and plastic pipes that he found in junkyards. Now, his story is a best-selling book and William got the education he wanted in the first place—he is a student at an Ivy League University. A lack of resources or support should never stop you from setting your goals high and going after the life that you want.

it. Take what you've learned in this book and put it into action. If you consistently do that, the awesome life that we described above will be a natural result.

Everything You've Learned... In One Word

In this book, we've taught you lots of things about how the brain works and how to take actions that will lead you to straight A's. But in reality, all of that advice boils down to one thing, and as long as you're doing that, you'll always be moving forward.

Metacognition.

"Metacognition" is just a fancy word for "thinking about thinking." What we've really shown you in this book is that you always can be and always need to be thinking about your own thinking process. Now, you can be aware of what your automaticity, attention, and emotions are doing while you learn. More importantly, during the process of learning, you can stop and consider whether what you're doing is the most effective method. Maybe you need to stop and make something Cake-Mix Clear...maybe you need a little more Box-Office success, or a little more terminating. If you're constantly analyzing your process, then you're always improving it. That's how people become better, faster, and more successful.

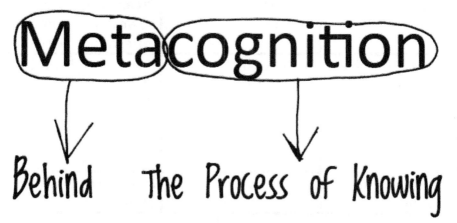

Perhaps the most crucial part of metacognition is accurate diagnosis. The best learners never let themselves get away with bad habits; they identify the problematic behaviors and then re-train themselves with *better* habits. If you can get good at identifying which specific behavior or thought is getting in your way, then fixing it is easy. To help you out on the path to becoming an expert problem-spotter, here's an easy reference chart.

You Think It's This	Really It's This	Do This
I'm just bad at this subject.	Stupichondria	RESET that shame about your mistakes. Start fixing.
I'll never get it as quickly as (sibling/friend/frenemy).	Unfair Comparisons	Recognize the unfair comparison. Remind yourself that with practice, you can be that automatic too.
I'm so frustrated.	Unrealistic Expectations	Give yourself a break! Learning takes as long as it takes. Do enough fix-it-focused practice and you will be not only right but lightning-fast.
I'm totally overwhelmed.	Attention Overload	Wipe your attention and pick one piece to start.
I'm drawing a blank!	You need to refresh the info	Break the problem down. Look up or refresh each piece.
School/This subject is stupid.	You're using "whatever" to avoid feeling disappointed.	If you feel this way, it's because you really do care. Find a RESET that will get you past "whatever" so you can get to work.
This subject makes no sense.	Your rules aren't clear.	Make them Cake Mix Clear.

You Think It's This	Really It's This	Do This
This is boring./I don't care about this.	You don't really understand the material.	Do some Sherlocking and you'll discover why it's interesting.
There's no way I can solve this.	You're Lestrade-ing it—expecting to see how to solve it before you've even started.	Just figure out what you can say. Take any little action you can, and the way forward will reveal itself.
This essay is boring. / I have nothing to say.	You haven't done enough research to find something interesting to say.	Take pity on your poor reader. Keep Sherlocking until you find claims that pass the "SO WHAT?" test.
I can't memorize all of this.	You're treating the facts like they're unrelated.	Find the meaningful connections and facts will be unforgettable.
It's so unfair. I always lose points for bonehead mistakes.	Your checking is too passive.	Go Cyborg. Don't wait for mistakes to find you... seek them out and terminate them.
My parents and teachers keep nagging me.	Your brand needs reinvention.	Listen to what your coaches have to say and take responsibility for improving your brand.
What's the point? This all just seems like a lot of work.	You need a goal.	Figure out why you are doing this for you. Connect what you're doing to what you want, and you'll never feel obligated.

As you can see from the first column in this chart, students are really good at diagnosing what's going on. After all, they say these things all the time without even thinking. Deep down, you know what's going wrong with your schoolwork. It's just that now, you have the tools to really *interpret* what is happening in your brain...and then do something about it.

By the way, doing this kind of diagnosis does *not* mean that your work should take more time. After all, your homework takes long enough without stopping every five seconds to think about *how* you're doing it. In reality, metacognition is about using your time more effectively. The more of it you do, the faster and more effective your process will become. Improving your process will become so automated that you'll be willing and able to diagnose problems in just seconds, instead of letting them mess up your schoolwork for years. You'll cut out all of the time-wasting that happened in the past.

Metacognition is an extremely powerful tool. In fact, by teaching you how to do this, we've given you almost everything that you need to get that awesome life. There's just one more ingredient, and it's totally up to you to make sure you have it. In order to make sure that you actually do analyze and improve your process every time that you're working, you'll need a compass—something that keeps you on track. So, let's talk about setting goals.

"With Great Power Comes Great Responsibility"

Spiderman knew it, and now you know it too. When you are given the power to do amazing things, which you now have, it becomes your responsibility to use those powers for good. Unlike Spiderman, though, you don't have to be responsible for keeping an entire city of people and a cute redhead safe. Your primary responsibility is to yourself. You are responsible for not letting your powers go to waste. Decide what you want to use them for, and then go after it.

Go after what? That's a big question that requires a surprisingly little answer. While it is important to know that you want things like "success," words like that don't necessarily *mean* anything. You can't actually picture what "success" looks like, or exactly how you look as a "success." That's why, when you're setting a goal, you need to get specific. Don't just say that you want to get "good grades"—say that you want to get straight-*A*'s! Don't just say that you want to do "something that helps people" when you grow up; say that you want to be a doctor or a teacher or the President.

Here's what that will do for you. A specific goal will pull you through every time. On a Tuesday afternoon, when you come home from school and find yourself procrastinating about starting your homework, reconnecting to your goal will give you a reason to turn off the TV and just get the homework done. And if you know exactly what you're shooting for, then you know exactly what the standards are for achieving it. You'll also know *exactly* the moment when you've accomplished what you set out to do. What classifies as "good grades?" All *B*'s? Some *A*'s? No *F*'s? There's no real answer to that, but there's only one possible interpretation of "straight *A*'s." If you know *exactly* what you're going for, then you won't let yourself off the hook until you've gotten it.

Now, keep in mind, setting a goal for the future can be a daunting task, especially in high school. We're not saying that you have to know at age fifteen or sixteen exactly what you want to do with your whole life—in fact, it's very unlikely that you will. But even if you don't know what you want to do for a job, you can already set goals like getting straight *A*'s or going to a specific college. For example, Hunter's goal throughout high

> ### Get What YOU Want
>
> We've been talking about noble "save the world" type goals, but don't be ashamed if what gets you fired up is a shiny red convertible or a huge mansion with a dollar-shaped swimming pool. It's cool. We get it. At this stage, any goal that gets you to take the necessary steps to become an influential, effective adult is great. After all, you need to be just as intelligent to make a lot of money as you need to be to save the world; you can decide how you apply that intelligence in the future. For now, just get yourself going.

school was to attend Harvard College. Every time he was faced with work he didn't feel like doing, he checked in with that goal: "If I want to go to Harvard, then I'd better do this and do it well." For Hunter, that goal was strong enough and important enough to him that it kept him on track in even his most hated classes.

Regardless of the direction your life ultimately takes during high school, college, and beyond, your goal will ensure that you are taking the kinds of actions that will set you up to do whatever you want to do in the future. Pursuing a particular goal doesn't close any doors to you, as long as you're doing excellent work in the process. You can switch paths at any time and still be in good shape to start working toward your new goal. The only thing that closes future doors to you is doing work poorly. If you aren't consistently doing excellent work, then you'd better figure out a goal that's worth working for.

Here's the bonus prize. Once you've set a specific goal, you will have freed yourself of the one thing that most slows you down: obligation. If you can picture a specific goal and use that as your compass, then you will start seeing all the little tasks necessary to help you get to that goal. With no goal in mind, it's easy to feel like those tasks—homework assignments, books to read, essays to write—are things that you *have* to do *for someone else*. There's no need to feel that way, because this is where you have a leg up on superheroes like Spiderman. They don't get to choose their goal, so they always *have to* face the bad guy or *have to* save the city. Often, they complain about how tough their job is, because they feel obligated to pull through, every time. But with a strong, personal goal that means a lot to you, you won't feel obligated; you'll feel excited.

Motivating yourself by choosing a specific goal is the *most important* thing that you can bring to your schoolwork. And *only you* can make that contribution. The goal can't come from anyone else; you can't do things just because your parents want you to go to college, or because your teachers expect you to get *A*'s. Your goal has to be for you. You choose it, you want it, and you go after it.

No One's Asking You to Fight a Sea Monster

If it feels really overwhelming to think about starting to pursue a goal that's far into your future...then, first of all, wipe your attention clean. (You know better than to let yourself get overwhelmed!) But secondly, don't worry. Yes, "becoming a doctor" sounds like a huge task. But in reality, going after any big goal is not about doing some gigantic, heroic, massively effortful thing. *Every* goal is achieved by just doing a series of little, tiny, simple actions. No *one* particular action is that major—they just really do add up over time. These little actions are things like always looking up words you don't know. Like checking your work. Like taking the time to Sherlock your reading. Those things may not seem like much in the moment, but they actually do put you closer and closer to getting exactly the life that you want.

After all, Edison didn't fight a sea monster to extract the long-protected secret of the "perfect" light bulb. He and his team just tested thousands of replacement parts, one by one. They never knew exactly what the next step was going to need to be until they saw how the current one turned out. They just trusted that each failed test was helping in some way. If there is any tiny, little thing that you can be doing to get better...DO IT.

"I'll Never Use This in Real Life Anyway."

"But do I *really* need to look up 'flummoxed'? Do I *really* need to have the first twenty elements of the periodic table memorized? I'll never use that in real life." A lot of students have this concern,

Mall Rats vs Bookworms

Maybe you're thinking, "What if this sounds like a lot of work and I'd kind of rather just hang out?" That's a totally valid question and fortunately, research provides an answer. In one particularly telling study, psychologist Mihaly Csikszentmihalyi (ME-high CHICK-sent-me-high-ee) took 500 teenagers and asked them to report their happiness at random intervals throughout the day. Half of these teenagers spent their time hanging out at the mall and playing video games. (We'll call them "mall rats.") The other half spent their time studying, doing homework, and participating in extracurriculars. (We'll call these kids "bookworms.") The kids who spent their time just hanging out reported that they were less happy by almost every measure than the kids who challenged themselves were.

That's because there's a big difference between what psychologist Martin Seligman calls "pleasures" and "gratifications." Pleasures are things like watching TV, eating ice cream, hanging out at the mall, and playing video games. They require very little of us, and they always seem like a more appealing choice in the moment. Gratifications are challenges that leave us feeling good about ourselves, such as learning new things, acing a test, and completing a big project.

The downside of pleasures is that they don't last. They make you happy for a few minutes, but you're never really satisfied. That first bowl of ice cream tastes amazing, but by the third you feel gross. On the other hand, the happiness you get from gratifications is just as good every time. You never get tired of accomplishing something awesome. It always feels good. And that happiness actually lasts years into the future; you can look back at that moment years later and it will still make you feel great. Gratifications are the key to feeling good about yourself.

In fact, the bookworms were happier than the mall rats by every measure except one: the bookworms *thought* the mall rats were having more fun. We all think that a bowl of ice cream or another half an hour of TV will make us happier, but really the key to happiness is in tackling new challenges.

You may feel like a mallrat on most mornings when your alarm is going off and your eyes are half-open and you're trying to drag yourself out of bed. Just remind yourself that getting your inner bookworm to school is what will ultimately make you happier. (That's a quick RESET!)

and on the surface, they're absolutely right. It's very unlikely that you'll use *every* fact that you ever learn in high school in your future career. If you're going to be a doctor, then you may not explicitly use your knowledge of Shakespeare on a day-to-day basis. But, if you try to end there then you're totally missing the point. A doctor has to dig in, search for clues, and logically analyze them to determine an outcome or diagnosis in the same way that a literary scholar analyzes Shakespeare. A doctor also has to do a TON of reading, so you might as well get good at that now. The facts that you learn in high school are just a means to a much bigger end. What you really learn in high school is how to think.

In chemistry, in English, in history, in all of your classes, you're learning how to draw out the underlying logic in different areas of life and synthesize it into useful solutions. You're learning how to think critically for any type of problem you might encounter. You're learning how to analyze. You're learning how to problem-solve. You're learning how to approach a new challenge and use those skills to get through it. It's not so much about the facts as it is about the process.

High school really is preparation for life. As an adult, you are going to be *much* further ahead if you've really done well in high school. Sure, there's the argument that if you have a good base of knowledge in lots of areas then you can pursue any job. But more importantly, you'll be ready to face *all* of the

Anything Could Be the Key

"Much of what I stumbled into by following my curiosity and intuition turned out to be priceless later on. (At Reed College) I decided to take a calligraphy class... I learned about serif and san serif typefaces... about what makes great typography great. It was beautiful, historical, artistically subtle in a way that science can't capture, and I found it fascinating. None of this had even a hope of any practical application in my life. But ten years later, when we were designing the first Macintosh computer, it all came back to me. And we designed it all into the Mac. It was the first computer with beautiful typography. Of course it was impossible to connect the dots looking forward when I was in college. But it was very, very clear looking backwards ten years later. Again, you can't connect the dots looking forward; you can only connect them looking backwards. So you have to trust that the dots will somehow connect in your future."

—Steve Jobs, co-founder of Apple Computer and Pixar Studios

challenges of being an adult. How do people figure out how to pay taxes, or own and maintain an apartment or house? How do people know how to raise children or avoid parking tickets...not to mention learning their jobs? Adult life is about constant goal-setting and metacognition, which work together as an inseparable team. You set goals and then you work toward them, improving your process as you go. When you reach those goals or realize that you actually want something else, you redefine your goal, change your path, and set off in a new direction. Anything you do requires constant adjustment of and attention to those two things.

So why is school valuable? *Because learning any new skill or subject works in exactly the same way.* That's right. Chemistry is no different from English, is no different from math or languages or music. And all of those are no different from learning to be a rock star or a lawyer or someone who can keep finances in order or someone who can plan a six-month trip backpacking across the world.

The Challenge Makes It Fun

The only reason that learning ever feels too difficult or frustrating is that we've been trained to place expectations on the process and how it should go. If you get a new video game, you might say that you're going to beat the whole thing that very night. But if you can't, you don't *give up* on it! If it turns out to be tougher and lasts even longer than you thought it would, you get *excited!* Each time you lose, you rush to start again with a new attempt. That's because you have no judgments on that process. Imagine if everyone took their attitudes from learning a new video game and applied it to learning something new in school...

In less than a decade, TVs have gone from being back-breakingly heavy to being wafer-thin, cellphones have gone from being a luxury to being a necessity, and Facebook has gone from not existing to having over 845 million users. In the 21st century, the world is constantly speeding up. If you're going to keep pace with all of those changes, you need to be really good at learning. Just eighty years ago, if you were a student, you would have been training to work in a trolley car or wireless telegraph factory. You were just going to have one job for your whole life and that was that. Today, your education may help you to start your own web company, sell it at 35, and spend the next ten years as a novelist, before deciding that you really need to go to medical school. And who knows what other fields may be invented while you're an adult? What if the robo-laser-nanotechnology sector becomes huge? You'll need to be ready to jump into that and become an expert in it very quickly. The only thing that you can depend on is that the people who get ahead are always the ones who are best at learning.

What Can Three Billion Geniuses Do?

You are poised to be the coolest generation that has ever lived. It took the rest of us thousands of years to invent math and transportation and agriculture. You'll probably accomplish three times that much in the next three decades.

That's because for Generation Genius, exceptional performance is no longer reserved for a small, special group of people. It's no longer a question of luck; it's a question of choice. No longer will genius potential be wasted because of self-doubt. Humanity could have had millions and millions of geniuses all along; instead, the history books only remember a few from each generation who actually trusted in their intelligence.

For the members of Generation Genius (of which you're one...we're totally jealous), the path to mastery is completely straightforward. There is no mystery; if you know your brain, then the process of becoming awesome is totally reliable. So, the question is, what are you going to do about it? Are you going to feel obligated and drag yourself through the work, or are you going to realize the incredible potential that you have, get fired up, and make the world the kind of place everyone has always wanted it to be? You are a member of a three-billion-man team that can cure every disease. Your generation has the power to create the coolest technology, eradicate hunger, solve the world's environmental problems, and maybe even figure out how to time travel. Who knows?

The bottom line is, you're among the first people ever to be able to harness the full learning power of your brain. In the short-term, go and use that to make school easier for you than it has been for anyone before you. But keep in mind that there are long-term benefits too. With that kind of limitless potential, there's nothing you can't do, today, tomorrow, and for the rest of your life.

We're so excited for you.

END NOTES

THE SCIENCE BEHIND
THE STRAIGHT-A CONSPIRACY

Congratulations! You've finished *The Straight-A Conspiracy* and you are now ready to take on the world, one assignment at a time! Neurology, psychology, and educational research provide the backbone for our view of education, and so for those of you who are interested, we wanted to give a shout-out to some of our favorite works and provide you with the opportunity to find out more. If there were chapters or ideas in this book that particularly piqued your interest, we encourage you to read on and take your new knowledge to the next level!

Stereotype Threat, Self-Theories, and Learned Helplessness

The goal of the first half of *The Straight-A Conspiracy* is to make students aware of just how many preconceived notions about intelligence they possess and just how damaging those ideas can be. Among psychologists, a large body of work exists on what is called "stereotype threat." Many stereotypes exist related to performance—white men are less athletic, women are bad at math, and African-Americans do less well in school. When test-takers are made to think of themselves in terms of one of those stereotypes, the thought tends to impede their performance to such a degree that they in essence "fulfill" that stereotypical belief. In one particularly telling study, stereotypes caused Asian-American women to do both better and worse in math. When they were primed to think about their gender, the women's math skills suffered relative to those who had not been primed at all; conversely, the women scored higher than the control group on the same test when primed to focus on the fact that they were Asian. The bottom line is that even having a negative stereotype is enough to affect performance for the worse.

Some of the students that we've met have been affected by these generalized stereotypes. But more often, students develop damaging theories about their own specific capabilities, like those that we present in the opening chapter. These "self-theories"—as Stanford psychologist Carol Dweck has termed them—have been shown to make students less motivated, less persistent, and less likely to seek help when they're struggling. Unsurprisingly, students who are less motivated, less persistent, and less likely to seek help tend to get bad grades, which in turn make their original self-theories seem all the more "accurate."

But to really appreciate the power of these academic self-theories, it is important to understand that they are one variety of the much larger field of psychology pioneered by Martin Seligman. In 1967, Seligman and his colleagues conducted an experiment in which dogs were placed in electrified kennels. One group of dogs was free to move, while another was chained in place. Predictably, the dogs that were free to move jumped out of the kennels to avoid being shocked. The other group strained to get away, but couldn't and eventually resigned themselves to being shocked. When those same dogs were subsequently unchained, Seligman's group found that although they now had the ability to jump out of the kennel, they simply lay down and accepted shock after shock. This state is now known as "learned helplessness" and has since been used to explain human behavior in a wide variety of contexts.

Crucially, in humans, this learned helplessness is triggered by how we explain what happens to us. If we view our circumstances as being in our control, we improve them. If we don't, we devote our energies to coming to terms with what we view as an unchangeable reality. What is important to note is that, when the dogs were unchained, they didn't even see the obvious things they could do to improve their situation. In studies of learned helplessness in humans, the same effect is observed. Students who feel like their level of intelligence is out of their control often don't even see that simple actions would allow them to get good grades. However, time and time again, studies have found that shaking students out of their state of "learned helplessness" is as simple as showing them just how much control they do have over how intelligent they become.

Read this: *Mindset* by Carol Dweck, *Learned Optimism* by Martin Seligman. See "Selected References" for further scientific reading on this and all sections.

Training-induced Neuroplasticity

One of the biggest problems in modern education is that people everywhere continue to believe that the brain is a fixed organ with a fixed capacity, despite the fact that in the last forty years, scientists have discovered that the brain is, in fact, incredibly flexible. Research has shown that myelination and increased area of activity are just two of the many ways in which the brain can become better able to perform a task. Training has also been observed to cause the growth of new neurons, the expansion of particular brain structures, and changes in the ways in which neurons interact with each other. It's not only the degree to which the brain can change that is impressive. It is also the speed with which those changes can happen. Amazingly, observable changes in the structure of the brain can happen in as little as five days.

Read this: *The Brain That Changes Itself* by Norman Doidge, *In Search of Memory* by Eric Kandel

The Illusion of Rationality (Heuristics and the Intersection of Emotion and Attention)

An equally massive shift in science has been our understanding of how we make decisions. On a physical level, we now know that structures like the amygdala, which process emotion, have a high level of connectivity with the part of the brain involved in rational thought. But in order to appreciate this on a functional level, it helps to know the story of a patient named Elliot. USC professor of neuroscience Antonio Damasio studied what happened to Elliot after doctors removed a tumor from his brain, and what he found has radically altered our understanding of the role of emotion in making everyday decisions.

Before his operation, Elliot was an upstanding citizen, successful businessman, and happy family man—thanks in no small part to his ability to make good decisions regularly and quickly. That all changed after doctors removed the small section of brain behind his nose. Suddenly, simple decisions proved insoluble. Elliot would spend hours trying to decide what restaurant to go to, only to realize that he'd been weighing his options for so long that lunchtime was over. In other words, the new Elliot could not make a decision. The operation had not affected his cognitive function at all; on an intelligence test, Elliot still scored in the 97th percentile. But then Damasio set up a test to measure Elliot's emotional responses, similar to a lie-detector test. When shown "emotional" images, such as that of a gun or a severed foot, most subjects would have an emotional response that could be measured through physiological signs, such as sweating palms. No matter how many of these pictures Elliot saw, he had no response whatsoever; Elliot had no emotions about anything.

Damasio concluded that Elliot's lack of emotion was the reason for his sudden inability to make good decisions. Most people can tell that they feel like eating a certain food for lunch, or might get a gut feeling about something being "not quite right" when they encounter a shady character. But Elliot couldn't access his "gut" feelings anymore, and so he either had to weigh options endlessly or just make a snap judgment, which often led to disastrous results. Sure enough, in a short period of time, Elliot lost his job and ran up a string of failed business ventures, his wife divorced him, and he had to declare bankruptcy after falling victim to a con man. Most of us would assume that taking emotion out of the equation would help us make better decisions, but that wasn't the case for Elliot at all.

Before scientists studied Elliot and cases like his, emotions were thought to be a mere intruder in the process of rational decision making. However, in recent years, scientists have realized that more often than not, we make emotional decisions that we then retroactively justify to ourselves through reason. In fact, as studies have shown, we are all very good at finding logic to explain all kinds of things about our lives: why our decisions are sound, why we're not at fault when we are in a fight with someone, and why it "makes sense" that we're not good at certain subjects. Psychologists have termed this tendency to believe that our feelings are facts "naïve realism." As shown in the Emotions chapter of the main text, our emotions often conspire to validate our self-theories. However, it is important to note that in various studies in this area, subjects who were made aware of how naïve realism distorts our view of reality were better able to do something about it. In other words, awareness facilitates progress.

On a more refined level, psychologists and behavioral economists have uncovered that our decision-making relies heavily on shortcuts known as "heuristics." (hyu-RIS-tiks) These shortcuts are generally helpful to our decision-making abilities. For example, doctors have to use mental shortcuts when diagnosing patients in emergency situations, but sometimes those shortcuts can lead to misdiagnoses. Rather than eliminating those shortcuts, people in the medical field work to make them better. In fact, one of the defining characteristics of experts in any field is that they use more effective heuristics than amateurs do. In school, the most easily recognizable heuristic is the way in which students consistently look to their peers' performances to determine how they should be performing—a shortcut which, as we have seen in this book, is not always productive. Much of this book's text—culminating in the chart used in Generation Genius— aims to help students find new, more productive shortcuts to enable them to quickly "diagnose" what is going wrong with their work and subsequently move forward in the best possible way.

Read This: *Thinking, Fast and Slow* by Daniel Kahneman, *Nudge* by Cass R. Sunstein and Richard H. Thaler

Schemas and the Importance of Prior Knowledge

On a test, it's clear that you will be expected to know the facts, and so it makes sense that many students try to simply cram those facts into their heads as quickly as possible. To these students, taking the time to understand the material seems like an unnecessary extra step. In reality, research has now shown that the "extra step" of working to make sense of the material actually saves time. As demonstrated in the chapter about London cabbies, by working to understand the material, students are digging beyond the surface facts to discover the framework that connects them. The framework may be the chronology of historical events or the causal relationship within a biological process. No matter the subject, taking advantage of the inherent "schemas"—as researchers usually call these frameworks—not only makes it easier to organize and memorize the material when it's new, but it also makes that information easier to retain over the long term.

The scientifically demonstrated contextual nature of human memory is the basis for the assertion in this book that "more is more." Study after study has shown that experts in a given field learn new facts related to their field extremely quickly. That's because they have such a rich context in which to anchor those facts. However, it takes them just as long as it would anyone else to learn new facts in fields unrelated to their field of expertise. This is why minimizing the amount of information you need to study, or relying exclusively on the broad outlines provided by book summaries and study guides is not actually the most effective way to speed up your study time—or to make it memorable.

Read This: *Moonwalking With Einstein* by Joshua Foer

Flow and Quality of Experience

While getting straight-*A*'s might be a goal worth aiming for, it's a hard sell if—as many teenagers assume—it's going to mean being miserable and stressed out. One of the most exciting findings about expert performance centers not on what it takes to acquire expertise but how it feels to acquire expertise. In the final chapter of this book, we mention Mihaly Csikszentmihalyi, who has focused his career on the study of "flow." Flow—also known as being "in the zone"—is the state that we experience when we are totally absorbed in a task. When we are working at something that is at the edge of our current abilities and draws fully on our skills in that area, we all have the experience of self-consciousness dropping away and time seeming to fly by. This is not to say that the work is "easy," but when you're in the zone and experiencing flow, the work is totally engaging and satisfying.

Students are correct to observe that getting straight-*A*'s does involve some anxiety, but they are disregarding the rest of the emotional experience—specifically all of the benefits. As Csikszentmihalyi has found, while top-performing students do experience slightly more anxiety, they also experience less boredom and far more flow. From a purely emotional perspective, being heavily engaged is a better choice. But flow comes with one other major benefit that should be of particular interest to teenagers. Flow has been shown to reduce self-consciousness. Thanks to researchers such as Csikszentmihalyi, the motivation to get great grades doesn't have to be far-distant college or career possibilities; it doesn't even have to be the grades themselves; doing well in school can be about improving the experience you're having right now.

Read This: *Flow* by Mihalyi Csikszentmihalyi

Acquisition of Expertise and the 10,000 Hour Rule

In the thirteenth century, noted scholar Roger Bacon argued that it would take a minimum of thirty to forty years to master the highest level of mathematical knowledge that existed at that time. Today, that level of mathematics is routinely taught to high school juniors. As we advance in any given field over time, we also get better at acquiring and sharing the existing knowledge in that field. That's why the average high school graduate in the twenty-first century is far more advanced than the leading experts of yesteryear.

What this teaches us is that practicing in a smarter way allows you to massively reduce the amount of time required to become an expert. Anders K. Ericsson and his colleagues studied the acquisition of expertise by current top performers in fields as diverse as music, physics, chess and sports; they have found that part of what separates experts from amateurs is about 10,000 hours of practice. However, in their work, the researchers also defined the universal characteristics of exactly what kind of practice it takes in order for those 10,000 hours to pay off. As it turns out, practice doesn't necessarily make perfect, if you're doing the wrong kind of practice.

The right kind of practice, which Ericsson calls "deliberate practice," is most easily understood through the example of classical musicians. For those of us who learned a musical instrument and didn't become the next Yo Yo Ma, practice mostly consisted of stumbling our way through the pieces assigned by the high school band director and using the time-honored technique of playing really softly when you're not totally sure what notes to play and coming in overly strongly when you know a section well. Either way, the primary goal was just to get all the way to the end of the piece. In contrast, performers who become truly excellent practice in a very stop-start way. When they run into difficulty with a particular section, they stop and slow their practice down—sometimes to an excruciatingly slow pace—until they can guarantee that they are practicing the exact notes. As they automate that section, they are able to move more and more quickly, but they do not move on to the next phrase until they are sure the current one is perfect. Musicians on the path to mastery do not spend their time playing the pieces they like or the ones that make them sound good. They spend their time playing scales and exercises and pieces that challenge specific aspects of their technique. Deliberate practice identifies areas of weakness in the most specifically targeted way possible and then develops activities to improve those specific aspects of performance. Fudging your way through pieces that you recognize may be more fun in the short-term, but the long-term benefits of being the best at what you do more than make up for all the self-discipline that deliberate practice requires.

For the purposes of introducing the concept of deliberate practice to teenagers, we have chosen the term "fix-it-focused practice," because fix-it-focused practice puts the student's attention on identifying his or her mistakes. Identifying and fixing mistakes is the most essential part of effective learning—and it's also the part of learning that self-theories make us most likely to avoid. Students who are currently doing their best to avoid their mistakes are generally not emotionally ready to be introduced to all of the vigors of Ericsson's deliberate practice. However, as we have found in case after case, if students can just begin to pay attention to their mistakes—and then engage with them—they will start to see the payoff of that work almost immediately. In time, the way in which they target areas of weakness in their work will become more and more specific, and eventually, they will be practicing just like the experts do.

Read this: *Outliers* by Malcolm Gladwell, *The Talent Code* by Daniel Coyle

Metacognition

Reviewing these disparate fields, it becomes possible to see that the key to maximizing your efforts in school is metacognition. In every field that we've discussed in this section and in the main text of the book, awareness of your thoughts, perceptions, and actions is the key to overcoming the things that are standing in your way. That the National Academy of Sciences chose to underscore metacognition as a unifying characteristic of effective teaching and learning in their report "How Students Learn" presents hope that a broad-based consensus can be built around this idea. In all of our thousands of hours of tutoring experience, what we have consistently observed is that the vast majority of the stress, frustration, shame, and "whatevering" that happens in school is a result of students' desire to not look at what's really going on—or, more specifically, going wrong—in their work. Stressed-out academic superstars and students who are failing have more in common than they realize. For them, school is a feat of endurance; they both devote a tremendous amount of energy to justifying a less-than-ideal experience rather than using that energy to improve it. The impulses to do well in school and to actually enjoy your life are both totally valid. With metacognition, they no longer work against each other; rather, they complement each other. Doing well generates enjoyment. Enjoyment generates greater engagement, which leads to better performance. By cultivating a deep-seated trust that our students can do well and an understanding that using their mistakes will get them there, we can help our students realize that doing well in school is actually the least stressful and most fun way to spend your teenage years.

SELECTED REFERENCES

**If you're interested in going beyond the readings suggested in "The Science Behind *The Straight-A Conspiracy*," here's a list of sources that further explicate the science and research that inspired the concepts presented in this book.

Carter, Rita, Susan Aldridge, Martyn Page, Steve Parker, Christopher D. Frith, Uta Frith, and Melanie B. Shulman. *The Human Brain Book*. London: DK Pub., 2009. Print. *(See pg. 150 for where we originally found MRI's of the reading brain.)*

Cohen, Marlene R., and John H R. Maunsell. "Attention Improves Performance Primarily by Reducing Interneuronal Correlations." *Nature Neuroscience* 12.12 (2009): 1594-600. Print.

Csikszentmihalyi, Mihaly. *Flow: The Psychology of Optimal Experience*. New York: Harper Perennial, 2008. Print.

Csikszentmihalyi, Mihaly, and Isabella Selega. Csikszentmihalyi. *Optimal Experience: Psychological Studies of Flow in Consciousness*. Cambridge: Cambridge UP, 1988. Print. *(The study mentioned in the Notes section appears on pg. 325 of this book.)*

Damasio, Antonio R. *Descartes' Error: Emotion, Reason, and the Human Brain*. New York: Putnam, 1994. Print.

Deary, Ian J., Lars Penke, and Wendy Johnson. "The Neuroscience of Human Intelligence Differences." *Nature Reviews Neuroscience*, 2010. Print. *(This article rigorously reviews any existing claims of scientists having found a gene for above-average intelligence and concludes that zero such genes have been found.)*

Donovan, Suzanne, and John Bransford. *How Students Learn: History, Mathematics, and Science in the Classroom.* Washington, D.C.: National Academies, 2005. Print. *(We have found that this provides the best review of the work on schema, prior knowledge and metacognition.)*

Dove, A., S. Pollman, T. Schubert, C. Wiggins, and D. Von Cramon. "Prefrontal Cortex Activation in Task Switching: An Event-related FMRI Study." *Cognitive Brain Research 9.1* (2000): 103-09. Print.

Draganski, Bogdan, Christian Gaser, Volker Busch, Gerhard Schuierer, Ulrich Bogdahn, and Arne May. "Neuroplasticity: Changes in Grey Matter Induced by Training." *Nature* 427.6972 (2004): 311-12. Print.

Dweck, Carol S. *Self-theories: Their Role in Motivation, Personality, and Development.* Philadelphia, PA: *Psychology*, 2000. Print.

Ekman, Paul. *Emotions Revealed: Recognizing Faces and Feelings to Improve Communication and Emotional Life.* New York: Times, 2003. Print. *(See page 63 for more on the physiological responses to anger and fear.)*

Elliot, Andrew J., and Carol S. Dweck. *Handbook of Competence and Motivation.* New York: Guilford, 2005. Print.

Ericsson, K. Anders. *The Cambridge Handbook of Expertise and Expert Performance.* Cambridge: Cambridge UP, 2006. Print.

Ericsson, Anders, Ralf Krampe and Clemens Tesch-Römer. "The Role of Deliberate Practice in the Acquisition of Expert Performance." *Psychological Review.* 100.3 (1993): 363-406. Print.

Fara, Patricia. *Newton: The Making of Genius.* Columbia Univ Press, 2004. Print.

Gawande, Atul. *The Checklist Manifesto: How to Get Things Right.* Picador USA, 2011. Print. *(Besides informing much of our thinking on checklists, Gawande's book also gave us the inside scoop on David Lee*

Roth and his brown M&M's test.)

Good, C. "Improving Adolescents' Standardized Test Performance: An Intervention to Reduce the Effects of Stereotype Threat." *Journal of Applied Developmental Psychology* 24.6 (2003): 645-62. Print.

Haidt, Jonathan. *The Happiness Hypothesis: Finding Modern Truth in Ancient Wisdom*. New York: Basic, 2006. Print.

Johns, M., T. Schmader, and A. Martens. "Knowing Is Half the Battle—Teaching Stereotype Threat as a Means of Improving Women's Math Performance." *Psychological Science* 16.3 (2005): 175-79. Print.

Kim, Yee Joon, Marcia Grabowecky, Ken A. Paller, Krishnakumur Muthu, and Satoru Suzuki. "Voluntary Direction of Attention Increases Response Gain." *Nature Neuroscience* 10.1 (2007): 117-25. Print.

Lewis, Michael, and Jeannette M. Haviland-Jones. *Handbook of Emotions*. New York: Guilford, 1993. Print.

Lewis, Michael. *Shame: The Exposed Self.* New York: Free, 1992. Print.

MacCulloch, Diarmaid. *The Reformation.* Penguin Group USA, 2004. Print.

Maguire, Eleanor A., David G. Gadian, Ingrid S. Johnsrude, Catriona D. Good, John Ashbruner, Richard Frackiowac, and Christopher D. Frith. "Navigation-related Structural Change in the Hippocampi of Taxi Drivers." *Proceedings of the National Academy of Sciences* 97.8 (2000): 4398-403. Print.

Marks, Susan. *Finding Betty Crocker: The Secret Life of America's First Lady of Food.* Univ. Of Minnesota Press, 2007. Print.

Mueller, Claudia M., and Carol S. Dweck. "Praise for Intelligence Can Undermine Children's Motivation and Performance." *Journal of Personality and Social Psychology* 75 (1998): 33-52. Print.

Mulligan, Neil W. "The Role of Attention during Encoding in Implicit and Explicit Memory." *Journal of Experimental Psychology: Learning, Memory, and Cognition* 24.1 (1998): 27-47. Print.

"National-Academies.org | Newsroom." *Under Construction.* Web. 10 Feb. 2012. <http://www8.nationalacademies.org/onpinews/newsitem.aspx?RecordID=9728>.

Öhman, Arne, Anders Flykt, and Francisco Esteves. "Emotion Drives Attention: Detecting the Snake in the Grass." *Journal of Experimental Psychology: General* 130.3 (2001): 466-78. Print.

Ophir, E., C. Nass, and A. D. Wagner. "Cognitive Control in Media Multitaskers." *Proceedings of the National Academy of Sciences* 106.37 (2009): 15583-5587. Print. *(This study is referenced in the box about multi-tasking that appears in the Attention chapter.)*

Ochsner, Kevin N., Silvia A. Bunge, James J. Gross, and John D. E. Gabrieli. "Rethinking Feelings: An FMRI Study of the Cognitive Regulation of Emotion." *Journal of Cognitive Neuroscience* 14.8 (2002): 1215-229. Print.

Pascual-Leone, Alvaro, and Fernando Torres. "Plasticity of the Sensorimotor Cortex Representation of the Reading Finger in Braille Readers." *Brain* 116.1 (1993): 39-52. Print.

Peterson, Christopher, Steven F. Maier, and Martin E. P. Seligman. *Learned Helplessness: A Theory for the Age of Personal Control.* New York: Oxford UP, 1993. Print.

Schlaug, G. "Increased Corpus Callosum Size in Musicians." *Neuropsychologia* 33.8 (1995): 1047-055. Print.

Scholz, Jan, Miriam C. Klein, Timothy E J. Behrens, and Heidi Johansen-Berg. "Training Induces Changes in White-matter Architecture." *Nature Neuroscience* (2009). Print.

Seligman, Martin E. P. *Authentic Happiness: Using the New Positive Psychology to Realize Your Potential for Lasting Fulfillment.*

New York: Free, 2002. Print. *(The Csikszentmihalyi study mentioned in Generation Genius originally came from pg. 117 of this book.)*

Shih, Margaret, Todd L. Pittinsky, and Nalini Ambady. "Stereotype Susceptibility: Identity Salience and Shifts in Quantitative Performance." *Psychological Science* 10.1 (1999): 80-83. Print.

Spencer, Steven J., Claude M. Steele, and Diane M. Quinn. "Stereotype Threat and Women's Math Performance." *Journal of Experimental Social Psychology* 35.1 (1999): 4-28. Print.

Steele, Claude M., and Joshua Aronson. "Stereotype Threat and the Intellectual Test Performance of African Americans." *Journal of Personality and Social Psychology* 69.5 (1995): 797-811. Print.

Stafford, William. *The Mozart Myths: A Critical Reassessment.* Stanford Univ Press, 1993. Print.

Stipek, Deborah, and Heidi Gralinski. "Children's Beliefs about Intelligence and School Performance." *Journal of Educational Psychology* 88.3 (1997): 397-407. Print.

Stross, Randall. *The Wizard of Menlo Park: How Thomas Alva Edison Invented the Modern World.* Three Rivers Press, 2008. Print.

Tracy, Jessica L., Richard W. Robins, and June Price Tangney. *The Self-conscious Emotions: Theory and Research.* New York: Guilford, 2007. Print.

Woollett, Katherine and Eleanor A Maguire. "Acquiring the Knowledge of London's Layout Drives Structural Brain Changes." *Current Biology* 21.24 (2011): 2109 - 2114. Print.

A NOTE TO PARENTS

Many parents who have read this book are excited by what it means for their children and what is possible for the future. They understand fully what their children need to do, but what they really want to know is what *they* can do. What's the best way for a parent to help?

Well, that's tricky. While school is almost universally a topic that brings up strong emotions between parents and children, each parent-child relationship is unique. We know some parents who are hyper-involved and communicate with their children constantly about what's happening in their classes. Others feel that their only hope of maintaining any sort of dialogue with their children is to avoid the subject of school altogether. Obviously, you are a parent who cares very deeply about your child's academic future; that's why you took the time to purchase and look through this book. No matter what kind of relationship surrounding "school" you currently have with your student, there is one parental action that we've seen make a big difference in every case. It's simple. Take the information in this book and apply it to *your own* experience in school. Imagine that you yourself had been armed with this information. How much less stress would school have given to you? How much easier would it have been if you had known that the straight-*A* students in your class didn't possess magical powers, but rather a concrete set of skills and behaviors that allowed them to develop into academic successes over time? How differently would you have approached your own work?

The reality is that you grew up in a time when there were basically two ways to explain students' academic results—and success in general: hard work and natural ability. As we've outlined in this book, this is a horrifically crude system, and the result of that thinking was an assumed lack of control over one's own successes and failures. And that thinking has stayed with most of us for our entire lives. Before you can help guide your child's experience, you have to make sense of your own experience in light of what we now know; it's time to face the truth about what you believed. Of course, that's not always easy. If you have always believed that you're just bad at math or languages or writing, or if you were someone who never did his or her homework, there's a tendency to want to push that aside and deny that it ever happened, in part because you don't want to consider the possibility that your genes may have doomed your children to suffer the same difficulties in school. As a parent, your hardships can be your best asset in understanding your child's academic experience; they are not something to hide away. Even if you were a brainiac, straight-A student yourself, remember to identify any areas (no matter how minor) in which you may have struggled. Telling your own story can help your child to understand how you did or didn't overcome obstacles in your past. Even if the experience isn't directly applicable, sharing it in an honest and humble way can open the door to a more open dialogue with your child.

We hope you see that whatever experience you had, it was likely a natural reaction to the incomplete and often incorrect information about the brain and learning that existed when you were in school. So, we suggest that you take some time and ask yourself the following questions:

1) When you were in school, did you feel like you were naturally bad at a certain subject? Do you still feel that way today?

2) Are there areas in which you feel that you are naturally better or more talented than most people? Has that belief made you confident or complacent?

3) Who was the person in your school that always seemed to "get it" right away?

4) When you read Part 3 of this book, did you find any study techniques that you used…or definitely didn't use? How did your approach to work go?

5) Even as an adult, are there any skills that you still view as "beyond you?" Are there skills that you believe are mostly the

product of natural talent, such as drawing, writing, or even being good with computers?

6) What, other than bad feelings, have you gotten from harboring these beliefs about your brain and its potential?

By seeing your own experience in a new light, it's likely that you will realize how much of your own personal successes and failures were due to the *actions* that you took each day, rather than to the worth of your brain. Think about how much *has been* possible for you all along, and how *not knowing* that possibility has shaped your life. Be honest with yourself in this process. Did you hate science class because you were bad at it? Or did you get bad grades in science because you hated it? Did you *really* put 100% effort into that class, even though you suspected that you'd never be good at it anyway? Isn't it possible that if you *had* taken the right actions, you might have actually done really well? And what about now? Do you believe that it is possible for school to be enjoyable? Do you believe that your child really can get straight-A's? You'd be amazed by how greatly your own beliefs and experiences are affecting how you talk to your child about school.

If you can understand how the things you *did* affected your own grades in school, then it becomes easier to see past the smokescreen of emotions and keep discussions of school focused on your child's *actions*. Instead of hiding your past, *use* it. In doing this, you will be able to provide what your child needs most: an objective partner to help troubleshoot academic problems, analyze mistakes and fix them for next time. Focus on changing your child's actions, and in time, the emotions will change too.

So be human—it's okay that you made your own mistakes or let yourself be led astray by false information about your brain and what it takes to be "smart." Now is the time to take a closer look at your past actions and beliefs and make them a part of the discussion. That way, you can speak from *experience* when you tell your child just how amazing his or her brain is and how much changing his or her actions now can not only improve school, but also the rest of his or her life.

We really are excited for what this generation of students can do.

If they are willing to rise to the challenge, the possibilities for success are endless. What today's students need most is the conviction that with the right actions, they can achieve anything. And before you can give your child that mindset, you need to believe in it yourself. Take the time now to clean out and clear up all of your past beliefs about learning, and you'll be in the best position possible to inspire your children to see beyond today's test, quiz, or essay to the amazing future that is theirs for the taking.

ABOUT THE AUTHORS

Katie O'Brien

A native New Englander, Katie graduated first in her class from Pinkerton Academy, a New Hampshire regional public school of 3200 students, nestled in the most Norman Rockwell-y part of small-town America that you can imagine. She arrived at Harvard College in the fall of 2000 and majored in English and American Literature and Language, ultimately graduating *magna cum laude*. At Harvard, she also co-directed CityStep—a program that integrates arts education into the Cambridge public middle schools—and after graduating and moving to New York, she continued that work with high schoolers in NYC, Oxford, London, and Edinburgh. During this time, Katie also teamed up with Hunter and two other Harvard classmates to form Overqualified Tutoring, a NYC- and LA-based educational services company. She has spent thousands of hours tutoring and home-schooling students of all ages, and in all subject areas. Katie currently resides in Los Angeles...but still roots for the Red Sox from afar.

Hunter Maats

Hunter isn't really a native of anywhere. Born in Saudi Arabia, he'd lived in Brazil, Greece and New York before his family moved to

England when he was eight years old. There he attended Eton College, England's most stodgy and prestigious all-boys boarding school. After high school, he pursued his love of science by spending a year doing tumor virus research at Cold Spring Harbor laboratory, where he lived in the basement of James Watson, Nobel Laureate and co-discoverer of the double helical structure of DNA. It was a no-brainer for Hunter to major in Biochemistry when he enrolled at Harvard College in the fall of 2000. While at Harvard, Hunter devoted his spare time and his electives to a mixture of pranks and foreign languages. Occasionally, he mixed the two. After graduating, Hunter moved to Los Angeles and helped to found Overqualified Tutoring. A current owner of comically overstuffed bookshelves, Hunter has enjoyed tackling the one aspect of science that he has always found unsettling: the gap between the research that exists and the public's knowledge. Today, Hunter spends his time finding more and more ways to bring those two together. When he's away from the aforementioned bookshelves, Hunter can be found at cross-fit, eating Nicole's food, or dreaming of Kansas City.